TRANSNATIONAL CIVIL LITIGATION

Principles and Prospects

GEORGE A. RUTHERGLEN
John Barbee Minor Distinguished Professor of Law
Barron F. Black Research Professor of Law
University of Virginia School of Law

CONCEPTS AND INSIGHTS SERIES®

FOUNDATION PRESS

Concepts and Insights Series is a trademark registered in the U.S. Patent and Trademark Office.

© 2016 LEG, Inc. d/b/a West Academic
    444 Cedar Street, Suite 700
    St. Paul, MN 55101
    1-877-888-1330

Printed in the United States of America

ISBN: 978-1-63459-500-1

TABLE OF CONTENTS

TRANSNATIONAL CIVIL LITIGATION

Principles and Prospects

INTRODUCTION: SCOPE AND THEORY

Transnational civil litigation, as its name implies, stands at the intersection of three different fields: first, transnational law as opposed to the law applied in wholly domestic cases; second, civil liability in contrast to criminal liability; and third, litigation rules of jurisdiction and procedure in contrast to substantive law. All of these fields extend far beyond transnational civil litigation, which is concerned primarily with claims between private parties that arise from events that cross national boundaries. These fields reach into the relation between sovereign nations, the divide between civil damages and criminal penalties, and the many distinctions that can be drawn between substance and procedure. The overlap between these three fields in transnational civil litigation might be regarded simply as the inevitable byproduct of identifying different kinds of litigation and distinguishing between cases that are wholly domestic and those that are not. Yet even that simple distinction does not do justice to the complexity of the American system of federalism, where a case may concern only events in this country, yet cross the borders of several different states. All legal fields share margins and boundaries with others, causing principles from neighboring fields to interact with each other and resulting in cases that must address a range of intersecting issues. Even so, the overlap among the fields that constitute transnational civil litigation takes these interactions to new and higher levels of sophistication, resulting in a series of issues, such as jurisdiction and the extraterritorial coverage of American law, that are systematically related to one another. Transnational civil litigation is a genuine subject in its own right and one with increasing significance as global activity becomes ever more intense in scope and far-reaching in its consequences, ranging across issues from commerce to human rights.

A few basic concepts unify this subject and frame the controversies within it: sovereignty, individual rights, and political accountability. The first concept, sovereignty, defines the scope of legitimate government action and accounts for the multifarious ways in which the term "jurisdiction" is deployed in international disputes. It bridges the gap between international and domestic law and between both of these sources of law and rules of jurisdiction. Competition between independent sovereigns, constituted as territorially defined states, forms the basis for international relations as we know them today. Sovereignty in this form is based primarily upon control over a defined territory exclusive of the power of other states. Notwithstanding criticism of this conception of sovereignty, as a relic of the nation states recognized in the Treaty of Westphalia in 1648, it constitutes the foundation for all ongoing developments in international law. Treaties, international organizations, and customary international law all begin from the consent and action of territorially defined states. International institutions supersede such states, and might eventually supplant them, only because of what the states themselves have done to establish those institutions. For now, the territory of each state primarily defines its power with respect to other states, which is not to deny that state power can extend beyond its own territory or that one state can recognize the power of another within its own territory. The latter issue goes under the indefinite heading of "comity": the accommodation that a state makes to a foreign state out of mutual respect but not as a limit on its own power. Comity counsels each nation to recognize other nations as co-equal sovereigns, and without requiring any nation do so, to take seriously the possible application of foreign law, the recognition of foreign judgments, and requests for foreign sovereign immunity.

The second concept, individual rights, protects the private interests at stake in civil litigation. In recent years, the focus has been upon human rights, defined as those owed to all human beings regardless of national law. Historically, however, economic rights to property and contract received greater protection in international law as they have in domestic law, and most prominently, in domestic constitutional law. Commerce among nations fostered the first regimes of private international law, such as the law of maritime transactions and accidents. The expansion to general human rights gained momentum in the latter half of the twentieth century, a development that followed and paralleled a similar expansion of individual rights under the American Constitution, from property and contract rights to political and civil rights. If individual rights put the "civil" in transnational civil litigation, they also connect it to jurisdiction and procedural rules, which have their foundation in American law through the Due Process Clauses in the Fifth and Fourteenth Amendments.

The third concept, political accountability, also echoes an important theme in constitutional law: the tension between judicial decision-making and democratic accountability through the political branches of government. In matters touching on foreign affairs, judicial deference to the executive and legislative branches has been even stronger than in constitutional law generally. Courts, and particularly the Supreme Court, have been reluctant to act unilaterally without the support of the public officials who set foreign policy and manage its implementation.[1] Seemingly unrelated issues,

---

[1]   United States v. Pink, 315 U.S. 203, 222–23, 229 (1942) (stating in relevant part, "the conduct of foreign relations is committed by the Constitution to the political

such as treatment of American nationals by a foreign country within its borders, or expropriation of assets by a foreign country, or the extent to which a foreign sovereign can be sued in an American court, have important implications for the nation's foreign policy.[2] The linkage between foreign policy and the law applicable to the acts of foreign sovereigns often does not follow the logic of legal principles, but instead requires compromises and ad hoc solutions more properly within the power of the political branches of government. Congress and the executive can respond more flexibly to such issues than the judiciary, which must rationalize decisions according to established rules of law and legal procedure. So, too, acceptance and implementation of international law as part of our law often requires explicit approval of the political branches, most obviously in agreement to and ratification of treaties. Likewise, legislation to protect and enforce private rights often is needed to improve upon the default rules of the common law. In the American system, reliance on the common law leads to particular complications surrounding the doctrine of *Erie Railroad Co. v. Tompkins*.[3] State law thus takes on an important role as the residual source for the law applied in international cases. If the political branches of the federal government have not acted to displace state law, and the federal Constitution does not otherwise require or provide, state law applies by default.

The concepts of sovereignty, individual rights, and political accountability play out across the full range of issues in transnational civil litigation. They are competing and complementary approaches to the subject that do not dictate outcomes in the manner of categorical imperatives. Instead, they provide the basis for opposing arguments and different perspectives. To see them as inflexible rules greatly diminishes their role in explaining the many controversies in this field and in justifying the various ways in which they can be resolved. To reduce their role to an all-or-nothing determination leaves unexplained the persistent disputes over issues such as personal jurisdiction and choice of law and minimizes the complications in resolving them. These concepts do not yield implications that can simply be turned or turned off, requiring conformity to one concept or the other as opposed to competing and complementary arguments. To go to the opposite

---

departments of the Federal Government; [and] that the propriety of the exercise of that power is not open to judicial review").

    [2]   Abbott v. Abbott, 560 U.S. 1, 15 (2010) (reasoning that "The Court's conclusion . . . is supported and informed by the State Department's view on the issue. . . . It is well settled that the Executive Branch's interpretation of a treaty 'is entitled to great weight.' There is no reason to doubt that this well-established canon of deference is appropriate here.").

    [3]   304 U.S. 64 (1938).

extreme and view these concepts factors always to be balanced against one another, runs the opposite risk of denying any structure to the field at all. The tendency toward case-by-case analysis of difficult issues already threatens to make decisions in this field overly dependent upon the exercise of judicial discretion. More must be accomplished by the applicable standards in this field to make the decisions in concrete cases predictable and consistent, and in doing so, to restrain judicial power and make it accountable. As a purely intellectual matter, it would be disappointing to find that the field amounted to nothing more than a collection of indeterminate standards. The goal instead must be to identify principles at the right level of generality, which can guide decisions by courts, planning by private parties, and the policy decisions of public officials. Those principles need to be placed in a theoretical structure that allows them to be compared and adjusted to one another, so that ultimate goals can be served by implementing rules in a hierarchy that identifies ends and means, leading to a kind of reflective equilibrium that best justifies the law as we have it today. The remainder of this book takes the first steps in this direction.

We begin with jurisdiction as the first area in need of clearer and more workable standards. The term jurisdiction itself has three different meanings, each of which will be discussed in a separate chapter in this book. Personal jurisdiction concerns judicial power over a defendant or any other party forced into litigation. Its focus has been on the connection between the forum, the defendant, and the lawsuit. The plaintiff, who has nearly always selected the original forum, has thereby consented to the exercise of its jurisdiction. Subject-matter jurisdiction concerns judicial power over the kind of dispute that has been placed before the court. In American law, its focus has been whether a case falls within the constitutional and statutory grants of jurisdiction to the federal courts. Only a small fraction of cases do, including those with international elements, because federal courts are courts of limited jurisdiction. The state courts, by contrast, are courts of general jurisdiction, and insofar as their jurisdiction is limited at all, those limits come mainly from statutes conferring exclusive jurisdiction on the federal courts. Defendants also can remove cases from state court to federal court, usually if the federal court could have originally exercised jurisdiction over the case. In the absence of exclusive federal jurisdiction or removal, state courts continue to play a significant role in transnational cases. A court's power to apply its own law to a controversy involves jurisdiction in a third sense, prescriptive jurisdiction. In transnational cases, it can be recast as limits on the power of a court to apply its own law, either state or federal, to cases with elements from overseas. These cases raise issues traditionally dealt with in conflict of laws, which often goes under the heading of "private international law." In the American system, again because of the *Erie* doctrine, most of this law is state law, subject only to very loose constitutional restrictions. A chapter therefore surveys the developments in that field and the peculiarly American reluctance to rely upon more definite choice-of-law rules. That reluctance turns out to derive from an approach similar to that used to determine personal jurisdiction, where abstract standards predominate over clear-cut rules.

Even this brief summary of the scope and meaning of "jurisdiction" in its various senses reveals how dependent jurisdictional issues are on the concept of territorial sovereignty. Limits on territorial sovereignty protect individual rights to escape the reach of a particular sovereign, and in so doing define the scope of the sovereign's power. In American law, many of these issues have been explored in purely domestic cases, where the power of one American state has been questioned insofar as it extends to parties or activities in a sister state. Exercising personal jurisdiction over parties and events wholly within the forum state rarely leads to any issue of jurisdiction worth litigating. Attempts to reach beyond the state's boundaries trigger territorial limits on state power and elicit the criticism that courts are acting in violation of individual rights and in excess of the authority granted to them as organs of the state. The results in interstate cases then carry over to international cases, where the defendant comes from a foreign nation or the plaintiff's claim involves activities there. Courts tend to cast the arguments in both domestic and foreign cases in constitutional terms,[4] but statutes often define the framework and determine the outcome of jurisdictional issues. The presumption against the extraterritorial application of federal statutes, for instance, can be overridden by clear language adopted by Congress.[5] On all these issues, territorial boundaries form the baseline for assessing individual rights and for defining sovereign power, subject to departures undertaken mainly by the political branches of government.

The interrelation among jurisdictional issues also supports treating them as different components of a single subject. Personal jurisdiction and subject-matter jurisdiction might be familiar from courses on civil procedure, but how they interact with issues of extraterritoriality brings in issues from conflict of laws. All three forms of jurisdiction come into play in transnational civil litigation because choice of forum and choice of law present far more

---

[4] International Shoe Co. v. Washington, 326 U.S. 310, 316 (1945) (requiring that there be "certain minimum contacts" for in personam jurisdiction, to ensure that " 'traditional notions of fair play and substantial justice' " are not offended).

[5] Morrison v. National Australia Bank Ltd., 561 U.S. 247 (2010).

consequential choices there than in domestic litigation. The distances, both literal and figurative, are greater between domestic and foreign legal systems. Just the cost of litigating in a geographically distant forum might affect legal strategy and tactics, and the cultural differences between legal systems,[6] starting with mundane issues such as the language used in a foreign court, can have a profound effect on the outcome of litigation. Laws and legal practice differ more across legal systems than they do within our own, where the common law origins of the law in most states has insured a degree of uniformity among them. At a conceptual level, identifying what counts as a contact with the forum state for purposes of personal jurisdiction presupposes a reference, certainly in close cases, to the applicable substantive law. And conversely, choice of forum often determines foreign law, as courts tend to apply their own law to cases before them. In a similar way, subject-matter jurisdiction is intertwined with substantive law, most obviously when the jurisdiction of a federal court depends upon the existence of a claim that arises under federal law. For other headings of federal jurisdiction, the influence typically runs in the opposite direction, where the basis for jurisdiction determines the applicable law. This is true in both admiralty and diversity cases, each of which invokes choice-of-law rules unique to its domain. Courts sitting in admiralty follow federal choice-of-law rules, while those relying upon diversity jurisdiction follow the rules of the state in which they sit. The deep connection between jurisdiction and substantive law resembles, in many respects, the relationship between adjudication and the political process. Substantive law forms the framework in which particular issues of personal jurisdiction and subject-matter jurisdiction are resolved and in which the consequences of those decisions are evaluated, both by the parties as a matter of strategy and by lawmakers as a matter of policy.

The connection between jurisdiction and substance becomes even tighter in the chapter on sovereign immunity and the act of state doctrine. For reasons similar to those that support the comity that one state accords another, sovereign immunity takes the form both of relief from liability on the merits and an exemption from subject-matter jurisdiction. Foreign sovereigns are relieved both of liability and, out of respect for their status as independent nations, of any need to subject themselves to the power of an American court. A jurisdictional finding of immunity, however, does not leave the plaintiff with the alternative of suing in a different court in this country, but forbids any future lawsuit here. The act of state doctrine,

---

[6]   *See* Asahi Metal Industry Co. v. Superior Court, 480 U.S. 102, 113–16 (1987) (holding that the burden on Japanese corporation of litigating in California on claim under contract with Taiwanese corporation alone was sufficient to deny due process).

by contrast, goes directly to the merits of a lawsuit, not necessarily involving a foreign sovereign, but also a private individual or firm that benefits from the actions of a foreign sovereign. The doctrine, if applicable, recognizes the legal validity of an act of a foreign sovereign within its own territory. It constitutes a choice-of-law rule that makes a foreign sovereign's action decisive on the legal issues within its scope, such as the legality of a seizure of property. The doctrine immunizes such issues from review by American courts. Decisions of the Supreme Court and legislation by Congress have progressively narrowed the effective scope of the act of state doctrine, resisting the tendency to expand the doctrine into a general principle of deference to foreign sovereigns and confining it, instead, to the validity of actions taken on behalf of a foreign sovereign under its own law within its own territory.[7] Where sovereign immunity is framed in terms of subject-matter jurisdiction, the act-of-state doctrine takes the form of choice-of-law rule.

The two doctrines resemble each other in implementing the otherwise nebulous concept of comity through more or less determinate legal rules. They also resemble each other in having important territorial elements, and in particular, as the activity of the foreign sovereign has greater contacts with American territory, it increases the exposure of the sovereign to suit and to liability in the courts of this country. Part of this process of implementation requires resort to the definite limits that the territorial boundaries of the modern state provide. Most of the exceptions to foreign sovereign immunity require both some kind of illegal action by the foreign state—whether that is a breach of contract, commission of a tort, or expropriation of private property—and some connection between that act and the United States. Just the commission of a civil wrong, or even a criminal wrong, alone does not usually abrogate the immunity of a foreign sovereign and subject it to jurisdiction and liability in this country. The wrongful conduct must somehow be connected to the United States, most commonly through commercial activity. Like sovereign immunity, the act-of-state doctrine applies most clearly to the acts of a foreign state within its own territory, without acts undertaken here. The adoption of territorial analysis on these issues reveals obvious affinities with personal jurisdiction and choice of law and the persistence, despite continued criticism in recent decades, of the essential territorial basis of modern state power. It cannot be replaced by arguments based on what is reasonable or just, independent of territorial connections. Especially on issues of sovereign immunity and acts of state, transnational civil litigation takes the existence of modern states for granted, as it does

---

[7] W.S. Kirkpatrick & Co., Inc. v. Environmental Tectonics Corp. Int'l, 493 U.S. 400 (1990).

the territorial basis for their exercise of power. This is not to say that the law on these issues must remain unchanged. In fact, the record of development reveals an incremental process of steady change, marked by the cumulative effect of decisions by all the branches of government over this century and the last.[8]

The development of the "restrictive theory" of sovereign immunity illustrates this process. Judicial decisions, assisted by opinions of the State Department, moved steadily in the twentieth century to denying immunity for liability arising from the commercial acts of foreign states, a position ultimately codified in the Foreign Sovereign Immunities Act of 1976.[9] A similar process now prevails in the field of human rights, with judicial and legislative decisions fitfully expanding tort liability for non-commercial acts to claims based on the denial of human rights. The ascendancy of human rights in public international law in the decades since World War II necessarily raises questions about the limits of sovereignty and, as a corollary, questions about the scope of sovereign immunity. Those questions have, so far, resulted in a patchwork of exceptions for human rights claims but they may yet coalesce into a general body of law analogous to domestic civil rights law, with corresponding limits on foreign sovereign immunity and the act-of-state doctrine. That development remains in the future, but it illustrates the potential of transnational civil litigation to grow to embrace new claims.

The next three chapters switch from the question of whether a lawsuit can be maintained to questions about what happens once it is pending. Service of process has the closest relationship to questions of jurisdiction, based on its historical function of acquiring personal jurisdiction over a defendant found within the forum state.[10] When the defendant is served elsewhere, however, service of process operates of its own force only to give notice of the pending action. It does not automatically result in acquisition of personal jurisdiction over the defendant. To do so would compromise a foreign nation's control over the issuance of effective legal process within its own borders. All forms of legal service, from notice of a newly filed lawsuit to execution of a judgment, carry an implicit threat of the use of force if the party served does not comply in timely fashion to appear in court. A default judgment, if it is upheld, can be enforced against the defendant wherever its assets can be found. Even if the threat is carried out elsewhere, it seeks to control activity within the boundaries of the foreign nation and triggers concerns over territorial sovereignty. So, too, simply as a matter of formality, service of

---

[8]   Verlinden B.V. v. Central Bank of Nigeria, 461 U.S. 480, 486–89 (1983).

[9]   28 U.S.C. §§ 1330, 1441(d), 1602–11.

[10]   Burnham v. Superior Court, 495 U.S. 604 (1990).

process carries with it the implication of government authority. Without its approval, one sovereign would not lightly confer such authority within its own territory to the acts of another sovereign. Hence foreign service of process rests on the most secure ground, and is most likely to result in a judgment recognized in the nation where service is effected, when it conforms to the practices of the foreign government or a treaty to which it has agreed.

The same can be said of another subject discussed later in the same chapter: discovery requests directed overseas. These give rise to especially pointed disputes when the foreign sovereign has protected the information sought from disclosure, by establishing a privilege, classifying a document as secret or confidential, or passing a "blocking statute" that specifically bars compliance with foreign discovery orders. These disputes become all the more frequent and intractable because the scope of American discovery so far exceeds that available in other countries. Private litigants here can seek information often denied in civil proceedings elsewhere. Even when public officials bring the underlying action, request for information can cause heated disputes. Tax and penal judgments have long been denied enforcement in other countries, yet requests for information to collect taxes or impose penalties, whether civil or criminal, could be construed as an attempt to circumvent this rule. In recent years, agreements to obtain information for tax and law enforcement have weakened the traditional resistance to investigation in foreign countries, although not to the point that civil discovery by private litigants has been routinely allowed to take place overseas. Transnational civil litigation remains in flux on this issue, as it has on so many others.

The third chapter in this sequence takes up the question raised by the pendency of an action itself: whether the action should remain pending or be dismissed in favor of an action elsewhere, and conversely, whether the action should take priority over a competing action through an injunction against litigation outside the forum. A court that dismisses an action pending before it, for instance, on grounds of *forum non conveniens*, reduces the risk of a conflicting judgment between the courts in different nations. But a court that enjoins a foreign action escalates that risk into direct interference with foreign legal proceedings. Which course to take, and at what expense to the litigants, implicates questions that go back to personal jurisdiction and choice of law as the means of striking a balance between assuring the plaintiff's access to justice and protecting the defendant from an abusive choice of forum. Wholly domestic cases have addressed the question of how to coordinate proceedings in different judicial systems, settling on a general rule of noninterference.[11] The commonly recognized exceptions are for injunctions needed to preserve the exercise of exclusive jurisdiction over property and to protect and effectuate a judgment already rendered. Another is for injunctions expressly authorized by Congress.[12]

Parallel proceedings can go forward unless an especially strong reason supports the need for a single court to exercise exclusive jurisdiction. A similar rule prevails in international cases, seemingly relying on the costs of multiple proceedings to deter most parties from conducting duplicative litigation. Yet here as elsewhere, the stakes are higher in transnational litigation and may lead parties to adopt more expensive strategies. Dismissing a case in favor of a foreign proceeding puts new hurdles in the way of a defendant who initially sought recovery in an American court under American law. Absent a strict system of coordination, such as the priority assigned to the first action filed in a proper court in the European Union, adjustments between competing proceedings, either pending or imminent, have to be made case by case. Dismissals for *forum non conveniens* require such an inquiry, but work in the opposite direction: in favor of proceeding in a foreign court rather than in the court chosen by the plaintiff in this country. The costs of such an inquiry might, in a single case, seem to outweigh the benefits, but the law does not seek, and probably could not find, an ideal solution. Instead, it seeks a workable compromise. The doctrine of *forum non conveniens* represents another such compromise, allowing dismissal of an action here if the balance of convenience tilts strongly in favor of litigation in a foreign court.[13] Paradoxically enough, however, the strict standard for granting dismissal on this ground triggers appellate review only for "abuse of discretion."[14] The same lenient standard of appellate review generally accompanies the strict standards for granting countersuit injunctions. The rationale for the disparity appears to lie in the fact-specific inquiry necessary to grant dismissal or to issue an injunction and in the comparatively better position of a trial court, rather than an appellate court, to make this determination.

The same pattern of adjustment based on experience with wholly domestic cases also appears in the last two chapters covered by this book: one concerned with recognition of foreign judgments,

---

[11]   Colorado River Water Conservation Dist. v. United States, 424 U.S. 800, 817 (1976) (stating that the "difference in general approach between state-federal concurrent jurisdiction and wholly federal concurrent jurisdiction stems from the virtually unflagging obligation of the federal courts to exercise the jurisdiction given them").

[12]   28 U.S.C. § 2283.

[13]   Piper Aircraft Co. v. Reyno, 454 U.S. 235, 249, 255 (1981).

[14]   *Id.* at 257.

the other with enforcement of arbitration agreements and arbitration awards. The two subjects resemble each other in deferring to the resolution of a dispute by an alternative system of adjudication, usually relieving American courts of any need to reexamine the merits of a claim. Recognition of foreign judgments follows the practice, if not the strict rules, established under the Full Faith and Credit Clause of the United States Constitution. That clause, and legislation enacted under it, allows American courts to refuse to recognize the judgments from courts of sister states only for a narrow range of reasons, primarily for lack of personal jurisdiction of the rendering court. Although the statutes governing recognition of foreign judgments recognize a much wider range of reasons for nonrecognition, American practice has been generally receptive to foreign judgments. A few exceptions stand out, especially judgments for libel, which are subjected to standards of free speech under the First Amendment, regardless of the law of the rendering forum.[15] Re-examining the basis for personal jurisdiction remains, however, the single most significant reason to deny recognition to a foreign judgment. More generally, procedural objections play a larger role in denying recognition to foreign judgments than substantive objections, particularly that a foreign judgment is "repugnant to the public policy of this state or the United States."[16] The latter ground rarely has been successfully invoked to prevent recognition of a foreign judgment.

The same could also be said of objections to arbitration, which seldom have invalidated arbitration clauses or prevented enforcement of arbitration awards. Arbitration has become a standard alternative to litigation, displacing it entirely in some areas, such as enforcement of bilateral investment treaties where investors from one country seek protection from adverse action, including judicial action, by the courts of the country in which they invest their money. This trend, too, follows one that has become established in domestic American law, and is based significantly on cases with international elements. Maritime law has given rise to several of these precedents, as have antitrust claims based on international markets. The argument for arbitration, while often based on the simplified and expedited procedures in arbitrations, rests more soundly on the parties' interest in replacing uncertain rules of personal jurisdiction and choice of law with a forum that they selected themselves and functioning according to rules that they control. Critics of the prevailing trend have argued that arbitration gives priority to freedom of contract over other values, particularly those of weaker parties to contracts of adhesion, but that criticism

---

[15] The SPEECH Act of 2010, 28 U.S.C. §§ 4101–4105 (2012).

[16] Uniform Foreign-Country Money Judgments Act § 4(c)(3) (2005).

loses force outside the domain of consumer and employment claims, which are relatively rare in transnational civil litigation. The real question posed by the prevalence of arbitration in this field comes from the lenient attitude that courts take toward enforcement of arbitration awards. With the gradual accumulation of precedent, both by courts and arbitrators, the law administered outside the courts might diverge from the law officially declared within them. The law in arbitration might become a wayward variation of the law actually on the books.

As these last two subjects illustrate, the law governing transnational civil litigation remains deeply intertwined with the law applicable to purely domestic disputes. It also invites a comparative assessment of its relation to the laws of other nations, both in how it fits with domestic law and how it fits with the laws of other nations. This book will not undertake a comprehensive account of the law of our major trading partners, but it must offer an analysis of the points of difference and friction between American and foreign law. What other nations do both informs an evaluation of our law and indicates ways in which it might be brought into greater conformity with the law elsewhere. Despite continued disputes over the weight to be given to foreign law as a precedent within our legal system, it has traditionally assumed a significant role in transnational cases. The same is true of international law as a coordinating device to assure a degree of harmony in resolving international disputes. Reliance upon it, especially in the form of customary international law, has proved to be controversial, but adaptation of American law to its requirements has been a principle dating back to the Marshall Court.[17] Ambivalence toward foreign law and international law has tempered their reception into American law, making approval and reconciliation dependent upon different issues and different contexts. This book addresses the salient issues on which these encounters have occurred.

The introduction in this chapter presents a whirlwind tour of the subjects covered by this book. It cannot do justice to the intricacy of the issues posed by each of them. Part of the intricacy derives from the interaction of the different sources of law just discussed. The parties can exploit the different sources of law and the different perspectives that can be brought to bear on a single case to obtain strategic advantages, not necessarily related to the purposes of the underlying law. The same incentives exist, of course, in domestic litigation, but they do not operate over the same range of issues and tactics. No matter how complicated, a purely domestic case does not raise the possibility of dismissal in favor of foreign proceedings and

---

[17]   Murray v. Schooner Charming Betsy, 6 U.S. (2 Cranch) 64, 118 (1804).

application of foreign law. This observation may amount to no more than a truism, but it is one that defines the field of transnational civil litigation. The range of issues in this field creates a striking contrast between high principle and low strategic interests. From considerations of sovereignty, individual rights, and political accountability, arguments can quickly be drawn that serve the immediate self-interest of the parties. General propositions, as Justice Holmes remarked, may not decide concrete cases, but they do generate more specific standards, which often are determinative.[18] The question of how to frame those standards is of crucial interest to the parties, to judges, and to all the institutions that make the law in this field.

Much of the effort, and most of the controversy, in international cases concern such questions of implementation of general principles in more, or less, determinate rules. Yet determinacy represents only one dimension in the assessment of legal standards, and only one extreme along that dimension. The capacity of the law to adapt and develop lies at the opposite extreme and constitutes a persistent feature of the law in this field. Legal principles need not have immediate effects to result in enduring consequences. The increasing protection of human rights, mentioned earlier, has resulted from a process of continued demands for immediate action, often in the face of urgent crises, but whether or not these demands have been met, the cumulative effect of repeated attention to the issue has resulted in fitful progress. The same could be said of the much less salient issue of discovery of information overseas. Repeated requests for information have led to a gradual accommodation between broad discovery in this country and broad protection of private documents elsewhere. Bank secrecy laws, for instance, have given way to cooperation in law enforcement and tax collection, no matter how grudging it has been on either side. International civil litigation must take account of all these shifting sources of law and policy, and reconcile them with established procedural rules. The reconciliation must come from both directions, adapting both procedure and substance to develop workable rules. Those rules need not be permanent, in the sense of precluding further change, but they must do more than offer Justice Robert's restricted railroad ticket, "good for this day and train only."[19]

The disturbing tendency in the field, perhaps drawn from developments in conflict of laws, is to rely upon flexible standards rather than determinate rules. Analysis of minimum contacts and the reasonableness of exercising personal jurisdiction exemplify this

---

[18] Lochner v. New York, 198 U.S. 45, 76 (1905) (Holmes, J., dissenting) (noting that "[g]eneral propositions do not decide concrete cases").

[19] Smith v. Allwright, 321 U.S. 649 (1944).

approach. It has been partially offset by the attempt to formulate presumptions, such as that against the extraterritorial application of federal statutes, which cast the burden of resolving doubts in close cases on the disfavored position. Presumptions of this kind, however, do not strictly follow the rules of evidence, since the issues to be resolved are matters of law rather than fact. In this analogical form, presumptions leave open the crucial issue of how strong an argument must be to overcome the force of the presumption. The attempt to bring determinacy to the field by these means can be only partly successful. This book seeks to identify more definite rules, where they can be found, and to concede the need for indeterminate standards, where they are necessary. In the process, the analysis offered here seeks to offer more than a snapshot of where the law is today. It also seeks to identify the trends that might take the law in another direction and shape its content for the future. We begin with personal jurisdiction as an example, as it is both familiar from courses on civil procedure and informative of the distinctive demands and developing changes in the field of transnational civil litigation.

Chapter I

PERSONAL JURISDICTION, TERRITORIAL POWER, AND INDIVIDUAL RIGHTS

Personal jurisdiction originates in concepts of territorial sovereignty and due process, familiar from civil procedure, and illustrates the inherent tension between power at the collective level of the nation state and rights at the level of individual entitlements. At the very beginning, these competing concepts provide a window into the fundamental questions that animate the law of international civil litigation and into the range of acceptable answers to those questions. They do the same in purely domestic cases as well, although not in the heightened form that comes with considering the power of national sovereigns. Personal jurisdiction in domestic cases has had to adapt to the complexities of American federalism and it was first modeled on Justice Story's theory of sovereign relations in his Commentaries on the Conflict of Laws.[1] International and domestic cases have shared a common analysis of personal jurisdiction that goes back to the beginning and to the foundations of modern procedure.

The Supreme Court overhauled those foundations in the middle of the twentieth century in *International Shoe Co. v. Washington*,[2] without, however, questioning the equivalence of the rules for personal jurisdiction in domestic and international cases. The abstract standard formulated by the Court required "only that in order to subject a defendant to a judgment in personam, if he be not present within the territory of the forum, he have certain minimum contacts with it such the maintenance of the suit does not offend 'traditional notions of fair play and substantial justice.' "[3] This standard for jurisdiction under the Due Process Clause has since taken more particular form, chiefly in the distinction between specific and general jurisdiction with roots in the opinion in *International Shoe*. Specific jurisdiction depends on relation between the defendant, the forum, and the cause of action. The defendant must have contacts with the forum related to the plaintiff's claim. General jurisdiction dispenses with this last component of specific jurisdiction and allows the assertion of any claim the plaintiff has against the defendant. To offset the breadth of general jurisdiction, the plaintiff

---

[1]   Pennoyer v. Neff, 95 U.S. 714, 722–23 (1878).

[2]   326 U.S. 310 (1945).

[3]   *Id.* at 316 (quoting Milliken v. Meyer, 311 U.S. 457, 463 (1940)).

must be "essentially at home" in the forum, either as an individual domiciled there or as a corporation with its place of incorporation or headquarters there, or some similar substantial connection.

International cases have figured prominently in the formulation of principles of general jurisdiction, and less so, but still significantly, in specific jurisdiction cases. This chapter therefore begins by examining general jurisdiction and then proceeds to specific jurisdiction. Other bases of jurisdiction then are taken up briefly, along with the procedures for raising objections to personal jurisdiction. These topics carry over to subjects discussed in later chapters and cross-references are made accordingly. Service of process within the forum and consent to jurisdiction constitute two crucial means of acquiring power over the defendant. The first is narrowly available against individuals, while the second has proved to be a widely adopted alternative to government-imposed rules. Both illustrate the utility of clearly specified means of acquiring personal jurisdiction. The methods of objecting to personal jurisdiction raise important issues about how much the defendant must accede to the power of the forum, even in order to challenge its assertion in a timely and sufficient manner. This chapter then turns to the role of statutory law in expanding and defining the appropriate scope of jurisdiction. Legislatures in the United States, and particularly Congress, have taken only an episodic and secondary role in identifying the cases suitable for the exercise of jurisdiction. This also ties into the discussion of the venue in a later chapter. This chapter concludes with a brief comparison of American procedures with those of the European Union.

The overriding theme throughout this chapter is the desirability and difficulty of distilling workable rules from the conflict between territorial sovereignty and individual rights. This conflict becomes especially acute when, as in many of the close cases on personal jurisdiction, the events giving rise to the claim took place overseas. In these cases, the extraterritorial reach of American jurisdiction can become the first step toward the extraterritorial application of American law. Both tendencies, although not precisely correlated with one another, raise the question of what the defendant could have done to insulate itself from the reach of American law and American courts. Existing law takes this issue of individual rights and merges it with a general inquiry into the overall fairness of exercising jurisdiction. An inquiry along these lines finds support in the reference to "fair play and substantial justice" in *International Shoe*, yet it does little to reconcile the collective concern over sovereignty with the individual concern over fairness. An analysis of the cases on general jurisdiction provides a way to bridge the gap between these very different considerations and we turn to those now.

A. General Jurisdiction

A nation's assertion of power over individuals and firms with strong and continuing connections to it presents the strongest case for legitimacy: for taking private persons to have acquiesced in the exercise of government authority over them. This argument has not, to be sure, persuaded all critics of government authority, who argue that an individual or a firm might have found itself within national territory for reasons wholly beyond its control and with little realistic prospect of exit.[4] The situation of residents nevertheless contrasts dramatically with the situation of nonresidents, whose ties to the forum state might be minimal or nonexistent. "Residents" in this context includes individuals who are citizens, domiciliaries, or resident aliens of the forum, and artificial persons who are incorporated, created, headquartered, or have similarly substantial ties there. "Nonresidents" include all other defendants. The case for asserting jurisdiction over them suffers from a serious weakness not present for residents. Nonresidents have already decided to distance themselves from the forum and its exercise of power by not becoming residents, and so jurisdiction over them must be judged by different standards. Otherwise, no one could ever take any steps to insulate themselves from the forum's power.

Most lawyers would find this conclusion to be obvious, but important implications follow from it. First, the category of general jurisdiction must be narrowly confined so that it does not sweep nonresidents into the power of a government they properly sought to avoid. Accordingly, in recent cases, the Supreme Court has emphasized the strict requirements for asserting general jurisdiction. It represents a difference in kind, not in degree, as *International Shoe* itself cautioned in warning against making jurisdiction a matter of "a little more or a little less." But second, where this difference in kind exists, it dramatically expands the scope of personal jurisdiction, creating a kind of "universal jurisdiction," over claims that might arise anywhere in the world. So corporations can be sued in their home state for any kind of claim that might have arisen anywhere. The availability of this form of jurisdiction puts more pressure on doctrines like *forum non conveniens* and choice of law, to be considered in later chapters. In purely procedural terms, dismissals for lack of personal jurisdiction give way to dismissals for *forum non conveniens* and dismissals on the merits as the dispositive ruling in litigation. And third, even within personal jurisdiction, the close cases shift from general jurisdiction to specific jurisdiction. As the former becomes narrower, the latter becomes more important. It

---

[4] A. JOHN SIMMONS, MORAL PRINCIPLES AND POLITICAL OBLIGATION 57–100 (1979).

must, however, respond to the same concerns over preserving the freedom of nonresidents to structure their activities to avoid contact with the forum. On this view, assessing whether the defendant properly took steps to limit its activities and their effects within the forum becomes the focus of jurisdictional analysis.

This theme appears repeatedly in the Supreme Court's decisions on general jurisdiction. It begins with a case upholding jurisdiction, *Perkins v. Benguet Consolidated Mining Co.*[5] The corporate defendant there ordinarily conducted most of its business in the Philippines, where it was also incorporated. During the Japanese occupation of the Philippines during World War II, however, the corporation shut down its ordinary operations and its president, general manager, and principal shareholder conducted its residual operations in Ohio during and after the war. The plaintiff sued the corporation there on a claim for failure to issue dividends and stock arising elsewhere. The Supreme Court upheld jurisdiction because virtually all of the corporation's activities took place in Ohio until its operations could be restarted in the Philippines. Having taken refuge in Ohio, the corporation submitted to its jurisdiction.

This decision, although recognizing general jurisdiction, set the tone for subsequent decisions that denied it. In *Helicopteros Nacionales de Colombia v. Hall*,[6] the plaintiff tried to obtain jurisdiction in Texas over a Colombian corporation that entered into contracts with Texas defendants, with respect to wrongful death claims from the crash of a helicopter in Peru. The Colombian corporation did business in Texas but not enough to "constitute the kind of continuous and systematic general business contacts the Court found to exist in *Perkins*."[7] The case proceeded on the assumption that the wrongful death claims did not arise from the corporation's activities in Texas, so that plaintiffs could not rely upon specific jurisdiction. Doing business with Texas residents did not, by itself, subject the corporation to jurisdiction on the same terms as the residents themselves.

"Doing business" nevertheless became a way of circumventing the strict requirements of general jurisdiction, widely used by the lower courts. Taking a phrase out of context from *International Shoe*, courts frequently upheld jurisdiction when the defendant engaged in "continuous and systematic" activities of the forum even if they were unrelated to the plaintiff's claim.[8] The opinion in *International Shoe*,

---

[5]   342 U.S. 437 (1952).

[6]   466 U.S. 408 (1984).

[7]   *Id.* at 416.

[8]   Mary Twitchell, *Why We Keep Doing Business with Doing-Business Jurisdiction*, 2001 U. CHI. LEGAL F. 171.

however, limited this phrase to cases of specific jurisdiction, in which the "continuous and systematic" activities "also g[a]ve rise to the liabilities sued on."[9] The courts seemed to be open to this misinterpretation of precedent partly as a means of avoiding the intricate analysis of the relationship between the defendant, the forum, and the cause of action required by specific jurisdiction. Partly, too, the general standard of "fair play and substantial justice" in *International Shoe* supported the conclusion that once a defendant corporation surpassed a certain threshold of activity in the forum, it could be fairly subjected to personal jurisdiction.

Two cases taking this broad view of general jurisdiction eventually made their way to the Supreme Court. In *Goodyear Dunlop Tires Operations, S.A. v. Brown*,[10] the Court refused to find general jurisdiction in North Carolina over the foreign subsidiaries of an American tire manufacturer with respect to a claim arising from a bus accident outside of Paris involving the blowout of a tire manufactured by one of the subsidiaries in Turkey. The Court reframed the test for jurisdiction to cases where the defendants' "affiliation with the State are so 'continuous and systematic' as to render them essentially at home in the forum State."[11] The American parent corporation did not challenge jurisdiction, although all of its activities in the forum were unrelated to the claim.[12] Those activities entered into the Court's analysis only by way of rejecting the plaintiffs' attempt to attribute the parent's activities in the forum to the subsidiaries. This attempt to "pierce the corporate veil" failed because the plaintiffs' had failed to raise it in the courts below and did so only belatedly in their briefs in the Supreme Court.[13] As a result, they were left with only the American parent as a defendant over whom they could acquire jurisdiction, but they had only the weakest claim against it on the merits because it was not involved at all in manufacturing or marketing the tire in question.

The subsequent decision, *Daimler AG v. Bauman*,[14] cast doubt even on the assumption that general jurisdiction could be acquired over a parent corporation in these circumstances. The plaintiffs there asserted human rights claims against *Daimler AG*, the German parent corporation of subsidiaries in both Argentina and in the United States. The plaintiffs accused the Argentine subsidiary of complicity in the "dirty war" by the Argentine military government against leftist and labor groups. The American subsidiary did

---

9 *Id.* at 182.

10 131 S.Ct. 2846 (2011).

11 *Id.* at 2851.

12 *Id.* at 2850.

13 *Id.* at 2857 & n.6.

14 134 S.Ct. 746 (2014).

substantial business in California, where the plaintiffs sued in federal court. The plaintiffs sought to use the acts of the Argentine subsidiary in Argentina to impose liability upon the German parent and the acts of the American subsidiary in California to assert general jurisdiction there. Essentially, the plaintiffs wanted to treat the subsidiaries as agents of the parent corporation. As in *Goodyear*, the Supreme Court rejected this attempt to ignore corporate structure for purposes of ruling on personal jurisdiction. Moreover, the Court went on to hold that even if the activities of the American subsidiary in California could be attributed to the German parent, those activities at most justified general jurisdiction over the American subsidiary, not the German parent, because of the magnitude of the latter's actions outside of California. *Daimler AG* was incorporated and had its principal place of business in Germany. For the same reason, the Court also cast doubt on the assumption, which it made only for purposes of this case, that the American subsidiary could be subjected to general jurisdiction based only on the business it did in California, since it was incorporated and had its principal place of business outside that state. The Court summarized its reasoning by emphasizing the principle that defendants should be able " 'to structure their primary conduct with some minimum assurance as to where that conduct will and will not render them liable to suit.' "[15]

As both *Goodyear* and *Daimler* illustrate, this principle gives corporations considerable freedom to adapt their corporate structure to limit their exposure to lawsuits. Plaintiffs have to exercise more care in identifying the correct component of the corporate structure to sue and in ascertaining where jurisdiction might be asserted over it. An element of jurisdiction by necessity enters into these calculations, but if this form of jurisdiction exists at all, it adds little to general jurisdiction, which itself serves to provide the plaintiff with at least one forum in which to sue.[16] Any argument for jurisdiction by necessity presupposes the absence of any alternative forum, including one that could exercise general jurisdiction. Hence, in *Helicopteros*, the plaintiffs argued unsuccessfully jurisdiction by necessity because the Colombian corporation could have been sued there or where the claim arose, in Peru.[17] If plaintiffs find forums such as these to be unacceptable, general jurisdiction no longer provides them with a broad basis for suing in the United States. The federal structure of American government also impedes resort to general jurisdiction in a particular state, because it is that state, and not the United States as a whole, in which the defendant must be

---

[15] *Id.* at 762 (quoting Burger King Corp. v. Rudzewicz, 471 U.S. 462, 472 (1985)).

[16] *Id.* at 760.

[17] *Helicopteros*, 466 U.S. at 419 & n.13.

"essentially at home." Even the federal courts largely rely upon state law in asserting personal jurisdiction and they remain bound by the limits imposed upon it, as in *Daimler*.[18] The division of the United States into separate states augments the division of private firms into separate corporations, making general jurisdiction available only in a few clearly defined forums. *Daimler* suggested, without quite deciding, that the place of incorporation and the principal place of business identified the only forums available for general jurisdiction.[19] Having done so, the Court emphasized that these limits had particular force in international cases because of the objections of other nations to the "exorbitant" exercise of jurisdiction.[20] Plaintiffs must now seek jurisdiction in alternative forums on grounds other than general jurisdiction, the most obvious ground being specific jurisdiction, to which we now turn.

B. Specific Jurisdiction

International Shoe itself upheld the exercise of specific jurisdiction, and in a series of subsequent decisions, the Supreme Court has elaborated on this holding, either finding a sufficient relationship between the defendant, the forum, and the plaintiff's claim to support jurisdiction on this ground or finding an insufficient relationship. Several of these decisions, like *International Shoe*, have "international" or "worldwide" in the name of a party and the title of the case, but they do not involve international cases. The Supreme Court has decided only a few cases of this kind and the distinctive issues that they raise, and this discussion focuses upon them. While the doctrinal standards nominally are the same for international and domestic cases, they differ in their implications, both practically and theoretically, in the international context. Practically, a foreign defendant might well face higher costs in litigating in an unfamiliar legal system far from home. And by the same token, if jurisdiction is denied, the plaintiff might be placed in the same position. Theoretically, the defendant might be frustrated that its attempts to insulate itself from the American legal system failed, and again, by the same token, if jurisdiction is denied, plaintiffs might find themselves submitting their claims to a foreign legal system.

The two decisions of the Supreme Court on specific jurisdiction in international cases both began by addressing the question whether putting goods into the stream of commerce was, by itself, sufficient to confer jurisdiction over a claim for death or injury from the use of the goods in the forum state. Neither case resulted in a majority opinion that either upheld or denied jurisdiction on this ground, so that the

---

[18] Fed. R. Civ. P. 4(k)(1)(A).

[19] *Daimler*, 134 S.Ct. at 761 & n.19.

[20] *Id.* at 761–62.

safest statement of the law now is that putting goods into the stream of commerce has never been held sufficient. The decisions concerned only jurisdiction under state law, so that contacts with the United States as a whole did not figure in the analysis. Hence the decisions offer the puzzling prospect of international civil litigation determined largely by the law governing interstate relations. The distinctive demands of international cases might, instead, require departure from the principles of due process applicable to interstate cases.

The first of these decisions, *Asahi Metal Industry Co. v. Superior Court*,[21] relied explicitly on the international features of the case, which arose from a motorcycle accident in California and involved a claim for indemnity by the Taiwanese manufacturer of the motorcycle tire, who had previously settled a wrongful death claim by the motorcyclist's next of kin, against the Japanese manufacturer of a valve that was incorporated into the tire. Because the claim for wrongful death had been settled, the case reduced to a claim between two foreign firms. The Supreme Court found no basis for jurisdiction consistent with "fair play and substantial justice," reasoning that "[t]he unique burdens placed upon one who must defend oneself in a foreign legal system should have significant weight in assessing the reasonableness of stretching the long arm of personal jurisdiction over national borders."[22] The territorial connection between the valve manufacturer and the California forum did not enter directly into this analysis because the Supreme Court was evenly divided on the question whether the Japanese valve manufacturer had sufficient contacts with California. Eight justices, on the other hand, endorsed a direct appeal to the "unreasonableness" of exercising jurisdiction.[23]

Although this reasoning resulted in a determinate outcome in *Asahi*, it introduced further indeterminacy into the test for personal jurisdiction under the Due Process Clause. Earlier decisions had identified the factors that went into finding reasonableness, using them to resolve close cases based on territorial contacts alone.[24] These factors include "the burden on the defendant," "the forum State's interest in adjudicating the dispute," "the plaintiff's interest in obtaining convenient and effective relief," "the interstate judicial system's interest in obtaining the most efficient resolution of controversies," and "the shared interest of the several States in furthering fundamental substantive social policies."[25] Yet those decisions also intimated that these factors operated in a one-sided

---

[21]   480 U.S. 102 (1987).

[22]   *Id.* at 114.

[23]   *Id.*

[24]   Burger King Corp. v. Rudzewicz, 471 U.S. 462, 476–78, 482–84 (1985); World-Wide Volkswagen Corp. v. Woodson, 444 U.S. 286, 292 (1980).

[25]   *World-Wide Volkswagen*, 444 U.S. at 292.

manner: mainly to defeat rather than to support jurisdiction. They "sometimes serve to establish the reasonableness of jurisdiction upon a less showing of minimum contracts than would otherwise be required. On the other hand, where a defendant who purposefully has directed his activities at forum residents seeks to defeat jurisdiction, he must present a compelling case that the presence of some other consideration would render jurisdiction unreasonable."[26] In order to support jurisdiction, the territorial threshold of minimum contacts still has to be met to support jurisdiction, if it can be watered down by consideration of these other factors. As in *Asahi*, however, these factors can defeat jurisdiction even if the existence of minimum contacts remains unclear.

The factors themselves contain a striking amount of indeterminacy in the analysis. They seem to include everything under the sun and to exclude nothing. They follow an approach characteristic of American Legal Realism in the early twentieth century, which tended to view definite rules as limited to the "law on the books," and to constitute misstatements of the "law in action," which was better captured by open-ended standards. That attitude, whatever its prevalence elsewhere in American law, dominated the "conflicts revolution" in personal jurisdiction and choice of law. The search for definite rules to handle admittedly hard cases gave way to an endorsement of broadly framed standards and multi-factor tests. The next chapter documents this trend with respect to choice of law, but it gained authoritative support from decisions like *International Shoe*, which led directly to the multiple factors that proved decisive in *Asahi*.

Read literally, *Asahi* places an added hurdle in the way of plaintiffs seeking to obtain jurisdiction in a forum with which the defendant has marginal contacts. Read more broadly, it creates greater uncertainty for both plaintiffs and defendants, leading them to agree to forum-selection clauses when they can. That alternative would have been available on the facts of *Asahi*, even though the case arose from a tort claim, because the indemnification claim that remained in the case derived from a contractual relationship. Genuine consent, as discussed in a subsequent section of this chapter, provides the firmest foundation for the assertion of government power over an individual or a firm. From this perspective, we might try to reconstruct the law of specific jurisdiction by considering what forum the parties would have agreed to if they could have entered into a contract. Such a hypothetical contract, however, might end up being as indeterminate as the existing analysis.

---

[26] *Burger King*, 471 U.S. at 477.

The second decision in an international context, *J. McIntyre Machinery, Ltd. v. Nicastro*,[27] also arose from an accident. The plaintiff was injured in New Jersey by a machine manufactured by the defendant, an English corporation with its operations there. The plaintiff sued in a New Jersey state court, but the Supreme Court found insufficient contacts between the defendant and the forum. The defendant had marketed its machines through an independent distributor for sale across the United States, but at most four of the machines, and perhaps only the one involved in the accident, were sold for use in New Jersey. The plurality opinion in the Supreme Court, for four justices, concluded that putting goods into the stream of commerce did not meet either of the applicable tests: whether that defendant "purposefully avails itself of the privilege of conducting activities within the forum State, thus invoking the benefits protections of its laws"[28] or whether "the defendant can be said to have targeted the forum."[29] A separate opinion for two justices held that the plaintiff had not met his burden of proving sufficient contacts with the forum, leaving open the question of exactly how they might have done so. Three justices dissented on the ground that marketing a product within the United States as a whole, with the result that it caused injury in the forum state, satisfied the requirement of minimum contacts with the forum.

Where *Asahi* raised the hurdles to finding personal jurisdiction cases based on reasonableness, *McIntyre* raised the hurdles based on contacts. Read together with the decisions on general jurisdiction, these decisions send the message to defendants that they can minimize their exposure to jurisdiction in the United States by restructuring their operations so that their products enter any particular state by the actions of a separate corporation. The corporation would have to be genuinely separate to foreclose the possibility of "piercing the corporate veil." A subsidiary corporation or an independent distributor would have to be outside the control of the defendant. Even that, of course, would not completely insulate the defendant from jurisdiction, as a simple variation on *McIntyre* makes clear. What if several hundred of the defendant's machines had been sold to buyers in New Jersey? For that matter, the defendant remained subject to jurisdiction in Ohio, where its American distributor had its principal place of business.[30]

---

[27]   131 S.Ct. 2780 (2011).

[28]   *J. McIntyre*, 131 S.Ct. at 2787 (2011) (opinion of Kennedy, J.) (plurality opinion) (quoting Hanson v. Denckla, 357 U.S. 235, 253 (1958)).

[29]   *J. McIntyre*, 131 S.Ct. at 2788 (plurality opinion).

[30]   Nicastro v. McInytre Machinery of America, Ltd., 987 A.2d 575, 592 (2010), *rev'd*, 131 S.Ct. 2790 (2011). For analysis of personal jurisdiction in these circumstances, *see* Burger King Corp. v. Rudzewicz, 471 U.S. 462, 478–87 (1985).

Yet the defendant has little to lose and much to gain by taking these precautions. Whether to take them depends upon the defendant's assessment of the overall costs and benefits, which may be determined largely by business considerations wholly apart from the cost of litigation. For operational reasons, the defendant may find it more efficient to structure its operations in one way rather than another. Courts cannot easily make this calculation, but even so, they can infer much from the defendant's failure to take such precautions. If, for instance, the defendant in *McIntyre* had distributed its machines itself in New Jersey, the courts there would have clearly had jurisdiction over it.[31] So, too, if the defendant had controlled the sale of its machines by the nominally independent distributor. Although some might decry the ability of multinational firms to profit from a national market by way of intermediaries, as the dissent did in *McIntyre*, most would agree on the converse proposition: multinational corporations that do not take precautions against engaging in activity in the forum should be subject to personal jurisdiction there over any resulting claims against them. The hard cases then come down to decisions about what the defendant could have done to avoid personal jurisdiction. As the Supreme Court has put it, defendants should be able "to structure their primary conduct with some minimum assurance as to where that conduct will and will not render them liable to suit."[32] Exactly how to preserve this freedom from jurisdiction cannot be determined in the abstract. For all their uncertainty, however, the recent decisions of the Supreme Court give some guidance about how defendants can protect themselves.

Conceptions of American federalism complicate the implications to be drawn from interstate cases in deciding international cases. The division of sovereignty into the national government and the government of the several states segments the division of jurisdiction, so that in most cases the applicable standards follow state boundaries. The limits on state power under the Due Process Clause of the Fourteenth Amendment effectively determine the exercise of most forms of personal jurisdiction by American courts. These limits apply of their own force to cases in state court and they are incorporated by reference in the main provision for personal jurisdiction in federal court, under the Federal Rules of Civil Procedure. Rule 4(k)(1)(A) authorizes the exercise of jurisdiction over a defendant "who is subject to the jurisdiction of a court of general jurisdiction in the state where the district court is located." State long-arm statutes therefore apply in federal court, and when they do,

---

[31] McGee v. International Life Ins. Co., 355 U.S. 220 (1957).

[32] *Burger King*, 471 U.S. at 472; *see* Daimler AG v. Bauman, 134 S.Ct. 746, 762 (2014).

the Due Process Clause of the Fourteenth Amendment applies as well.[33]

A separate Due Process Clause, in the Fifth Amendment, limits the power of the federal government. While that clause has been interpreted like its counterpart in the Fourteenth Amendment, it presumes a different set of territorial boundaries: those of the entire nation rather than any separate state. Accordingly, the defendant's contacts with the United States as a whole determine the scope of personal jurisdiction, supplemented by the reasonableness factors from *Asahi*. The Fifth Amendment applies whenever a federal statute or a Federal Rule of Civil Procedure provides for jurisdiction, without reference to state law. The antitrust laws, notably among federal statutes, provides for jurisdiction over a corporation "in any district wherein it may be found or transacts business" and process may be served "wherever it may be found," extending to claims that might arise anywhere in the world.[34] Even more broadly, Federal Rule 4(k)(2) creates a form of jurisdiction by necessity. If the plaintiff files a federal claim and if the defendant is not subject to jurisdiction in any state court, then any federal district court can exercise jurisdiction "consistent with the United States Constitution and laws."[35] If this provision had applied in *McIntyre*, the Court could have upheld jurisdiction based on the defendant's contacts with the entire United States.[36]

Nevertheless, the plurality opinion raised the possibility that a federal statute could have conferred jurisdiction, most plausibly by providing for federal subject-matter jurisdiction and then providing for personal jurisdiction under terms similar to the antitrust laws. In that scenario, the fact that the defendant marketed its products throughout the United States would have been decisive. The reasonableness factors from *Asahi* could not have defeated jurisdiction with respect to an injury in the United States from a product marketed here. Yet Congress has passed few such statutes and the Federal Rules have only a few provisions that extend personal jurisdiction to the full extent allowed by the Fifth Amendment.[37] All have very limited scope, confined to particular claims, as under the antitrust laws, or to exacting conditions, like jurisdiction by necessity under Rule 4(k)(2). Federal power to exercise personal jurisdiction remains more potential than actual

---

[33] *See Burger King*, 471 U.S. at 463–64.

[34] 15 U.S.C. § 22.

[35] Fed. R. Civ. P. 4(k).

[36] There was, however, no federal claim in *McIntyre*, and the defendant apparently could have been sued in state court in Ohio under the theory of *Burger King*.

[37] Fed. R. Civ. P. 4(k)(1)(B)–(C) & (2).

because it falls so far short of the constitutional limits on the power of the federal government. Yet it enables Congress to address particular problems that arise in international litigation, such as suits against foreign sovereigns, with broad provisions for personal jurisdiction when a claim falls within the exceptions to sovereign immunity.[38] Statutes like this one demonstrate that Congress could readily expand the scope of personal jurisdiction beyond that has currently conferred on the federal courts. Here as elsewhere in international civil litigation, what the law might become must be sharply distinguished from what it now is.

C. Presence and Consent

These added grounds for acquiring personal jurisdiction raise the question of how they are related to specific and general jurisdiction. Presence of the defendant within the forum, coupled with personal service of process, constituted the traditional paradigm for bringing the defendant within the power of the court. For several decades after *International Shoe*, scholars argued that that decision supplanted the traditional paradigm with contacts analysis and they almost succeeded. The Court itself went so far as to say that " 'traditional notions of fair play and substantial justice' can be as readily offended by the perpetuation of ancient forms that are no longer justified as by the adoption of new procedures that are inconsistent with the basic values of our constitutional heritage."[39] Yet in a unanimous decision, in *Burnham v. Superior Court*,[40] the Supreme Court revived personal service on an individual defendant as a sufficient means of acquiring personal jurisdiction. No opinion in *Burnham* commanded a majority of justices, but most of the justices took care to endorse *International Shoe*, finding its approach to be sufficient for acquiring personal jurisdiction, if not strictly necessary.[41]

The opinion makes a difference, particularly in human rights litigation, because personal service within the forum often is the only way to acquire personal jurisdiction over individuals who have engaged in human rights violations. If the violation has occurred overseas, without any activity in the United States, the court cannot assert specific jurisdiction over the defendant. The court might acquire general jurisdiction if the defendant resides in the forum state, but that form of jurisdiction closely resembles jurisdiction based on presence; both require the defendant to be present in the

---

[38]   28 U.S.C. § 1330(b).

[39]   Shaffer v. Heitner, 433 U.S. 186, 212 (1977).

[40]   495 U.S. 604 (1990).

[41]   Burnham v. Superior Court, 495 U.S. 604, 610 (1990) (opinion of Scalia, J.); *id.* at 629 (Brennan, J., concurring in the judgment).

forum, for general jurisdiction on a regular basis, and for presence, at the time of service of process. In fact, presence could be analyzed as a kind of general jurisdiction because it applies to any claim against the defendant, regardless of its connection to the forum, and both presence within the forum and residence there constitute a traditional form of acquiescing in the forum's exercise of power within its boundaries. Still, presence at the time of service of process hardly makes the defendant "essentially at home" at home in the forum. After *Burnham*, however, it does facilitate the acquisition of jurisdiction over defendants who otherwise remain beyond the forum's power.

This line of reasoning does not work as well, if it works at all, for corporations and other artificial persons.[42] If they have appointed an agent for service of process within the forum, they have effectively consented to personal jurisdiction and the validity of the consent remains as the only issue to be resolved.[43] The situation is more complicated, and the courts are divided, when the state requires the defendant to appoint an agent for service of process.[44] The state's power to require appointment of an agent must first be settled before the appointment can be taken to be valid. If they have not appointed an agent for this purpose, but they have other agents in the state, then the situation comes close to the facts of *International Shoe*, where salesmen of the defendant were served inside the forum. That opinion rejected the fiction of corporate presence as a sufficient means of acquiring jurisdiction and substituted the now-familiar analysis in terms of contacts. That analysis, or the validity of consent, now governs virtually all problems of personal jurisdiction over corporations and other artificial persons.

Consent as an independent basis for jurisdiction also must avoid the strictures against the fictions found in *International Shoe*, where the Court refused to hold the corporation subject to personal jurisdiction "by resort to the legal fiction that it has given its consent to service and suit, consent being implied from its presence in the state through the acts of its authorized agents."[45] More recent decisions have relied upon actual consent in the form of a contract and then evaluated the validity of the contract, typically on grounds

---

[42] *See* Martinez v. Aero Caribbean, 764 F.3d 1062, 1066–69 (9th Cir. 2014), *cert. denied*, 135 S.Ct. 2310 (2015).

[43] For an example of appointment of an agent for service of process by individuals, *see* National Equipment Rental, Ltd. v. Szukhent, 375 U.S. 311, 316 (1964).

[44] Note, *Registration Statues, Personal Jurisdiction, and the Problem of Predictability*, 103 COLUM. L. REV. 1163 (2003). Since the state has required appointment of agent, the defendant has not unambiguously consented to service in the state.

[45] *International Shoe*, 326 U.S. at 318.

of unconscionability: that the contract was one of adhesion that unfairly imposed procedural burdens upon the weaker party. The Supreme Court has addressed these questions mainly in admiralty cases, which almost invariably have an international dimension. The Court in *Bremen v. Zapata Off-Shore Co.* upheld a forum-selection clause in a contract of towage, which required any dispute between the parties to be brought in the High Court in London.[46] The Court found "compelling reasons why a freely negotiated private international agreement, unaffected by fraud, undue influence, or overweening bargaining power, such as that involved here, should be given full effect."[47] That contract was between business firms, but the Court later extended the reasoning of *Zapata* to a contract between passengers and a cruise line. In *Carnival Cruise Lines, Inc. v. Shute*,[48] the voyage went from Los Angeles to Puerto Vallarta, Mexico, and one of the plaintiffs was injured when she slipped and fell during a tour of the ship. She and her husband sued in federal court in Washington State, but the court granted summary judgment to the defendant because the contract provided that all disputes had to be litigated in Florida, where the defendant had its principal place of business.[49] The Supreme Court found this clause to be enforceable, although it was in a form contract, because it met the requirements of "fundamental fairness."[50]

The clauses at issue in *Bremen* and in *Carnival Cruise Lines* were mandatory, but presumably the Court would take at least as lenient an approach toward enforcement for clauses that simply allowed, but did not require, litigation to be brought in the selected forum. That approach has carried over to related issues, like the validity of choice-of-law clauses and of arbitration clauses. The former often accompany choice-of-forum clauses, to assure that the chosen forum can apply its own law to the disputes, and the latter effectively are choice-of-forum clauses, although they designate a private forum rather than a public forum to resolve the dispute. The presumption of validity accorded to these clauses depends fundamentally upon freedom of contract, both as an efficient means of resolving otherwise contested issues in litigation and as a right of the parties to structure their relationship. We have already seen how consent provides the firmest foundation for the legitimate exercise of government power. The cases upholding these contractual clauses take consent several steps further: first, in providing a substitute

---

[46]   407 U.S. 1 (1972).

[47]   *Bremen*, 407 U.S. at 12–13.

[48]   499 U.S. 585 (1991).

[49]   Today, the proper form for enforcing a forum-selection clause is a motion to transfer under 28 U.S.C. § 1404. Atlantic Marine Constr. Co. v. U.S. District Court, 134 S.Ct. 568 (2013).

[50]   *Atlantic Marine*, 134 S.Ct. at 596.

forum and often specifying the law to be applied; second, in narrowing the grounds for challenging formal consent by a written contract; and third, by giving parties in a strong negotiating position the incentive to use it to obtain advantageous terms for resolving disputes. Subsequent chapters on choice of law and arbitration take up the implications of these steps. They all began, however, with the endorsement of forum-selection clauses. These resolve the inherent uncertainty in the cases in which personal jurisdiction is doubtful, but they also raise the question whether one party has gone too far in resolving those doubts in its favor. Present law generally answers that question in the negative, but it remains to be seen if the concept of "fundamental fairness," deployed in *Carnival Cruise Lines*, can impose some effective constraints.

The trend in favor of enforcing forum-selection clauses, evident in these decisions of the United States Supreme Court, has carried over to European Union law and to international law. The Brussels Regulation endorses the validity of forum-selection clauses selecting a Member State "unless the agreement is null and void as to its substantive validity under the law of that Member State."[51] These clauses are mandatory in the sense that they confer exclusive jurisdiction on the selected Member State, unless they provide expressly to the contrary. They cannot, however, be included in all contracts. Contracts marked by a systematic imbalance in bargaining power, such as those with consumers and employees, are excepted, as are contracts where the regulation itself provides for exclusive jurisdiction in another Member State.[52] In international law, the Hague Choice of Court Convention establishes very similar rules for enforcing exclusive choice of court agreements, although with a lengthier list of excepted contracts.[53] The Convention, however, has yet to achieve a sufficient number of ratifications to go into force. When it does, it will also give enhanced preclusive effect to judgments rendered by a court whose jurisdiction derives from a valid exclusive choice of court agreement.[54]

D. Statutes and Rules on Personal Jurisdiction

State "long-arm statutes" have made the greatest legislative contribution to the law of personal jurisdiction. Paradoxically, they have done so by reinforcing the predominant role of the Due Process

---

[51] Regulation (EU) 1215/2012 of the European Parliament and of the Council of 12 December 2012 on jurisdiction and the recognition and enforcement of judgments in civil and commercial matters (recast). Official Journal, OJ 20 December 2012, L 351/1, art. 25(1).

[52] *Id.* art. 25(4).

[53] Convention on Choice of Court Agreements (Concluded 30 June 2005) arts. 2–3.

[54] *Id.* arts. 8–9.

Clause of the Fourteenth Amendment in jurisdictional analysis. Federal courts, as noted earlier, typically rely upon state law to determine the scope of their own jurisdiction. That jurisdiction, to the extent that it extends beyond service of process inside the state, must be conferred by the legislature. State long-arm statutes accomplished this extension in the wake of *International Shoe*, extending the "long arm" of the state law beyond the state's borders.

Long-arm statutes come in three varieties: those, as in California and Rhode Island, that by their terms extend personal jurisdiction to the constitutional limits; those, as in Virginia and Texas, that have more restrictive provisions but that have been interpreted to reach to the constitutional limits; and those that have similar restrictive provisions, as in New York and Florida, but stop short of the constitutional limits.[55] The details of these statutes need not concern us, since they vary from state to state, but they all have in common an explicit or implicit reference to the Due Process Clause, which sets the terms of the debate over their effects. Long-arm statutes extend expressly or by implication as far as the Due Process Clause allows, or not quite as far. Consequently, due process dominates the analysis of jurisdiction in international cases, going so far as to be adapted to foreign legal systems in the concept of "international due process." As discussed in the chapter on recognition of foreign judgments, that concept figures prominently in the evaluation of personal jurisdiction and fair procedures in foreign courts.

The Due Process Clause of the Fifth Amendment takes on a subsidiary role to the Due Process Clause of the Fourteenth Amendment. This is not because the Fifth Amendment imposes more limits on the federal government than the Fourteenth Amendment does on the states, but because it applies only to those few instances in which the federal government has asserted personal jurisdiction beyond the boundaries of state authority. Federal Rule of Civil Procedure 4(k) creates or recognizes most of those instances of extended jurisdiction, beyond those from state courts adopted by cross-reference in Rule 4(k)(1)(A). Subdivision (B) provides for joinder of needed parties who can be served within 100 miles of the federal courthouse. It accomplishes a modest extension of power beyond service within a state, but does not, in any event, provide for service outside the United States, since the rule requires service "within a judicial district of the United States." Subdivision C recognizes the force of federal statutes to extend jurisdiction, as it must to prevent a conflict between the Federal Rules and federal legislation. The federal antitrust laws, as noted earlier, and the federal securities

---

[55] Douglas D. McFarland, *Dictum Run Wild: How Long-Arm Statutes Extended to the Limits of Due Process,* 84 B.U.L. REV. 491 (2004).

laws[56] furnish the most prominent examples of federal statutes asserting power over defendants outside the United States. By referring to federal statutes, subdivision C does finesse the question of whether the Federal Rules can affect personal jurisdiction at all, since Rule 82 provides that the rules "do not extend or limit the jurisdiction of the district courts or the venue of actions in those courts." This reference to "jurisdiction," however, has long since been interpreted to mean only subject-matter jurisdiction.[57]

Nevertheless, Rule 4(k)(2) does achieve a significant expansion of personal jurisdiction, particularly in international cases. When the plaintiff sues on a federal claim and when "the defendant is not subject to jurisdiction in any state's courts of general jurisdiction," the jurisdiction of a federal court extends to the limits those imposed by "the Constitution and laws." Strong arguments in theory support jurisdiction by necessity under the conditions specified in this provision, but they have proved awkward to implement. In theory, when a plaintiff has a claim under federal law, she should have the opportunity to present it to an American court. If no state court has jurisdiction, then no federal court has jurisdiction under Rule 4(k)(1)(A). In the absence of a federal statute providing for jurisdiction, a plaintiff can sue in this country only under Rule 4(k)(2). The rule, however, forces plaintiffs to make the strong showing that no state court of general jurisdiction has power over the defendant. Some courts have tried to alleviate this burden by switching part of it to the defendant, in particular, the identification of a state court in which it could be sued.[58] The defendant then waives any argument that it could be sued in any state that it does not identify. Exactly how this burden shifting works in practice can become complicated, revealing just how exacting the conditions for establishing jurisdiction by necessity are. Once those conditions are met, the Fifth Amendment then allows the plaintiff to rely upon all of the defendant's contacts with the United States in order to establish jurisdiction.

The relative scarcity of federal statutes extending personal jurisdiction overseas conforms to the subordinate role taken by statutory law in this area. Congress and the state legislatures have been content to leave the main outlines of the subject to be determined by the court as a matter of due process. Most cases come down to the application of constitutional standards to the particular

---

[56]   15 U.S.C. § 77v.

[57]   Fed. R. Civ. P., Adv. Comm. Notes, 39 F.R.D. 98–99 (1966); Benjamin Kaplan, *Continuing Work of the Civil Committee: 1966 Amendments of the Federal Rules of the Civil Procedure* (pt. 1), 81 HARV. L. REV. 356, 380–84 (1967).

[58]   United States v. Swiss American Bank, Ltd., 191 F.3d 30, 41–42 (1st Cir. 1999).

facts of the case. In the abstract, clear-cut rules would do a much better job of defining the scope of personal jurisdiction, leaving it to legislatures to frame such rules within the bounds of due process. Yet as a matter of experience, state long-arm statutes reveal the difficulty of drafting clear-cut rules and of applying them to stop short of the constitutional limits. Congress also has not enacted rules in this form. Instead, it either has not acted at all, leaving plaintiffs with the terms of Rule 4(k) and primarily its reference to state law in subdivision (1)(A), or it has simply provided that the defendant may be served wherever it may be found, implicitly accepting only the limits on jurisdiction under the Due Process Clause of the Fifth Amendment. Congress could refine the standards for personal jurisdiction in the federal courts in the future, but based on past experience, it is far more likely to engage in selective expansion for particular causes of action.

E. Objecting to Personal Jurisdiction

The rules on acquiring personal jurisdiction have generated further rules on how to object to it, either in the original proceeding in which jurisdiction was asserted or in collateral proceedings attacking any resulting judgment. Objections to personal jurisdiction have historically been tangled up with the presence in the forum as a basis for jurisdiction. Consequently, in the original proceeding, a defendant could object to personal jurisdiction only by way of a "special appearance": if they only objected to personal jurisdiction, they were not considered present in the forum for purposes of service of process. That rule has weakened, but still retains considerable strength, particularly in requiring motions to dismiss for lack of personal jurisdiction to be made early in the proceedings. In the federal system, the defendant waives any objection to personal jurisdiction if it is not made in the first set of motions or in the answer, whichever comes first.[59] Some states go further and impose a waiver of the objection if it is overruled and the defendant fails to take an immediate appeal, but instead defends on the merits.[60] Foreign nations impose similar limits on objections to personal jurisdiction.[61]

The modern rationale for the rule departs from the literal implications of presence to the desirability of promptly determining the court's jurisdiction. A finding of no jurisdiction results in the invalidation of all that preceded it in the litigation, wasting all the expense and effort that the parties and the court have put into the

---

[59] Fed. R. Civ. P. 12(h)(1).

[60] *E.g.,* Cal. Code Civ. P. § 410.10.

[61] Somportex Ltd. v. Philadelphia Chewing Gum Corp., 453 F.2d 435, 442 (3d Cir. 1971), cert. denied, 405 U.S. 1017 (1972).

case without making progress towards a resolution on the merits. After a dismissal for lack of jurisdiction, the plaintiff remains free to re-file the action in a court that has jurisdiction. Requiring a prompt objection meets constitutional requirements, so long as it does not deprive the defendant of a fair opportunity to object to personal jurisdiction. That opportunity derives from the fundamental right of a defendant to protect itself from the power of the forum. The defendant must submit to the power of the forum only to the limited extent of adjudicating its objections to personal jurisdiction. It need not waive those objections in the very act of making them.

Yet because the standards for personal jurisdiction are so indeterminate, litigation of that issue can become protracted and complicated. In *Insurance Co. of Ireland v. Compagnie des Bauxites de Guinee*,[62] it resulted in discovery orders that the defendant refused to obey. As a sanction, the district court took the objection to personal jurisdiction to be waived, a ruling eventually upheld by the Supreme Court. This decision stands for the unexceptional proposition that a court always has jurisdiction to determine jurisdiction. Although it appears to be slightly paradoxical for a court determine its own jurisdiction if it doesn't *have* jurisdiction, that same court usually is the tribunal in the best position to resolve this question. From the defendant's point of view, by lodging an objection with the court, the defendant has agreed to have it resolved according to the forum's rules.

On the other hand, if the defendant does not make a special appearance and object, the rules for collateral attack on any resulting judgment come into play. These rules protect the defendant from the burden even of litigating the issue of personal jurisdiction in the forum. In purely domestic cases, the defendant can fail to appear in the forum and then take a default judgment. When the plaintiff seeks to enforce the judgment, wherever the defendant has assets that can satisfy the amount assessed against him, the defendant can then raise the objection to personal jurisdiction in those proceedings. Note that this form of collateral attack only applies to default judgments. If the defendant appears in the initial proceedings, and either waives the objection to personal jurisdiction by failing to make it in a timely manner or loses on the resolution of that objection, the resulting judgment precludes him from raising the issue again.[63]

In international cases, the rules for recognition of judgment allow greater scope for collateral attack. The strict rules for recognition of sister-state judgments under the Full Faith and Credit Clause do not apply, and several exceptions allow the enforcing court

---

[62]   456 U.S. 694 (1982).

[63]   Baldwin v. Iowa State Traveling Men's Ass'n, 283 U.S. 522, 525–26 (1931).

to disregard the judgment of the rendering court. Among these exceptions is lack of personal jurisdiction, which the defendant can invoke in the enforcing court even if the rendering court determined that it had jurisdiction.[64] This exception is hemmed in by a number of qualifications, and even more so, by the strong tendency of American courts to recognize foreign judgments.[65] The courts here often entertain objections to foreign judgments based on lack of personal jurisdiction, but most of the time, they overrule the objection and recognize the judgment.[66] The flexibility of the resulting practice protects residents, and others with assets in this country, from instances of truly excessive jurisdiction exercised by courts elsewhere.

F. Exorbitant Jurisdiction Under European Union Law

In the European Union, excessive extension of personal jurisdiction goes under the heading of "exorbitant" jurisdiction, which corresponds to a denial of due process in American law. The Brussels Regulation determines the effect of judgments within the European Union: judgments by a court of a member state sought to be recognized in another member state. The Regulation performs the same function as the Full Faith and Credit and Due Process Clauses in the United States Constitution, although it does so in more elaborate terms that leave less room for judicial interpretation. In this respect, the Regulation follows the European tradition, from civil law countries, of depending more on statutes and rules than on judge-made law. Since the Regulation covers the United Kingdom as a member state, this tendency now has carried over to and partially superseded the common law in its country of origin.

The greatest contrast between the Regulation and American law lies less in content than in form. European courts exercise jurisdiction along lines broadly similar to American courts, relying upon the location of the defendant's actions and their effects; the defendant's residence, domicile, nationality, and their analogues for corporations; and giving effect to a wide range of forum-selection clauses. The Regulation deploys these concepts, however, in rules far more definite than the abstract standards of *International Shoe*. The regulation also distinguishes between different types of claims, for instance, increasing the scope of jurisdiction for claims of personal injury and decreasing the scope of forum-selection clauses, to exclude

---

[64] Uniform Foreign-Country Money Judgments Recognition Act § 4(a)(2) (2005).

[65] *Id.* § 5.

[66] *See* Chapter 7.

consumer and employment contracts.[67] For nationals from member states, jurisdiction generally depends upon domicile, with the addition of a "white list" of accepted additional bases of jurisdiction, for instance, in tort cases, "for the place where the harmful event occurred or may occur."[68] The Regulation also contains a "black list" of prohibited bases of jurisdiction, citing particular provisions in the laws of member states that the Regulation takes to be exorbitant. Often cited as a notorious example of exorbitant jurisdiction, the French Civil Code provides for personal jurisdiction over any defendant sued by a French national, regardless of where the claim arose.[69] The black list also includes a dozen other provisions of national law. It does not, however, prevent the exercise of jurisdiction over defendants not domiciled within the European Union, who can be sued as allowed by the law of member states.[70]

The same sharp distinction applies to recognition of judgments. The Regulation allows limited grounds for collateral attack, but only as to judgments rendered by the courts of member states.[71] In this respect, it follows the model of the Full Faith and Credit Clause, although it differs in detail from American law, for instance, in allowing nonrecognition based on the public policy of the enforcing state.[72] Also, like the Full Faith and Credit Clause, the Regulation covers only judgments rendered by courts within the union, not those outside it. As elaborated more fully in the chapter on recognition of judgments, those from American courts receive heightened scrutiny before they are recognized in the European Union. The Regulation nevertheless does have an indirect effect on recognition of American judgments. If the judgments are based on the exorbitant exercise of personal jurisdiction under the black list, then they are not likely to be recognized, because to do so would be to treat them better than the judgments of member states in the European Union. Fortunately, those occasions have rarely surfaced because of the broad similarity between the Regulation and the American law of due process. The disparities, such as they are, mostly concern the treatment of forum-selection clauses in consumer and employment contracts, which face much sterner prohibitions in European law than in American law.

---

[67] Regulation (EU) 1215/2012 of the European Parliament and of the Council of 12 December 2012 on jurisdiction and the recognition and enforcement of judgments in civil and commercial matters (recast). Official Journal, OJ 20 December 2012, L 351/1, arts. 5, 15–21.

[68] *Id.* art. 5(3).

[69] *Id.* arts. 14 and 15.

[70] *Id.* art. 4(2).

[71] *Id.* arts. 33–37.

[72] *Id.* art. 34(1).

Chapter II

CHOICE OF LAW AND THE EXTRATERRITORIAL APPLICATION OF AMERICAN LAW

Many of the leading decisions on choice of law, like those on personal jurisdiction, come from international cases, where the stakes are higher on choice-of-law issues because the differences are greater. Foreign law tends to differ more from American law than the law of any one American state tends to differ from the law of any other. The relative generosity of American tort recoveries, particularly for punitive damages and noneconomic loss, create a striking contrast with the rest of the world. Such differences raise the stakes in international cases as compared to purely domestic cases because the higher return from applying American law diverges so sharply from the recovery available under foreign law. The higher stakes also tend to increase the use of motions to dismiss for *forum non conveniens*, which often rely upon the difficulty faced by American courts in applying foreign law. Nevertheless, the doctrine and overall approach to choice of law nominally remain, the same in domestic and international cases. The same principles govern choice of state law and choice of foreign law, despite the very different context in which these issues arise.

The disparity between domestic and international cases raises concerns that the simple doctrinal equivalence of principles applied across-the-board masks real differences in outcome and justification. The varied, and relatively flexible, approach to choice of law taken by American courts might be entirely acceptable in a federal system with differences in state law confined within the shared traditions of the common law. It might be less workable for the larger differences between American and foreign law, which extend beyond substantive law to choice of law itself. The American suspicion of clear rules on this choice of law, although not universally shared among all American states, nevertheless contrasts with the general acceptance of such rules elsewhere. The varied approaches to choice of law taken by the states, and to a limited extent, the federal government, only heighten the uncertainty of the outcome of any choice-of-law decision. It depends upon the forum selected by the plaintiff, and most of the time, it depends upon state law, even in international cases. Since there is no general federal approach to choice of law, American choice of law fragments mostly into the rules and principles adopted in different states.

This situation has led critics of American choice of law to complain that the whole field is "a mess."[1] Part of the disarray derives from the "choice-of-law revolution" in the middle of the twentieth century and, in particular, the work of Brainerd Currie in discrediting definite choice-of-law rules, like those found in the First Restatement of Conflict of Laws.[2] In the opinion of many scholars of conflict of laws, he demonstrated that such rules did not serve the purpose for which they were designed, let alone the purpose of the law that they purported to choose. Whatever certainty they offered was illusory, and in any event, came at too great a cost in implementing substantive policy. The first section of this chapter recounts this development, but its outcome has been clear for some time. The choice-of-law revolution swept away the old rules without generating a consensus about what would replace them.

The second section of this chapter turns to the implications of the choice-of-law revolution for international civil litigation and how, in particular, it has led to attempts to expand American law overseas. Constitutional restrictions on choice of law, just like those on personal jurisdiction, became looser as a variety of different approaches took hold in American law. The Supreme Court adopted a variant of the contacts analysis from *International Shoe* to determine when a case had a sufficient relationship to the forum to allow application of its law. This variant imposed even weaker restrictions than the contacts analysis of personal jurisdiction because it counted contacts with the forum of the entire case, not just those of the defendant. Contacts of the plaintiff with the forum, for instance, could support choice of the forum's law.[3] As a result, a court usually acquired the power to apply its own law to the case if it acquired personal jurisdiction over the defendant. In addition to these weak constraints on state law, the Constitution does very little to constrain of federal law. Due process requires only some contact of the entire case with the entire United States, and the federal government has a variety of powers—from the treaty power, to regulation of international commerce, to the war power—to expand the reach of federal law.

The prospect of nearly limitless expansion of American law generated a search for limiting principles, discussed in the third section of this chapter. In the Supreme Court, this search took the form of renewed emphasis upon a "presumption against extraterritoriality" in the interpretation of federal statutes. The

---

[1]   Christopher A. Whytock, *Myth of Mess? International Choice of Law in Action*, 84 N.Y.U. L. REV. 719, 721 (2009).

[2]   *See* BRAINERD CURRIE, SELECTED ESSAYS IN THE CONFLICT OF LAWS (1963).

[3]   Allstate Ins. Co. v. Hague, 449 U.S. 302, 313–14 (1981) (opinion of Brennan, J.) (decedent worked in forum state).

Court presumed that Congress, in the absence of clear statutory language to the contrary, meant to limit the coverage of federal statutes to the territorial boundaries of the United States.[4] Congress itself has sometimes acted to override this presumption, and because it depends upon general principles of statutory interpretation, it does not always yield a clear answer to the question of coverage of a federal statute. State courts have taken steps in the same direction, but because many claims in state court have their roots in the common law, but not in a statute, the state analysis of extraterritoriality often returns to general questions of choice of law. Because of its direct effect on only federal law, the presumption against extraterritorial application of federal statutes does little to ameliorate the general indeterminacy of American choice of law.

Parties have reacted to the uncertainty in choice of law, as they have with the uncertainty over personal jurisdiction, by contracting around it in the form of choice-of-law clauses. Like forum-selection clauses, these clauses receive a large degree of judicial deference and courts routinely enforce them so long as the case has some colorable relation to the country whose law is chosen. The fourth section of this chapter takes up the treatment of these clauses, both in American law and in European Union law. The latter takes the same categorical approach as it does with respect to choice-of-forum clauses, allowing them in contracts between businesses but not in contracts with parties who have presumptively less bargaining power, like consumers or employees. In those situations, European Union law reverts to ordinary choice-of-law rules, which bear a striking resemblance to the rules of the First Restatement of Conflict of Laws. These rules confirm the contrast between European approaches to conflict of laws and the modern American approaches, as the European approaches seek to frame fairly clear rules and reach fairly determinate outcomes.

A. The Choice-of-Law Revolution

The change in the American approach to choice of law came about as part of the Legal Realist movement, which challenged sharply defined legal rules as a manifestation only of "the law on the books" rather than "the law in action." The same intellectual trends that led to decisions on personal jurisdiction like *International Shoe*, which criticized the fictions of corporate presence and constructive consent, also led to decisions on choice of law that looked behind legal rules, both those on choice of law and those of substantive law, to ascertain the purpose that they served. The First Restatement of Conflict of Laws adopted a very different perspective and sought to achieve very different goals. It sought to frame rules that minimized

---

[4]   Morrison v. National Australia Bank, Ltd., 561 U.S. 247, 255 (2010).

the factors that went into making choice-of-law decisions and to narrow the range of resulting decisions. The form that the law took, in the sense of its specific doctrinal terms, mattered more to the First Restatement than to the approaches that sought to displace it. Those approaches looked far more to the purposes, cast by Brainerd Currie as the "interests," that were served by applying the law of different states.

The most famous of the rules of the First Restatement adopted the principle of *lex loci delicti* for tort cases: applying the law of the place of the wrong, or more specifically, "the state where the last event necessary to make an actor liable for an alleged tort takes place."[5] This rule, which persists today in Europe and in those states that still follow the First Restatement, illustrates both the strengths and the weaknesses of the First Restatement. The strengths become most apparent in fairly routine cases, where the conduct and parties involved in a tort all cluster around the place where the injury occurred. *Lex loci delicti* captures the intuition that the location of injury provides the natural focal point for ascertaining the applicable law. The weaknesses of the First Restatement become apparent when the facts grow more complicated and the salience of the place of injury must compete with alternative locations, such as the place where the wrongful conduct occurred, which might govern the standard of care, or the place where the plaintiff resides, which might govern the amount of compensation. Any case that raises serious choice-of-law issues involves at least two states whose law arguably could apply to the facts of the case. Rules designed for simpler cases, in which the choice of one state's law is clear, do not necessarily contribute to the resolution of harder cases, in which the law of two or more states could apply. And, indeed, the First Restatement includes several qualifications and clarifications of its basic rule, for instance, for cases of poisoning, defamation, or privilege.[6]

More generally, the First Restatement acknowledged the possibility of characterizing cases in different terms, for instance, as involving issues either of tort, contract, or procedure, and thus triggering the application of different choice-of-law rules. The dominant rule for contracts was the law of the place where the contract was made, or the *lex loci contractus*,[7] and for procedure, the law of the place where the action was brought, or the *lex fori*.[8] Thus, a dispute arising from a contractual relationship could be governed by the law from any of these sources of law: where the injury occurred, if the case goes under the heading of torts; where the

---

[5]   RESTATEMENT (FIRST) OF CONFLICT OF LAWS § 377 (1934).

[6]   *Id.* § 377; *see also* §§ 379, 382.

[7]   *Id.* § 311.

[8]   *Id.* § 585.

contract was made, if it is characterized as one of contract; or the law of forum for issues characterized as procedural. The First Restatement tried to sort out these competing characterizations,[9] but courts that were uneasy with the results dictated by the specific rules of torts, contracts, or procedure could shift among these domains and re-characterize the nature of the disputed choice of law. The First Restatement also contained an explicit exception for claims under the law of another state that would violate the public policy of the forum.[10]

These examples form only a small subset of the competing provisions in the First Restatement, and of the devices available to evade the seemingly obvious consequences of the rules it contained. Judges could use these safety valves in hard cases to reach results that they found to be more satisfactory. For instance, a court might characterize a case arising from an accident involving a rental car as one arising from the rental contract, and therefore based on the law of the state where the parties entered into the contract, rather than the law of the state where the accident occurred.[11] The Legal Realists concluded from this observation that the First Restatement neither adequately described existing legal practice nor furnished useful standards for decisions in the future. Although their position certainly contained a grain of truth, the Legal Realists perhaps made too much of it. All legal rules suffer from lack of fit with the purposes they seek to accomplish, being both too broad or too narrow in some respect or other: going too far beyond their underlying purpose or failing to go far enough.

More telling was the Legal Realists' criticism that the rules of the First Restatement often lost sight of the purposes underlying the substantive law. The choice-of-law rules selected different laws regardless of whether doing so served the purposes for which they were designed. Tort cases, for instance, purport to further policies of both deterrence and compensation, the former supporting application of the law of the place of wrongful conduct and the latter supporting the law of the plaintiff's residence. Neither policy supports the law of the place of injury selected by the First Restatement, except insofar as that place coincides, by chance, with the place of wrongful conduct or the plaintiff's residence. The law of the place of injury could be selected based on the expenses that might be incurred there in caring for the plaintiff, but that rationale also applies only coincidentally with all the cases covered by the rule of the First Restatement.

---

[9] *See id.* § 584 (discussing whether a given question is one of substance or procedure).

[10] *Id.* § 612.

[11] *See, e.g.,* Levy v. Daniels' U-Drive Auto Renting Co., 108 Conn. 333, 143 A. 163 (1938).

Critics of the First Restatement took advantage of these defects to propose an entirely different approach to choice of law. They relied upon the purposes of competing laws, or in Brainerd Currie's terms, the "interests" of each state in having its law applied. Currie's version of the choice-of-law revolution presented it as a form of purposive statutory interpretation, which looked to what the legislature sought to accomplish in passing a particular law and reasoned from the ends it had in view to the conclusion that the means—either of applying or not applying forum law—were appropriate. So, for instance, if the state of the plaintiff's residence followed the common law rule of a complete defense based on contributory negligence, while the state where the accident occurred followed the new rule of comparative negligence, the court should apply the latter rule because the case presented a "false conflict." The state of the plaintiff's residence had no obvious interest in denying recovery to its residents, while the state where the accident took place had an interest in deterring unsafe conduct by both the plaintiff and defendant only as reflected in its rule of comparative fault. So the courts of both states, if suit had been brought there, should have applied the rule of comparative fault.

If, on the other hand, the legal rules had been reversed, the case would have generated a "true conflict": one between the law of the plaintiff's residence and the law of the place of the accident. On this version of the case, the state of the plaintiff's residence follows the rule of comparative fault and favors compensation of the plaintiff, while the state of the accident subordinates any interest in compensation to deterring negligence by potential plaintiffs. Neither state's interests could be accommodated with the other's. In such a case, Currie would have had the forum state, whether it was the residence of the plaintiff or the place where the accident took place, apply its own law. The courts, on his view, had no authority to depart from otherwise valid state interests simply because a case had an interstate element.

As this simplified example illustrates, everything in Currie's "interest analysis" depends on identifying the interests at stake. To alter the example again, suppose that both states assert an interest in fairly allocating the costs of accident, regardless of the residence of the plaintiff and regardless of where the accident occurred. With their interests characterized in this way, the conflict between the law of contributory negligence in one state and comparative negligence in another always generates a true conflict. The courts of each state would accordingly apply their own law to any case that came before them. Interest analysis depends heavily on the accurate discovery and formulation of the underlying purpose of competing laws. This raises real difficulties in the absence of reliable evidence of the legislative intent behind a statute or an authoritative statement of the purpose served by a common law rule. These difficulties become all the more challenging in international cases, where foreign law might not lend itself to interpretation in light of its underlying purpose, which might, after all, be to serve competing goals.

A leading case, *Babcock v. Jackson*, illustrates the problem.[12] That case arose from an automobile accident in Ontario, Canada, and gave rise to a claim by a New York passenger riding in the car as the guest of a New York driver. Ontario barred recovery of claims by guests against their drivers, apparently to prevent fraudulent claims by the guest in collusion with the driver at the expense of the driver's insurer. The New York Court of Appeals accepted this as the purpose of the Ontario "guest statute," as it was called, but then dismissed its relevance to any claim between New York parties.[13] Any fraud that they might practice was "scarcely a valid legislative concern of Ontario simply because the accident occurred there."[14] The court refused to recognize any broader interest of Ontario beyond preventing fraud by its residents.[15] That might well be the correct result, but it depends less on what Ontario saw as its interests than on what the New York Court of Appeals defined its legitimate interests to be.

As the opinion turned out, the court adopted its own variation on interest analysis, called the "center of gravity" or "grouping of contacts" doctrine.[16] The court just added up all the contacts of the cases with New York, including the parties' residence there, where their journey began and was supposed to end, and where the driver obtained his insurance, and found that these contacts outweighed the contact with Ontario, where the accident occurred.[17] The court accordingly applied New York law, which allowed recovery by the plaintiff guest, rather than Ontario law, which did not. The court's subjective assessment of contacts candidly revealed the uncertainty surrounding the many factors that go into a correct choice-of-law decision, but it implicitly diminished the weight of Ontario's interests by emphasizing factors such as where the trip began and ended. Interest analysis, and the several variations upon it, owned up to the difficulty of making choice-of-law decisions, which the First Restatement had largely concealed behind its array of rules, but this

---

[12]   12 N.Y.2d 473, 191 N.E.2d 279, 240 N.Y.S.2d 743 (1963).

[13]   *Id.* at 482–83.

[14]   *Id.* at 483.

[15]   *Id.*

[16]   *Id.* at 485 (Van Voorhis, J., dissenting).

[17]   *Id.*

mode of analysis then went on to invite even more indeterminacy by multiplying the factors that courts needed to consider.

In another leading decision, *Lauritzen v. Larsen*,[18] the Supreme Court also took into a variety of different "connecting factors"[19] for and against application of American law. A Danish seaman had filed a claim under the Jones Act for injury aboard a Danish ship that occurred in Cuban waters.[20] The Court examined a variety of factors, but found none of them sufficient for application of the Jones Act: the place of the wrongful act; the law of the vessel's flag; the allegiance of domiciles of the plaintiff; the allegiance of the defendant ship owner; the place of contract; the inaccessibility of a foreign forum; and the law of the forum.[21] Because the case concerned a federal statute, the Supreme Court addressed these factors as a matter of federal law, invoking the maxim, for instance, that "an act of Congress ought never to be construed to violate the law of nations if any other possible construction remains."[22] The factors identified in the opinion thus served as a catalogue of the considerations that entered into an analysis of what the law of nations required. The opinion, although persuasive on the precise question before the Court, hardly yields a determinate answer on the general question of the extraterritorial reach of federal statutes.

As these decisions illustrate, the new approaches to choice of law sacrificed simplicity for intense analysis, making the result less predictable in routine cases but more nuanced in exceptional cases. This trade-off had the undesirable side effects of detracting from the ex ante guidance that choice-of-law rules can offer parties before a dispute arises, and inviting manipulation of competing interests and relevant factors once a dispute makes its way to court. Even if courts coalesce around a particular outcome on particular facts, it does the parties no good ex ante if their conduct presents a different set of facts or if they cannot ascertain the pattern of results that courts have reached. The divergence among modern approaches only heightens the tendency towards manipulation ex post. One scholar went so far as to advise courts to apply "the better law" among the competing alternatives, as a candid acknowledgment of what they did in practice.[23]

---

[18] 345 U.S. 571 (1953).

[19] *Id.* at 592.

[20] *Id.*

[21] *Id.* at 583–92.

[22] *Id.* at 578 (quoting Murray v. The Schooner Charming Betsy, 6 U.S. (2 Cranch) 64, 118 (1804)).

[23] Robert A. Leflar, *Choice-Influencing Considerations in Conflicts Law*, 41 N.Y.U. L. REV. 267 (1966). Robert A. Leflar, *Conflicts Law: More on Choice-Influencing Considerations*, 54 CAL. L. REV. 1584 (1966).

The Second Restatement of Conflict of Laws tried to break the intellectual stalemate resulting from the stark choice between sharply framed rules in the First Restatement and the open-ended standards advocated by critics of such rules. It sought to strike a balance between the two approaches by articulating presumptively applicable rules and then qualifying them by an appeal to general principles. It follows the model of its predecessor to this extent, for instance, in the rule on validity of conveyances of land, which looks in most cases to the law of the *situs* of the property.[24] Such definite rules, however, yield to more abstract standards in a wide range of cases, such as those in torts, where the court should apply the law of the state that "has the most significant relationship to the occurrence and the parties under the principles stated in § 6."[25] Section 6, in turn, lists seven considerations in framing choice-of-law principles, and Section 145(2) lists four contacts relevant specifically to tort cases. The "law of the place where the injury occurred" accounts for only one consideration, out of a total of eleven which are not meant to be exclusive, and all of which bear on choice of law in tort cases. Similar qualifications apply to the rule for contract cases.[26] As the standards in the Second Restatement become more and more fully articulated, they become less and less definite.

The compromise attempted by the Second Restatement failed to achieve any widespread support and instead succeeded only in adding another modern approach to the alternatives already available. The resulting cacophony of doctrine in different states and at the federal level undermined any prospect in the short term for a coherent synthesis of American choice of law. Most states have abandoned crucial parts of the First Restatement without putting any single alternative in its place.[27] The sophistication of the modern approaches choice of law, fitted to the facts of each case, exceeded the capacity of the common law system of adjudication to generate workable new rules accessible to most lawyers and judges. The scholars who undermined the old system of choice of law proved unable to put a new system in its place. The consequent doctrinal disarray in American law constitutes one of the conditions under which international civil litigation must go forward, at least for the present time. The next section looks at its implications for constitutional law.

---

[24] Restatement, *supra* note 5, § 223.

[25] *Id.* § 145(1).

[26] *Id.* § 188.

[27] 4 SYMEON C. SYMEONIDES, THE AMERICAN CHOICE-OF-LAW: PAST, PRESENT AND FUTURE (2006).

B. Constitutional Limits on Choice of Law

Over the course of the twentieth century, what courts should do as matter of state or federal choice of law became more contested, as did what they were required to do as a matter of constitutional law. The absence of consensus on the correct approach led to increasingly lenient constitutional restrictions on what was minimally acceptable for a court to do in choosing between forum law and that of another state or nation. Some precedents from the era of the First Restatement survived, but many were superseded by decisions that admitted the existence of competing state interests and the inability of choice-of-law rules to reconcile conflicts between them. With few surviving constitutional limits, the state courts remained free to choose among the variety of available approaches, and the federal courts followed their lead, either because they were required to so in diversity cases under the *Erie* doctrine[28] or because of the flexibility inherent in decisions such as *Lauritzen v. Larsen.*[29]

One of the enduring precedents from the old era, *Home Insurance Co. v. Dick*, arose in a transnational setting.[30] The plaintiff, a citizen of Texas, filed suit based on an insurance policy on a tugboat in Mexico. The defendant insurance companies had re-insured the risk of loss on a tugboat in Mexico, where the original insurance policies and the re-insurance policies had been issued. Nothing involving the insurance or the re-insurance agreements had occurred in Texas. The original insurers did not do business there and jurisdiction was acquired over them only by garnishing the obligations owed to them by the reinsurers. Dick, for his part, went to Mexico and obtained the right to recover under the original insurance policy, which required any suit on the original insurance policy to be filed within one year. The policy also contained a clause making it subject to Mexican law, which upheld the validity of the contractual time limit. Texas law, by contrast, made the time limit invalid, which became an issue in the case because Dick waited more than a year to be sued after the loss.

The Supreme Court held that application of Texas law would violate the Due Process Clause of the Fourteenth Amendment.[31] The Court reasoned that "nothing in any way relating to the policy sued on, or to the contracts of reinsurance, was ever done or required to be done in Texas."[32] Only the plaintiff's residence counted in favor of application of Texas law, but his residency generated no contacts

---

28 Klaxon Co. v. Stentor Electric Mfg. Co., 313 U.S. 487 (1941).

29 345 U.S. at 582–92.

30 281 U.S. 397 (1930).

31 *Id.* at 408.

32 *Id.*

relevant to the case.[33] As the Court would reason later in *International Shoe*, the Due Process Clause does not permit a state to exercise jurisdiction over a defendant "with which the state has no contacts, ties, or relations."[34] Cases of no contacts at all with the forum admittedly lie at one extreme, and appear to be as easy as to resolve as wholly domestic cases, but a finding of no relevant contacts introduces an element of circularity into choice-of-law analysis. How can a contact be dismissed as irrelevant without some reference to the substantive law to be chosen? Any adequate answer to this question presupposes constitutional limits on the contacts that a state can count towards applying its own law, even in seemingly easy cases like *Home Insurance*.

Shortly after this decision, the Supreme Court gave up on adjudicating disputes between states whose laws generated a true conflict in their underlying purposes. The Full Faith and Credit Clause imposed only limited obligations on one state to recognize the law of a sister state, and in particular, to subordinate its own interests, supported by relevant contacts, to those of another state. The Court reached this conclusion in *Pacific Employers Insurance Co. v. Industrial Accident Commission*,[35] another decision that prefigured the jurisdictional analysis in *International Shoe*. Justice (and later Chief Justice) Stone authored both opinions, and in *Pacific Employers*, he frankly acknowledged the direct conflict between the workers' compensation statutes of two states: Massachusetts, where the injured worker resided and entered into his contract of employment; and California, where he was injured and filed a compensation claim.[36] The Court made a gesture towards the territorial limits on state power, but only in order to narrow the state's constitutional obligations: "Full faith and credit does not here enable one state to legislate for the other or to project its laws across state lines so as to preclude the other from prescribing for itself the legal consequences of acts within it."[37]

Some decades later, the Supreme Court made explicit what the Due Process Clause embodied, in the process seeming to dilute those standards even further. In *Allstate Insurance Co. v. Hague*,[38] the Court upheld the application of Minnesota law to insurance policies issued in Wisconsin, based on contacts with Minnesota that were scarcely more relevant than those with the forum in *Home Insurance*. The plaintiff in *Allstate Insurance* had moved to Minnesota after the

---

[33] *Id.*

[34] International Shoe Co. v. Washington, 326 U.S. 310, 319 (1945).

[35] 306 U.S. 493 (1939).

[36] *Id.* at 504.

[37] *Id.* at 504–05.

[38] 449 U.S. 302 (1981).

death of her husband in an accident in Wisconsin and her residence there furnished the principal contact with the forum. The Court nevertheless held that Minnesota could apply its own law, effectively increasing the coverage available to the plaintiff under the Wisconsin insurance policies.[39] In addition to the plaintiff's residence in Minnesota at the time of suit, the Court relied upon the fact that State Farm did business in Minnesota and that the decedent worked for a Minnesota employer, although he was not killed in the course of employment or while commuting.[40] A plurality adopted this reasoning and the decisive concurring opinion simply concluded that the forum could select its own "unless that choice threatens the federal interest in national unity."[41] Doubts persist over the precise constitutional standard the two opinions adopted, but whatever it is, the decision represents a decided weakening of the constitutional restraints on choice of law.

The last decision in this series, *Phillips Petroleum Co. v. Shutts*,[42] departed from the trend towards weakening constitutional restraints but mainly as an exception that proves the rule. The case concerned the right to payments on oil and gas leases brought on behalf of the owners of real property where the oil and gas the wells were located. The Supreme Court held that the law of the place of the property determined the amount of the interest on delayed payments, following the general rule that *situs* of property determined the applicable law. The case was exceptional in restricting the forum's choice of its own law for out-of-state leases, but it provided the rule that where a consensus on choice of law exists, constitutional law follows. The disintegration of consensus elsewhere has inhibited the Supreme Court from insisting on effective constitutional constraints. Instead, the Court has been forced to look elsewhere to limit the reach of American law, for instance, by imposing restrictions on personal jurisdiction, as noted in the previous chapter, or by limiting the coverage of federal statutes, as discussed in the next section of this chapter.

C. The Presumption Against Extraterritoriality

The Constitution established the federal government as one of limited powers so that, in theory, a federal statute that applied extraterritorially could be held unconstitutional as in excess of those powers specifically given to Congress. Yet several of those powers specifically apply to foreign commerce and foreign affairs, such as the

---

[39] *Id.* at 320.

[40] *Id.* at 317–18.

[41] *Id.* at 323.

[42] 472 U.S. 797 (1985).

power to "regulate Commerce with foreign Nations,"[43] the war power, and the power to "define and punish Piracies and Felonies committed on the high Seas, and Offences against the Law of Nations,"[44] not to mention the power of the Senate to ratify treaties.[45] All these powers contemplate legislation that could or that necessarily does apply overseas and all are augmented by the Necessary and Proper Clause. Any restraint on the reach of federal statutes must therefore come from some other clause in the Constitution. The Due Process Clause of the Fifth Amendment constitutes a possible source of restraint,[46] but as with its impact on personal jurisdiction, it does little to prevent a federal statute from applying to conduct or to a party that has any contact with the entire United States. The Supreme Court has never held a federal statute unconstitutional on this ground.[47] To do so would have the ironic consequence that the statute could not apply extraterritorially because the Due Process Clause did does apply extraterritorially. The Clause, on this interpretation, would protect "any person" in the world, regardless of his status as citizen or alien or his location inside or outside the United States. The Supreme Court has been reluctant to recognize such universal coverage of the Constitution.[48]

The Court has avoided the constitutional question by interpreting federal statutes not to cover conduct overseas unless Congress explicitly provides otherwise. This presumption against extraterritoriality requires a clear statement by Congress for a statute to reach overseas. By implication, it also applies to the exercise of federal common law outside certain areas, such as admiralty, where federal courts traditionally have made law that applies outside the boundaries of this country.[49] The presumption developed partly to implement general principles of comity, designed to prevent conflicts between the enforcement of American law and the law of foreign nations. Such conflicts are particularly likely to arise if American law purports to cover activity within the boundaries of a foreign nation. They also implicate the *Charming Betsy* canon, which requires that an "act of Congress ought never to be construed to violate the law of nations if any other possible construction

---

[43] U.S. CONST. art. I, § 8, cl. 3.

[44] U.S. CONST. art. I, § 8, cl. 10.

[45] U.S. CONST. art. II, § 2, cl. 2.

[46] Lea Brilmayer & Charles Norchi, *Federal Extraterritoriality and Fifth Amendment Due Process*, 105 HARV. L. REV. 1217 (1992).

[47] *Id.* at 1219–20.

[48] *E.g.*, United States v. Verdugo Urquidez, 494 U.S. 259, 269 (1990).

[49] Kiobel v. Royal Dutch Petroleum Co., 133 S.Ct. 1659, 1667–69 (2013) (refusing to recognize federal cause of action for human rights violations inside the boundaries of another country).

remains."[50] International law admits only a few exceptions to the principle that a nation exercises exclusive jurisdiction within its own territory.[51]

A further implication of the presumption against extraterritoriality turns back to domestic principles of separation of powers, based on the superior ability of the political branches of government to deal with foreign affairs. Federal statutes often fail to specifically limit their coverage to American territory, as, for instance, in the original version of the antitrust laws. Section 1 of the Sherman Antitrust Act prohibits all conspiracies "in restraint of trade or commerce among the several States, or with foreign nations."[52] Read literally, it would extend to conspiracies in international commerce that have no connection at all with the United States. Under the traditional rule of *lex loci delicti*, however, it was read to exclude conduct that was legal in the foreign country where it occurred.[53] No wrong had occurred in this country, because the anticompetitive activity occurred elsewhere, and no wrong had occurred in another country, because the anticompetitive activity was legal there. That interpretation of the statute persisted for several decades, without any intervention by Congress to expand its scope. Strict adherence to the presumption against extraterritoriality would have left this interpretation intact partly because Congress could decide, better than a court could, how aggressively to enforce the antitrust laws in foreign countries.

The broader developments discussed in the previous section eventually eroded a narrow interpretation of the Sherman Act, establishing what became known as "the effects test" for extending coverage. The terms of the Act do reach foreign commerce, so that courts could fairly ask how far the act extended overseas. The leading decision, *United States v. Aluminum Co. of America*,[54] seemed to answer "very far," although the facts and reasoning of the opinion support a more cautious answer. Among the other defendants in *Alcoa* (as the case is known) was a Canadian producer of aluminum that had joined an international cartel to fix prices in the world market for this metal, including in the United States. All the acts relating to the cartel occurred outside the United States, but the government clearly established the existence of the cartel and its intent to restrict imports into this country. The Second Circuit found sufficient evidence to prove intent and effects on the American

---

[50] Murray v. The Schooner Charming Betsy, 6 U.S. (2 Cranch) 64, 118 (1804).

[51] ANDREW CLAPHAM, BRIERLY'S LAW OF NATIONS, 206–07, 235–301 (7th ed. 2012).

[52] Sherman Antitrust Act, 15 U.S.C. § 1 (2012).

[53] American Banana Co. v. United Fruit Co., 213 U.S. 347 (1909).

[54] 148 F.2d 416 (2d Cir. 1945).

market. This finding shifted the burden of proof to the defendant to prove the absence of effects, which it failed to carry.[55] The Second Circuit's emphasis upon effects caused *Alcoa* to become known for establishing "the effects test": the proposition that effects on the American market were sufficient for coverage under the Sherman Act, not just a necessary element of coverage. For several decades the "effects test" remained the dominant interpretation of the Act, despite the fact that anticompetitive practices anywhere in the world could easily have effects within the United States. The many connections between national markets assured that actions in restraint of trade elsewhere arguably affected markets here. The scope of the antitrust laws tended to expand accordingly, as did the "effects test" when it was applied to other federal laws, such as those regulating securities.

When a reaction eventually set in, it was cast in terms similar to the Second Restatement of Conflict of Laws, invoking a list of multiple factors that restricted coverage of the Sherman Act.[56] The Supreme Court initially accepted this approach, identifying it as a matter of comity to avoid conflicts with the laws of other nations.[57] But the Court defined "conflicts" very narrowly to include only situations in which compliance with the Sherman Act required a party to violate foreign law.[58] That decision seemed to leave the effects test intact in any case in which foreign law allowed a defendant to engage in conduct, which if done in the United States and direct to economic activity here, violated the Sherman Act. This result naturally followed from the indefinite standards of the First Restatement and the flexible concept of comity, which were not likely, in any event, to generate sharply defined limits on the scope of federal law. Those standards instead invited the same kind of case-by-case determinations as "the effects test" itself, leading to application of American law in any case with apparently sufficient contacts with the United States.

As this line of cases reveals, identifying which contacts were sufficient remained a vexed question. At almost the same time, Congress tried to address this question in the Foreign Trade and Antitrust Improvements Act (FTAIA). This statute sought to define and limit the overseas coverage of the antitrust laws but it was ultimately framed in terms that left confusion in its wake. The key provision of the FTAIA limited the antitrust laws to conduct with "a direct, substantial, and reasonably foreseeable effect" either on (i)

---

[55] *Id.* at 444.

[56] Timberlane Lumber Co. v. Bank of America, N.T. & S.A., 549 F.2d 597 (9th Cir. 1976).

[57] Hartford Fire Ins. v. California, 509 U.S. 764 (1993).

[58] *Id.* at 798–99.

"trade or commerce which is not trade commerce with foreign nations," (ii) "on import trade or import commerce with foreign nations", or (iii) "on export trade or export commerce with foreign nations, of a person engaged in such trade or commerce in the United States."[59] Translating from the awkward phrasing of these provisions, which actually take the form of a double or triple negative, the requisite effect must be on either (i) commerce within the United States, or (ii) import commerce to the United States, or (iii) export commerce from the United States. The clause identified above as (i) seemed to leave open coverage in the most problematic cases under the effects test: where anticompetitive activity overseas has domestic effects solely because of the connections between national and international markets.

Exactly this case came up in *F. Hoffman-La Roche Ltd. v. Empagran S.A.*,[60] where foreign participants in an alleged conspiracy to raise the price of vitamins abroad argued that they did not meet the coverage requirements of the FTAIA. Because they did not do any business in the United States, they did not meet the requirements of either (i), (ii), or (iii). The plaintiffs, however, argued that (i) was satisfied because the price of vitamins in this country depended in part on their price elsewhere. Yet the plaintiffs sought relief only for the losses they suffered because of the higher price of vitamins abroad. The Supreme Court acknowledged that the alleged price-fixing "significantly and adversely affects both customers outside the United States and customers within the United States," but it found nevertheless that "the adverse foreign effect is independent of any adverse domestic effect."[61] The Court might have offered that finding as a gloss on the need for a "direct" effect under the FTAIA, yet it narrowed its holding by relying on the plaintiffs' claim only for damages resulting from sales overseas.

Critics of the presumption against extraterritoriality might find the end result of judicial decisions and congressional intervention under the FTAIA to be highly unsatisfactory. The promised certainty of the presumption, like that promised by the First Restatement of Conflict of Laws, did not materialize. Foreign companies could evade the antitrust laws by carefully restricting their activities to those outside the United States. The statute itself, whatever the advantages of congressional involvement in foreign affairs, adds a further layer of complexity to an already complex inquiry. Despite these drawbacks, the existing compromise over the scope of the antitrust laws has the virtue of reining in the effects test with rules that might eventually prove to be workable. For instance, lower

---

[59] Foreign Trade and Antitrust Improvements Act, 15 U.S.C. § 6a (2012).
[60] 542 U.S. 155 (2004).
[61] *Id.* at 164.

courts have left open the ability of the Justice Department to bring criminal actions under the antitrust laws based on the total accumulation of effects here, rather than just those that would affect a private plaintiff, of anticompetitive conduct elsewhere.[62] And several agreements between the United States and the European Union seek to coordinate antitrust enforcement to reduce conflict between the competition laws in both jurisdictions.[63] The details of these arrangements resist summary in simple terms, but they reflect both the complexity of achieving optimal enforcement of different laws and the political will to work out an appropriate settlement.

The same pattern of extension, restraint, and congressional action also figured in the interpretation of the federal securities laws. Section 10(b) of the Securities Exchange Act generally prohibits any form of fraud in connection with the purchase or sale of security "by use of any means or instrumentality of interstate commerce or of the mails, or of any facility of any national securities exchange."[64] As the quoted phrase indicates, Section 10(b) contains no geographical restriction on its scope, nor does the implementing regulation in Rule 10b-5. The federal courts of appeals, led by the Second Circuit, imposed very loose limits on these provisions, adopting a variation on the effects test used in interpreting the antitrust laws, coupled with a conduct test: "whether the wrongful conduct had a substantial effect in the United States or upon United States citizens" or "whether the wrongful conduct occurred in the United States."[65] The economic effects of securities fraud, just like those of anti-competitive activity, can easily ripple through worldwide financial markets and have significant effects within the United States. For the same reason, conduct related to a foreign fraud often can be found in the United States, either in the securities markets here or in related economic transactions. The limits on Section 10(b) and Rule 10b-5 might turn out to be no limits at all.

The Supreme Court took this view in *Morrison v. National Australia Bank Ltd.*,[66] a case denominated in the securities bar as "foreign cubed." First, it was brought by foreign plaintiffs; second, it involved the sale of securities in a foreign corporation; and third, the sale took place on a foreign securities exchange. In all these respects, the case had ties only with Australia. The American connection,

---

[62] Motorola Mobility LLC v. AU Optronics Corp., 775 F.3d 816, 825–27 (7th Cir. 2014), *cert. denied,* 135 S.Ct. 2837 (2015).

[63] JOACHIM ZEKOLL, MICHAEL G. COLLINS & GEORGE A. RUTHERGLEN, TRANSNATIONAL CIVIL LITIGATION 588–90 (2013); *see also Motorola,* 775 F.3d at 825–27.

[64] Securities Exchange Act of 1934, 15 U.S.C. § 78j(b) (2012).

[65] SEC v. Berger, 322 F.3d 187, 192–93 (2d Cir. 2003).

[66] 561 U.S. 247 (2010).

apart from the place of suit, derived only from a wholly owned American subsidiary of the Australian corporation that issued the securities in question. By means of the presumption against extraterritoriality, the Court turned the absence of territorial limits in Section 10(b) into an absence of extraterritorial effect, at least on the facts presented. Private actions under American law, which tend to favor plaintiffs more than foreign law, threaten to interfere with foreign regulation of foreign securities exchanges.

Moreover, other provisions of the Securities Exchange Act specifically provide for extraterritorial application under regulations promulgated by the Securities and Exchange Commission (SEC) to prevent evasion of the act.[67] These were later augmented by the Dodd-Frank Act,[68] which revived the effects and conduct test for public actions. The Act provided for federal courts to have jurisdiction over fraud claims brought by the SEC or the United States based on "conduct occurring outside the United States that has a foreseeable substantial effect within the United States."[69] The resulting compromise does not simplify the law, but it does reflect the control that the political branches of government exercise over public enforcement actions, facilitating coordination with the authorities in other nations. Private actions, by contrast, escape political control, which has advantages when American law clearly applies to a claim, but disadvantages when it conflicts with the laws of foreign nations. The government cannot control actions brought by private individuals and firms and so cannot coordinate those actions with the enforcement policies of other countries.

The Court has invoked the presumption against extraterritoriality in a wide range of cases, from admiralty to labor law to employment discrimination to human rights.[70] Sometimes Congress has acted in response to extend the reach of federal law, accepting the Court's invitation to make a clear statement endorsing the extraterritorial coverage of the statute. In the context of human rights, *Kiobel v. Royal Dutch Petroleum Co.*,[71] illustrates both the hazards and the benefits of invoking the presumption. The plaintiffs there alleged violations of international law by the government of Nigeria, aided and abetted by the corporate defendants in the case. All of the alleged violations occurred in Nigeria, and, in fact, also

---

[67]   15 U.S.C. §§ 30(b), 78dd(b).

[68]   The Dodd-Frank Wall Street Reform and Consumer Protection Act, Pub. L. No. 111–203 § 929P(b)(2), 124 Stat. 1376 (2010) (codified at 15 U.S.C. § 78aa(b)(2)).

[69]   *Id.*

[70]   EEOC v. Arabian American Oil Co., 499 U.S. 244 (1991); McCulloch v. Sociedad Nacional De Marineros De Hond., 372 U.S. 10 (1963); Romero v. International Terminal Operating Co., 358 U.S. 354 (1959).

[71]   133 S.Ct. 1659 (2013).

constituted alleged violations of Nigerian law. Seeking a more effective remedy, however, the plaintiffs sued in this country under the Alien Tort Statute (ATS), which gives the federal courts subject-matter jurisdiction over "any civil action by an alien for a tort only, committed in violation of the law of nations or a treaty of the United States."[72]

The Supreme Court held that the presumption against extraterritoriality required dismissal of the complaint, even though claims under the ATS rest ultimately upon international law.[73] International law, by definition, applies across national boundaries, and insofar as it protects individuals from abuse by their own government, it applies within the territory of foreign nations. The Court apparently reached the paradoxical result that the presumption counteracted the international reach of international law.[74] As the presumption itself is framed, the reference in the ATS to "the law of nations" could be taken as a clear statement by Congress of the statute's extraterritorial coverage. As the next chapter explores in more detail, however, little about the ATS is clear. It originated in a section of the First Judiciary Act listing a compendium of cases over which federal courts could exercise jurisdiction, including jurisdiction in admiralty. In an apt phrase of Judge Henry Friendly, it is a "legal Lohengrin . . . no one seems to know whence it came."[75] It directly addresses only federal subject-matter jurisdiction, leaving open the way in which international law comes to be adopted and enforced by a federal court. From this perspective, *Kiobel* imposes territorial limits on federal remedies under the ATS, not on the underlying international law.[76]

This way of looking at the case also avoids tension between the presumption against extraterritoriality and the *Charming Betsy* canon that American law should be interpreted, if possible, to be consistent with international law. Denying a federal remedy for violations of international law does not itself violate international law. On the other hand, as the Court emphasizes, granting a remedy

---

[72] 28 U.S.C. § 1350 (2012).

[73] *Kiobel*, 133 S.Ct. at 1665.

[74] *Id.* at 1664.

[75] IIT v. Vencap, Ltd., 519 F.2d 1001, 1015 (2d Cir. 1975).

[76] The Court reached a similar result in RJR Nabisco, Inc. v. European Community, 136 S.Ct. 2090 (2016), where it found that Congress clearly intended the criminal prohibition in the Racketeering-Influenced and Corrupt Organizations Act (RICO), 18 U.S.C. § 1962(b), (c), to apply extraterritorially. RICO applies extraterritorially if the predicate crimes that are an element of a RICO violation themselves apply extraterritorially. But no such clear congressional intent accompanies the private damage remedy for a RICO violation under § 1964(c). The plaintiffs stipulated that they did not seek any damages from losses in the U.S. and their claims therefore were extraterritorial and fell outside the focus of § 1964(c) on domestic losses.

might well interfere with the laws of the foreign nation where the tort occurred. On the facts of the case, the inadequacy of remedies under Nigerian law is a matter, first of all, for the government of Nigeria, and then for the political branches of our government, which can legislate or enter into a treaty to address this issue. Without such action by the political branches, American courts cannot undertake to redress the inadequacies of other legal systems.

This view of the presumption also responds to the analogy, advanced in Justice Breyer's concurring opinion,[77] between human rights violations and torts upon the high seas, piracy prominently among them, which historically have been covered by American admiralty law. On the high seas, however, admiralty does not conflict with the laws of other nations but fills a gap that would otherwise exist. The high seas constitute waters outside the boundaries of any state and so they have traditionally been the subject of admiralty jurisdiction, in other countries as well as our own. The example of admiralty does nevertheless reveal the capacity for growth in judge-made law, especially as supplemented by federal legislation that codifies and revises traditional maritime law. Several of the opinions in *Kiobel* left the door open to adapting the presumption against extraterritoriality to accommodate an approach along these lines.

All of the cases discussed in this section concern interpretation of federal statutes or federal common law based largely upon federal statutes. Those sources of federal law, together with the Constitution, create the structure and most of the content of federal law. They do not, however, automatically displace state law, and in particular, state choice-of-law rules. State courts remain free to reach their own decisions on whether to apply state law extraterritorially, so long as they conform to the loose constitutional restrictions on choice of law under the Due Process Clause. Few states have adopted a presumption against extraterritoriality explicitly. Far more commonly, states have turned to general principles of choice of law.[78] That raises the possibility that in cases like *Morrison* or *Kiobel*, state courts could use their own statutes or common law to regulate conduct beyond the reach of federal law. Moreover, if this attempt were successful, federal courts would be bound to follow it in diversity cases, including those brought by or against aliens.[79] Few state courts have aggressively expanded their own law in this way, partly because of the limited contacts that the defendant or the entire case has with the state. Absence of contacts of the defendant prevents the assertion

<hr>

[77] *IIT*, 519 F.2d. at 1674–75.

[78] Caleb Nelson, *State and Federal Models of the Interaction between Statutes and Unwritten Law*, 80 U. CHI. L. REV. 657, 690–91 (2013).

[79] *Cf.* Patrickson v. Dole Food Co., 251 F.3d 795 (9th Cir. 2001) (no federal question jurisdiction in such a case), aff'd on other grounds, 538 U.S. 468 (2003).

of personal jurisdiction and absence of contacts of the case limits the grounds for applying forum law, even on variants of interest analysis or the Second Restatement. On the facts of *Kiobel*, for instance, a state court would have to search the record thoroughly to find any state interest furthered by preventing human rights violations overseas or to find the weight of all reasonable factors to support the choice of its own law. Nevertheless, some residual uncertainty remains and increases in magnitude as the contacts of the case with the forum increase. For that reason, the parties might want to anticipate choice-of-law issues by selecting the applicable law by contract, if they can. The next section of this chapter takes up this possibility.

D. Choice-of-Law Clauses

The variety and disarray in American approaches to choice of law contrasts with the European approach, which has steadfastly adhered to a rule-based approach similar to the First Restatement of Conflict of Laws. For cases solely with European contacts, that approach gives greater weight and a better chance to achieving uniformity and predictability. But in cases with both European and American contacts, the contrast between these different regimes further increases the uncertainty over choice of law. The two regimes do share, however, a favorable attitude towards enforcing choice-of-law clauses.[80]

The same arguments that support enforcement of choice-of-forum clauses have led courts also to accept choice-of-law clauses. Courts defer to the revealed preferences of the parties; they are relieved of difficult choice-of-law decisions themselves; they show comity and deference to the laws of foreign nations insofar as they enforce such clauses. A further resemblance to choice-of-forum clauses lies in the categorical approach of European Union law to restrict or prohibit such clauses in certain kinds of contracts, particularly in consumer and employment contracts.[81] As noted earlier in this chapter, Europe generally takes a more categorical approach to choice-of-law questions, facilitating the exclusion of particular kinds of contracts from the presumed validity of choice-of-law clauses. By regulation, the European Union has reconciled and adjusted the principles of freedom of contract, which favor the validity of such clauses, and principles that protect parties in a relatively weak bargaining position, such as consumers and employees.

---

[80] Regulation (EC) No 593/2008 of the European Parliament and of the Council of 17 June 2008 on the Law Applicable to Contractual Obligations, 2008 O.J. (L 177) 6, art. 3.1.

[81] *Id.* at arts. 6.2, 8.1.

Choice-of-law and choice-of forum clauses share more than similarity in enforcement and interpretation. Such clauses frequently appear together in the same contract. The simultaneous appearance of both raises questions about which should be addressed first by a court, but since the two clauses typically receive the same treatment, this theoretical question hardly ever makes a real difference. The forum court must begin by applying its own law (either its own choice-of-law rules or its own contract rules) to assess the validity of one or both clauses, since to do otherwise, would be to beg the question of validity. At that point, the court must decide which clause to evaluate first. No problems arise if both are valid or if both are invalid under both the law of the forum and the law chosen by the parties. If they are valid, the court does what the contract says; if they are invalid, the court ignores what the contract says. If one is valid and the other invalid, the court should address the validity of the choice-of-law clause first because it determines what law governs the choice-of-forum clause. If the contract chooses the law of the forum, the result again is straightforward; the forum court then evaluates the choice-of-forum clause under its own law. Complications arise only if the contract selects foreign law and a foreign court and where foreign law invalidates the forum-selection clause. That leaves the case in the forum, but subject to foreign law, which might seem odd but which nevertheless accords with what foreign law requires.[82] These cases fortunately are rare.

Courts generally uphold choice-of-law clauses absent concerns about the validity of the contract as a whole. An unconscionable contract cannot be saved even if it selects foreign law that would otherwise make it enforceable. Some suspicion therefore attaches to choice-of-law clauses in consumer and employment contracts, as reflected in the provisions of European Union law, noted earlier, that limit choice-of-law clauses in such contracts. The inclusion of these clauses might represent an attempt to evade the mandatory terms of protective legislation, designed to address systematic imbalances in bargaining power between the parties to a contract.[83] Choice-of-law clauses in contracts between businesses, by contrast, generate no such suspicions and the strong trend favors enforcement of their terms. A representative case is *Nedlloyd Lines B.V. v. Superior Court of San Mateo County (Seawinds Ltd.)*,[84] where the California Supreme Court enforced a clause selecting Hong Kong law to govern the agreement between the parties. The agreement created a joint

---

[82] For a case along these lines, but also raising questions of federal-state choice of law, *see* Albemarle Corp. v. AstraZeneca UK Ltd., 628 F.3d 643 (4th Cir. 2010).

[83] *E.g.*, DeSantis v. Wackenhut Corp., 793 S.W.2d 670 (Tex. 1990), cert. denied, 498 U.S. 1048 (1991) (choice-of-law clause cannot be sued to avoid restrictions on employee covenants not to compete).

[84] 3 Cal. 4th 459, 834 P.2d 1148, 11 Cal. Rprr.2d 330 (1992).

venture involving two Hong Kong corporations, one of which was the plaintiff in the case. Although the plaintiff had its principal place of business in California, the court found sufficient connection to Hong Kong as the place of incorporation of two of the parties. The court essentially found these attenuated contacts to be sufficient, just as forum-selection clauses have been upheld simply on the ground that they are not arbitrary or abusive. Pursuing that analogy, the court also pointed to the choice-of-forum clause in the contract, which selected Hong Kong law as a non-exclusive forum for resolving disputes under the agreement.[85] The plaintiff could not be surprised in any way by the application of Hong Kong law.

Turning to the argument of public policy, the court also found no violation of any fundamental public of policy of California. In particular, the court found no such policy based on an implied covenant of good faith and fair dealing, which formed the gravamen of the plaintiff's complaint. The dissent did not directly contest the validity of the choice-of-law clause, but would have interpreted it literally only to cover the actual agreement between the parties and not the implied covenant of good faith and fair dealing. That distinction, however, appears to be artificial given the essentially contractual relationship between the parties. Most contracts in the modern world trigger the coverage of regulatory statutes that give rise to claims or defenses available to the parties. Limiting choice-of-law clauses strictly to enforcement of the contract itself does not make sense against this background of pervasive regulation. It does remain true, of course, that a clause that clearly excludes non-contractual claims should be given effect according to its terms. Choice-of-law clauses perform the signal function of giving certainty to a notoriously uncertain part of the law, and their contribution should not be compromised by a narrow and technical interpretation.

---

[85]　Nedlloyd, 3 Cal.4th at 491–493.

Chapter III

SUBJECT-MATTER JURISDICTION

This topic comes most naturally after choice of law, and not after personal jurisdiction, because the existence of subject-matter jurisdiction in the federal courts often depends upon the choice of federal law. Moreover, the sometimes confusing use of the term "jurisdiction" leads these two issues to be conflated: whether the court has power to decide the controversy before it ("subject-matter jurisdiction"); and whether the legislature or other lawmaking authority has power to make the law governing the controversy ("prescriptive jurisdiction"). Once these confusions in terminology are cleared up, the relationship between these different kinds of jurisdiction can be simply stated. A federal court has subject-matter jurisdiction to hear a case "arising under the Constitution, laws, or treaties of the United States" only if those sources of federal law provide an arguable basis for the plaintiff's claim.[1] Many other issues surround the existence of "arising under" jurisdiction, notably the precise role that federal law plays in defining the plaintiff's claim. Some of these come up in connection with sovereign immunity, to be discussed in the next chapter. This chapter emphasizes the relationship between the coverage of federal law and the existence of federal jurisdiction.

The federal courts can also exercise jurisdiction on other grounds. Admiralty historically served as the first and most prominent basis for federal jurisdiction over international cases. It depends on either maritime subject matter for contract cases, or location on navigable water and significant connection with traditional maritime commerce for tort cases. Both branches of admiralty jurisdiction readily extend overseas, although as with claims arising under federal law, claims within the admiralty jurisdiction must have a reasonable basis in American law.[2]

Diversity jurisdiction extends overseas for a different reason: it depends upon the citizenship of the parties, either state citizenship for American citizens or foreign citizenship for aliens. At its core, alien diversity jurisdiction covers controversies between citizens of a state on one side and aliens on the other side. Along the periphery, the details of diversity jurisdiction complicate any simple account of its scope. The general principle still holds, however, that the diversity jurisdiction is narrowly construed, for instance, in the requirement

---

[1]   28 U.S.C. § 1332 (2012).

[2]   Romero v. International Terminal Operating Co., 358 U.S. 354, 379–80 (1959).

of complete diversity. In most cases, although not quite all, the presence of aliens on both sides of a case defeats diversity jurisdiction.

A. Claims Arising Under Federal Law

This form of federal jurisdiction usually goes under the heading of "federal question" jurisdiction, although that phrase misleadingly implies that a single federal issue is sufficient for a claim to arise under federal law.[3] Established case law rejects this conclusion as an interpretation of the general "federal question" jurisdiction under § 1331.[4] Paradoxically, a single federal issue is not sufficient to establish jurisdiction under this statute, but it usually is under the corresponding provision in the Constitution, which covers all cases "arising under this Constitution, the Laws of the United States, and Treaties made, or which shall be made, under their Authority."[5] Even so, to invoke this provision in the Constitution, Congress must also act to grant the jurisdiction to the federal courts, as part of its power to "constitute Tribunals inferior to the Supreme Court."[6] In interpreting the grant of jurisdiction in § 1331, the Supreme Court has required federal law to play a larger role than in the constitutional provision for "arising under" jurisdiction, either in defining the elements of the cause of action or in conferring the right to bring the cause of action on the plaintiff.[7] Exactly how large a role federal law must play remains a matter of some uncertainty. For instance, a federal defense is not sufficient, but if federal law completely preempts any claim under state law, the entire cause of action becomes federal, and jurisdiction follows accordingly.[8]

In international cases, Congress has often avoided the intricacies of § 1331 and enacted a statute that specifically confers jurisdiction on the federal courts, for instance, over claims under the securities or antitrust laws. Congress usually, although not always, defines an entire cause of action and confers it upon the plaintiff, easily satisfying the constitutional minimum for jurisdiction. In the typical case, the only question of jurisdiction derives from the question of extra-territorial coverage: Is there an arguable basis for finding coverage of federal law?[9] At this point, subject-matter

---

[3] Paul Mishkin, *The Federal "Question" in the District Courts*, 53 COLUM. L. REV. 157 (1953).

[4] 28 U.S.C. § 1331 (2012).

[5] U.S. CONST. art. III, § 2.

[6] U.S. CONST. art. I, § 8; art. III § 1.

[7] Gully v. First Nat'l Bank, 299 U.S. 109, 112 (1936) (federal law must create an essential element of the cause of action); American Well Works Co. v. Lane & Bowler Co., 241 U.S. 257, 260 (1916) (federal law must create the cause of action).

[8] Beneficial Nat'l Bank v. Anderson, 539 U.S. 1, 6–11 (2003).

[9] Bell v. Hood, 327 U.S. 678, 683–84 (1946).

jurisdiction can easily become confused with prescriptive jurisdiction, but they remain distinct. If an arguable basis for coverage exists, then so does subject-matter jurisdiction. In procedural terms, the court cannot dismiss the case for lack of subject-matter jurisdiction, although it might later dismiss for failure to state a claim if coverage does not actually exist. The different grounds for dismissal make a real difference in the effect of the resulting judgment, since a dismissal for lack of subject-matter jurisdiction leaves open the possibility that the plaintiff can sue on the same claim in a different court, while a dismissal for failure to state a claim bars any subsequent suit. And, of course, the existence of an arguable basis for coverage depends upon the state of the law when the court decides the issue of subject-matter jurisdiction. An authoritative holding, for instance, that a federal statute does not extend overseas eliminates any arguable basis for finding that a claim that arises overseas also arises under federal law.

The Supreme Court seems to have lost sight of these distinctions in *Hartford Fire Insurance Co. v. California*,[10] where it correctly found jurisdiction over an antitrust claim arising in the United Kingdom but then went on to conclude that coverage followed for the same reason. That inference works, but only in the opposite direction, from coverage to jurisdiction.[11] The Court should have framed its holding that the Sherman Act did not generate a true conflict with British law in terms of coverage: that the Sherman Act reached the conduct alleged in the complaint in the absence of any contrary British law. Jurisdiction, on this view of the case, would have followed either from actual coverage or, if coverage had not been found, from an arguable basis for coverage. But coverage could not have followed from jurisdiction because the latter could have rested simply on an arguable basis for coverage. By eliding the difference between arguable coverage and actual coverage, the Court erroneously framed its holding on the merits in jurisdictional terms. The Court's use of the term "prescriptive jurisdiction" only confuses this issue.

The tangled web of connections between adjudicative and prescriptive jurisdiction nevertheless persists, apparently as a reflection of the comprehensive and absolute nature of sovereignty. One form of jurisdiction follows from another, even if in particular cases, courts might draw distinctions between them. The Foreign Sovereign Immunities Act (FSIA) provides an illuminating example.[12] The terms of the legislation make the question of

---

[10]   509 U.S. 764, 795–99 (1993).

[11]   *See id.* at 800–21 (Scalia, J., dissenting).

[12]   94 Pub. L. No. 583, 90 Stat. 2891 (1976) (codified at 28 U.S.C. §§ 1330, 1332, 1391(f), 1441(d), and 1602–11 (2012)).

immunity of a foreign state both a matter of a defense to liability on the merits and, simultaneously, a matter of subject-matter and personal jurisdiction. If the immunity exists in the former respect, it defeats jurisdiction in the latter respect. The confluence of all these forms of jurisdiction might simply reflect an extended version of comity, demonstrating respect for foreign sovereigns by relieving them of any semblance of submission to the jurisdiction of our courts when immunity exists. Still, concerns of respect and comity should be allowed to confuse the conceptual distinctions between the different forms of jurisdiction.

Some residual conceptual puzzles remain. In the FSIA, subject-matter jurisdiction gets tangled up in the removal provisions of the statute, which allow any case against a foreign sovereign or its agencies or instrumentalities to be removed from state court to federal court.[13] If the federal court then finds that the defendant has immunity, it must dismiss the case for lack of subject-matter jurisdiction.[14] This section of the FSIA also extends to personal jurisdiction.[15] In such a case, the FSIA creates federal jurisdiction for removal but then, paradoxically, denies it if the defendant has immunity on the merits. Practically speaking, the removal provisions assure a federal forum for resolving the issue of immunity for foreign sovereigns sued in state court. Hence removal jurisdiction of the federal court really depends on an arguable basis for asserting immunity. Under the axiom that a court always has jurisdiction to determine jurisdiction, the federal court can then go ahead and decide whether the defendant actually has immunity, and if not, to go on and reach the merits of the case.

The Supreme Court tried to sort out this paradox, and to reconcile the jurisdictional provisions of the FSIA with the Constitution, in *Verlinden B.V. v. Central Bank of Nigeria.*[16] The plaintiff in that case was a foreign corporation, as was the defendant, so no diversity jurisdiction existed under the Constitution. The Court thus turned to the constitutional grant of jurisdiction over claims arising under federal law. That clause could not, of course, be satisfied by the presence of a federal issue concerned only with jurisdiction, since that circular argument would leave Congress without any constraint on the claims that it could bring within the jurisdiction of the federal courts. The Court reasoned, instead, that the FSIA created a "comprehensive scheme" that "codifies the standards governing foreign sovereign immunity as an aspect of substantive federal law . . . and applying those standards will

---

[13]   28 U.S.C. § 1441(d) (2012).

[14]   *Id.* § 1604.

[15]   *See id.* § 1330.

[16]   461 U.S. 480 (1983).

generally require interpretation of numerous points of federal law."[17] In effect, the Court presumed that the presence of a foreign sovereign as a defendant would always generate a federal issue on the merits, if it was also an issue of subject-matter jurisdiction.

This reasoning goes only so far, however, towards finding a federal issue that would sustain federal jurisdiction. Under existing law, a single federal issue on the merits would be sufficient to meet the constitutional requirements for "arising under" jurisdiction.[18] But the probability that a federal issue will arise does not guarantee that one will, notably in cases in which the foreign sovereign has clearly waived its immunity to suit, an exception specifically recognized in the FSIA.[19] In those cases, the entire basis for the plaintiff's claim could rest entirely on state law. The Court therefore required something less than an actual federal issue on the merits, seemingly finding that Congress established a sufficient federal interest in suits against foreign sovereigns to support federal jurisdiction. This reasoning comes close to a theory of "protective jurisdiction": the theory that Congress can confer federal jurisdiction whenever it has "an articulated and active federal policy regulating a field, the 'arising under' clause of Article III apparently permits the conferring of jurisdiction on the national courts of all cases in the area—including those substantively governed by state law."[20] The Court nevertheless refused to base its decision on this ground.[21]

For reasons discussed more fully in the next chapter, on sovereign immunity, the result in *Verlinden* might be regarded as a foregone conclusion. After many years of consideration, Congress had adopted the "restrictive theory" of sovereign immunity, exposing foreign sovereigns to liability for their commercial acts. The Supreme Court would hardly have wanted to undo this historic legislation by declaring the crucial provision on jurisdiction unconstitutional. The alternative would have been to relegate sovereign immunity to the uncertainty that pre-existed the FSIA and to the risk that state courts would exploit that uncertainty to the detriment of foreign sovereigns. Because the federal government has nearly plenary power over international commerce and foreign relations, giving jurisdiction to the federal courts over claims against foreign sovereigns seemed to follow naturally from the balance of power in our federal system. Such considerations explain the decision in

---

[17] *Id.* at 497.

[18] Mesa v. California, 489 U.S. 121, 137–38 (1989).

[19] 28 U.S.C. § 1605(a)(1) (2012).

[20] Mishkin, *supra* note 3, at 193.

[21] *Verlinden*, 461 U.S. at 491 n.17.

Verlinden, even if they do not fully reconcile the opinion with other decisions on the scope of "arising under" jurisdiction.

Another leading decision on this form of federal jurisdiction, *Sosa v. Alvarez-Machain*,[22] yields a similarly equivocal verdict. In that case, a Mexican national sued agents of the Drug Enforcement Agency (and other Mexicans working with them) under the Federal Tort Claims Act (FTCA)[23] and the Alien Tort Statute (ATS).[24] The Supreme Court eventually held that both claims should be dismissed on the merits, but only after it upheld jurisdiction over them.[25] That could have been accomplished in a simple and straightforward manner, by relying upon the grant of jurisdiction under the FTCA, which creates a federal claim against federal officers that plainly arises under federal law. Once the Court found jurisdiction on that basis, it could have upheld jurisdiction over the ATS claim as a form of supplemental jurisdiction, since all the claims arose out of the same transaction and occurrence, involving the alleged kidnapping of the plaintiff.[26] Yet the Court felt compelled to address longstanding questions about the ATS, which grants jurisdiction over "any action by an alien for a tort only, committed in violation of the law of nations or a treaty of the United States." Insofar as the statute supports jurisdiction over claims by aliens against aliens, without the presence of any American citizens (as were some of the defendants in *Sosa*), it cannot be based upon the constitutional grant of diversity jurisdiction. That left only "arising under" jurisdiction and a question similar to that in *Verlinden*: What source of federal law generated the plaintiff's claim?

The Court's answer was that international law, as incorporated into federal law, formed the basis for the plaintiff's tort claim under the ATS. As noted earlier, however, the Court went on to hold that the plaintiff's claim failed on the merits. He failed to prove a violation of "a norm of international character accepted by the civilized world and defined with a specificity comparable to the features of the 18th century paradigms" established when the ATS was passed in the Judiciary Act of 1789.[27] Essentially, the Court made the question of jurisdiction easy by addressing the harder question of how international law became part of the federal law. If a treaty had been violated, that question would also have been easy, since the

---

[22]   542 U.S. 692 (2004).

[23]   28 U.S.C. § 1346(b) (2012).

[24]   *Id.* § 1350 (2012).

[25]   *Sosa*, 542 U.S. at 703–38.

[26]   28 U.S.C. § 1367 (2012) (codification of supplemental jurisdiction of federal courts).

[27]   *Sosa*, 542 U.S. at 725.

Constitution equates treaties with federal law in several clauses.[28] But the plaintiff alleged a violation only of customary international law, which lacks a definitive source in official acts of the political branches, such as legislation, executive agreements, or treaties. In its holding on the merits, the Court drastically narrowed the scope of customary international law adopted as federal law, but it left open the possibility that the scope might expand as international consensus settled on more specific norms.

In the long run, creating that possibility might be the most important consequence of *Sosa*. Customary international law, particularly as it protects human rights, might become a significant feature of federal law. The Court certainly went out of its way to leave this possibility open, by refusing to decide the case on narrower grounds. Without addressing the constitutionality of the ATS, it could have upheld jurisdiction on other grounds and then gone on to address the merits of the ATS claim in light of its holding that the FTCA did not provide any relief to the plaintiff. In passing the FTCA, Congress set definite limits on the liability of federal agents and those acting in concert with them. Those limits certainly supported the implication of similar limits on any claim under the ATS. As the law stands now, however, the jurisdictional provisions of the ATS have generated a freestanding, if quite limited, claim under federal law.

One last point about "arising jurisdiction" concerns its effect on the subject-matter jurisdiction of state courts. As a general matter, it has no effect at all. Unless Congress has conferred jurisdiction exclusively on the federal courts, the state courts remain free to go forward on state or federal claims within their own grants of jurisdiction. Plaintiffs have the option of suing in federal court, but they can also go to state court. In state court, defendants might remove the case, as they have the right to do under the FSIA and other removal statutes.[29] The choice to sue in state court generally remains with the litigants.

B. Admiralty Jurisdiction

Admiralty and maritime cases offer an instructive contrast to cases arising under federal law. The Constitution identifies "all Cases of admiralty and maritime Jurisdiction" as a separate heading of jurisdiction, which has been implemented, in turn, by a separate statute.[30] Section 1333 grants jurisdiction over such cases to the federal courts, "exclusive of the courts of the States."[31] This last

---

[28] U.S. CONST. art. VI.

[29] 28 U.S.C. § 1441 (2012) (statute governing removal jurisdiction).

[30] U.S. CONST. art. III, § 2, cl. 1.

[31] 28 U.S.C. § 1333 (2012).

clause, however, is immediately qualified by the "Saving Clause," which creates an exception in these terms "saving to suitors in all cases all other remedies to which they are otherwise entitled."[32] In effect, the Saving Clause makes jurisdiction over most admiralty cases concurrent with the state courts, with only a few exceptions, such as for actions *in rem* directly against a vessel or some other object in maritime commerce. The state courts otherwise remain free to grant the litigants "all other remedies to which they are otherwise entitled."[33] This recourse to state remedies, or to other forms of federal jurisdiction, such as diversity, makes a practical difference mainly in giving the parties the right to jury trial, which is not available in admiralty.

Admiralty and maritime law is federal law, but somewhat paradoxically, claims under this source of federal law do not "arise under" federal law for purposes of jurisdiction. The separate basis for admiralty jurisdiction in the Constitution, and in statutes dating back to the Judiciary Act of 1789, justifies the historical separation of these forms of jurisdiction.[34] As a functional matter, the separation also preserves the distinctive procedures in admiralty, such as a seizure of a vessel or other object by maritime arrest or attachment and, as just mentioned, the absence of a right to jury trial. Many of the seminal cases on international litigation in American courts arose in admiralty and involved suits against vessels. Thus, *The Charming Betsy*[35] established the proposition that American law should be interpreted, if at all possible, to conform to international law, and *The Schooner Exchange v. McFaddon*[36] first recognized the doctrine of foreign sovereign immunity. Many of the modern cases, for instance, on forum selection clauses and arbitration, also arose in admiralty.[37]

The reason for admiralty's prominence in this field has to do with a departure from the presumption against extra-territoriality that has been evident since American courts first exercised admiralty jurisdiction. That jurisdiction operates predominantly (although not entirely) on the high seas, which by definition are waters outside the territorial boundaries of the United States or any other country. From the beginning, maritime law has filled a vacuum where no law otherwise could apply on strictly territorial principles. Recognizing the need for some law to apply on the high seas, seagoing nations

---

[32] *Id.*

[33] *Id.*

[34] Romero v. Int'l Terminal Operating Co., 358 U.S. 354, 379–80 (1959).

[35] Murray v. The Schooner Charming Betsy, 6 U.S. (2 Cranch) 64, 118 (1804).

[36] The Schooner Exchange v. McFadden, 11 U.S. (7 Cranch) 116 (1812).

[37] Vimar Seguros y Reaseguros v. M/V Sky Reefer, 515 U.S. 528 (1995); The Bremen v. Zapata Off-Shore Co., 407 U.S. 1 (1972).

have settled on fairly uniform principles to govern maritime commerce. The law of different nations does diverge in important particulars, but it retains broad similarity, fostered in recent years by conventions on such issues as collision, salvage, and damage to cargo. So, for instance, the Supreme Court could recognize the extension of the Alien Tort Statute to cases of piracy based on the longstanding condemnation of piracy by all the nations of the world.[38] In this respect, admiralty provides more than a precedent for international civil litigation. It also offers a model for future developments as nations settle on widely shared principles to address common needs.

The precise scope of admiralty jurisdiction has created several persistent problems, but confined mainly to cases arising near the shore and in undisputed territorial waters. These cases do not have a significant international dimension. They, instead, concern the boundary between maritime law and the law that would ordinarily apply on land. Tort claims for injury on or near land have been the most troublesome. For instance, injuries to longshore workers on the dock, on a vessel, and on a gangplank have generated a long and complex line of decisions.[39] The general test is that the injury must have occurred on or next to navigable water and must have "a significant relationship to traditional maritime commerce."[40] In contract cases, admiralty jurisdiction depends upon "the nature and subject-matter of the contract."[41] This test embraces all ordinary maritime contracts, such as for carriage of cargo or passengers; towage, salvage, and charter parties; and repair of and supplies to a vessel. Two surprising exceptions are contracts to build a vessel and contracts to sell a vessel, both justified on the ground that both transactions have substantial components on land. These exceptions, like the problematic tort cases, illustrate that the uncertainty over admiralty jurisdiction intensifies as the underlying facts come closer to the shore, not as they go further out to sea.

Admiralty jurisdiction does reach claims arising in the territorial waters of another nation, but such claims have given rise to few disputes over the applicable law. The claims might be dismissed on grounds of *forum non conveniens*, or to enforce a choice-of-forum clause, or because American and foreign law might be essentially the same, or because one source of law rather than another might clearly apply. On the last point, a choice-of-law clause

---

[38] Sosa v. Alvarez-Machain, 542 U.S. 692, 715 (2004).

[39] *See, e.g.,* Sun Ship, Inc. v. Pennsylvania, 447 U.S. 715 (1980); Gutierrez v. Waterman Steamship Corp., 373 U.S. 206 (1963); Southern Pacific Co. v. Jensen, 244 U.S. 205 (1917).

[40] Executive Jet Aviation, Inc. v. City of Cleveland, 409 U.S. 249, 268 (1972).

[41] Insurance Co. v. Dunham, 78 U.S. (11 Wall.) 1, 26 (1871).

might dictate this result, or local law—for instance, establishing maritime traffic separation schemes—might be determinative. In theory, national laws still might conflict in any particular maritime case, but in practice, the parties and the courts have devised workable solutions to resolve any outstanding differences. As it has been exercised by American courts, admiralty jurisdiction yields the hopeful lesson that federal courts can fashion federal law, with the assistance of Congress and the executive branch, to effectively deal with a significant segment of international civil litigation.

C. Diversity Jurisdiction

The Constitution provides for diversity jurisdiction over controversies "between a State, or the Citizens thereof, and foreign states, Citizens or Subjects."[42] The general diversity statute, § 1332, implements this grant of jurisdiction in several different subsections, which stop well short of giving the federal courts the power to hear any case involving an alien. As noted in the discussion of *Verlinden*, Article III does not extend to claims by aliens against aliens. Moreover, even when the case involves citizens of the United States, the absence of complete diversity of citizenship can defeat jurisdiction. Complete diversity is a statutory requirement. Under longstanding decisions of the Supreme Court, it prevents jurisdiction under § 1332 if any plaintiff and any defendant are from the same state. The constitutional requirement of minimal diversity goes to the opposite extreme. It supports jurisdiction if any plaintiff and any defendant are from different states, or if one is a citizen of a state and another is an alien. Certain statutes, such as those governing large class actions and multiparty, multi-forum cases, incorporate the constitutional requirement of minimal diversity.[43] These cases, because of their very size, can extend to aliens, who can be added as parties once diverse citizenship has been satisfied by any pair of plaintiffs and defendants.

The statutory requirement of complete diversity does not work in exactly the same way for aliens as it does for citizens. It is weaker in some respects and broader in others. So, for instance, when complete diversity exists between state citizens, aliens can be added to both sides of the case without defeating jurisdiction.[44] On the other hand, aliens admitted for permanent residence in the United States are treated as citizens of the state in which they are domiciled, for purposes of defeating jurisdiction by breaking up the requirement of complete diversity if an opposing party is a citizen of the same state.[45]

---

[42]   U.S. CONST. art. III, § 2.

[43]   28 U.S.C. §§ 1332(d), 1369(3) (2012).

[44]   *Id.* § 1332(a)(3).

[45]   *Id.* § 1332(a)(2).

Complications also surround the treatment of dual citizens. The emerging consensus in the courts of appeals treats these individuals as American citizens and looks to their state of domicile to determine state citizenship.[46] It follows that, if they are domiciled abroad, they are not citizens of any state, just as American citizens domiciled abroad have no state citizenship. The presence of any party in this posture automatically defeats diversity jurisdiction, on the presumed rationale that neither the Constitution nor § 1332(a) recognizes diversity jurisdiction over nonresident citizens.

Most of the intricacies can be subsumed under the general principle that diversity jurisdiction is narrowly construed to limit it, as far as possible, to the avowed purpose of preventing prejudice to out-of-staters in state court. Complete diversity serves this purpose by excluding from federal jurisdiction cases in which citizens from the same state are on both sides in the litigation. The state court in such cases would not, so to speak, know which side to be prejudiced against. The jurisdictional amount required under § 1332(b) gives another indication of the narrowness of diversity jurisdiction. A plaintiff's claim must exceed $75,000, and although plaintiffs with tort claims can usually seek damages that exceed this amount,[47] those with contract claims for damages well below this amount cannot easily get around this requirement. Still further requirements limit removal of diversity cases by defendants originally sued in state court. For instance, all defendants must agree to removal; additionally, strict time limits, not to exceed one year, apply to the petition for removal.[48] A last restriction on diversity jurisdiction appears in the statute on supplemental jurisdiction, which largely prevents parties in a diversity case from adding claims that arise out of the same transaction or occurrence, unless those claims have an independent basis in federal jurisdiction.[49] No such bar applies to suits based on claims arising under federal law.

A further limitation on diversity jurisdiction does not concern the terms under which it is granted but the law applied when it is exercised. Under *Erie Railroad Co. v. Tompkins*,[50] a federal court sitting in diversity must apply state law to most of the substantive issues in the case. Questions governed by the Federal Rules of Civil Procedure, or by any applicable federal statute, remain governed by federal law, but the existence of a cause of action, the elements that must be proved, the burden of proof, affirmative defenses (including the statute of limitations), and the extent of available remedies, all

---

[46] *E.g.*, Coury v. Prot, 85 F.3d 244, 250 (5th Cir. 1996).

[47] St. Paul Mercury Indem. Co. v. Red Cab Co., 303 U.S. 283, 289 (1938).

[48] 28 U.S.C. § 1446(b), (c) (2012).

[49] *Id.* § 1367(b).

[50] 304 U.S. 64 (1938).

are matters of state law. Hence aliens who get their cases into federal court based on diversity do not convert them into cases governed by federal law. That leaves state law to play a dominant role in any international case not based on the Constitution, federal statutes, treaties, or federal common law.

Indeed, the *Erie* doctrine casts doubt upon most forms of federal common law. The opinion famously declared, "There is no federal general common law," and that principle has allowed federal judge-made law to survive only as "special federal common law," which draws its force from other sources of federal law.[51] Special federal common law, in this sense, amounts to extended interpretation of the Constitution, federal statutes, and treaties. These sources reflect the outcome of the political process and the judgment of the political branches of government in formulating basic federal policy. After *Erie*, federal common law only implements policies settled elsewhere, an implication that has particular significance in international cases. The fact that the federal government has plenary authority over international commerce and foreign relations does not support the conclusion that federal courts have similarly broad lawmaking authority.[52]

D. Jurisdiction of the State Courts

The preceding discussion of federal jurisdiction presupposes that most cases filed in federal court might also have been filed in state court. As a general rule, the federal courts exercise jurisdiction concurrently with the state courts.[53] Some forms of federal jurisdiction are exclusive, as in certain admiralty cases and claims under the federal antitrust laws, but most forms are concurrent; the plaintiff can choose between filing in federal court and filing in state court.[54] If the plaintiff files in state court, the defendant can usually remove if the case could have been brought in federal court,[55] although the rules on removal have complicated exceptions and qualifications. Removal does not guarantee that a case that could have been brought in federal court will end up there. In vastly many more cases, the action simply falls outside the limited jurisdiction of the federal courts and can only be brought in state court. State courts

---

[51] *Id.* at 78.

[52] Curtis A. Bradley & Jack L. Goldsmith, *Customary International Law as Federal Common Law: A Critique of the Modern Position*, 110 HARV. L. REV. 815, 840 (1997).

[53] Tafflin v. Levitt, 493 U.S. 455, 458–59 (1981).

[54] Marrese v. American Academy of Orthpaedic Surgeons, 470 U.S. 373, 379–80 (1985).

[55] 28 U.S.C. § 1441(a) (2012).

of general jurisdiction have inherent power over all such cases, just as state law governs all issues not covered by federal law.

These principles hold in international civil litigation as they do in domestic litigation, leaving plaintiffs with access to state court, even though their claims arise partially or wholly overseas. Moreover, unlike federal jurisdiction over claims arising under federal law, state-court jurisdiction need not have an arguable basis in state substantive law. It can exceed the coverage of state law if the state's choice-of-law principles point to the application of foreign law, even if the state's own substantive law could not reach so far. As discussed in the previous chapter, few of the limits on the extra-territorial application of state law come directly from the Constitution, so that most such limits must be based on the state's own choice-of-law rules. When these lead to foreign law, other limitations on the state court's exercise of jurisdiction might come into play, such as lack of personal jurisdiction or the doctrine of *forum non conveniens*. A combination of federal law and judicial self-restraint—either in choosing to apply foreign law or in dismissing for *forum non conveniens*—imposes most of the practical limits on state subject-matter jurisdiction.

This chapter began with the questions raised by *Verlinden* and *Sosa* over the scope of federal jurisdiction for claims "arising under" federal law. Just beneath the surface of those opinions, however, the Supreme Court had to engage with the limited power of the federal courts to make law. State courts do not have to cope with such limits except insofar as they are restrained by federal law. The next chapter returns to those issues in a detailed discussion of foreign sovereign immunity, human rights, and the act of state doctrine.

Chapter IV

SOVEREIGN IMMUNITY, THE ACT OF STATE DOCTRINE, AND HUMAN RIGHTS

As modern nation states have expanded the range of their activities, they have exposed themselves to a wider range of lawsuits and thus have greater occasion to invoke the defense of sovereign immunity and the act of state doctrine. The commercial activities of sovereign nations led to the first transformation of the law of sovereign immunity. The argument gradually gained force that sovereign states and their instrumentalities should be treated like other actors in the commercial world. That position, called "the restrictive theory of sovereign immunity," eventually was codified in the Foreign Sovereign Immunities Act (FSIA).[1] During the same period, the current version of the act of state doctrine became part of federal law. This doctrine recognizes the legitimacy of official acts of foreign sovereigns according to their own laws within their own territory, even if those acts violate international law. The act of state doctrine, like foreign sovereign immunity, has narrowed in scope since the leading modern decision on the subject, *Banco Nacional De Cuba v. Sabbatino*,[2] which involved expropriation of property, allegedly in violation of international law. Although the violation involved property rights, the presence of international law points to the second transformation of sovereign immunity in the modern era: the expanded protection of human rights. Decisions under the Alien Tort Statute, discussed in previous chapters, exemplify this trend. If claims are brought against foreign nations or their instrumentalities, they must fall under an exception in the FSIA, which has special provisions for human rights violations. These provisions, although usually narrow in scope, have accumulated in number and significance as human rights violations have been more widely publicized and condemned. If recent developments are any guide, current trends strongly favor further protection for human rights.

Human rights, like commercial activity, reveal how the modern understanding of sovereignty has expanded the dimensions of international civil litigation. As the power of sovereign nations has grown, their immunity from suit has diminished. Sovereignty has changed from the absolute terms in which it was previously conceived, as the exclusive power of a single government within the territory it controlled, to a highly qualified and complicated issue

---

[1]   94 Pub. L. No. 583, 90 Stat. 2891 (1976) (codified at 28 U.S.C. §§ 1330, 1332, 1391(f), 1441(d), and 1602–11 (2012)) [hereinafter FSIA].

[2]   376 U.S. 398 (1964).

which opens the door to claims against government officials for human rights violations committed against the government's own people within its own boundaries. In American law, the same trends have become familiar in domestic government litigation, where contract, tort, and civil rights claims against the government and government officials have spawned intricate procedures and complicated forms of immunity. International litigation against foreign sovereigns and foreign officials has initiated a parallel process of doctrinal elaboration, which has only begun to address all the implications of any program of effective enforcement of human rights.

The movement from enforcement of commercial and property rights, which dominate the terms of the FSIA, to enforcement of human rights also resembles the pattern of development of American law, particularly with respect to constitutional rights. Early in the nation's history, most constitutional claims protected rights to property and contract, and only in the twentieth century did protection extend to other constitutional rights, such as freedom of speech, religion, and privacy. Restraints on government that protected property and commercial interests only later spread to a range of individual rights that everyone could enjoy. Those who could initially afford the expense of taking on the government paved the way through legal doctrine and procedure for those with fewer resources. In the process, constitutional rights expanded accordingly. Litigation under the FSIA exhibits the same trend, from commercial disputes dealing with foreign sovereigns and their instrumentalities to human rights claims recognized as a matter of tort or statutory law. The latter have not yet developed into a full-fledged system of protecting individual rights, a development which must await international agreements and initiatives undertaken by the executive and legislative branches of government. Most of the cases in this chapter concern commercial and property disputes, and relatively few concern human rights, yet both types of cases are intimately connected by the legal doctrine common to both of them. Existing law recognizes the potential for broad protection of human rights, even if it has yet to be realized.

A. The Restrictive Theory of Foreign Sovereign Immunity

Foreign sovereigns acquired immunity from the jurisdiction of American courts early in the nineteenth century in *The Schooner Exchange v. McFadden*.[3] That decision brought the customary international law of immunity into American law, analogizing the treatment of property owned by a sovereign to the immunity enjoyed

---

[3]   11 U.S. (7 Cranch) 116 (1812).

by foreign diplomats. Sovereign immunity followed from the need to accommodate the dignity of foreign sovereigns to the mutually exclusive absolute power that each sovereign exercised within its borders. The Supreme Court framed the immunity in similarly absolute terms, finding it "to be a principle of public law, that national ships of war, entering the port of a friendly power open for their reception, are to be considered as exempted by the consent of that power from its jurisdiction."[4] As the name of the case implies, *The Schooner Exchange* was an admiralty case arising from the seizure of a French warship in an American port, and it was followed by a series of admiralty cases that extended immunity to commercial vessels owned by foreign sovereigns.[5]

That view began to change, as critics of existing doctrine argued that immunity for state commercial activities gave foreign nations and their wholly owned companies a competitive advantage over private firms. The proliferation of commercial activities of socialist nations, and others with mixed capitalist and socialist economies, gave added force to this argument. The Supreme Court responded by suggesting that the views of the State Department, if given in a particular case, would be dispositive on the issue of sovereign immunity.[6] This suggestion soon became standard practice, but it raised as many problems as it solved. The Court did invite the participation of the executive branch in a sensitive question with implications for foreign policy, but the Court did not require executive participation in every case. Where a foreign sovereign did not seek a letter from the State Department, the courts were on their own. And when a letter was granted or denied, the parties had few means of appeal through the bureaucracy of the State Department. If, on the other hand, the parties continued to litigate the act of state issue through the courts, that issue itself raised further issues of separation of powers. Should the courts defer to the views of the State Department, at the risk of abdicating the role of determining what the law is? Or should they resist deference and seemingly spurn the expertise of the executive branch on issues of foreign affairs?

The State Department addressed some of these concerns in the "Tate Letter," which stated that it would generally follow the restrictive theory of sovereign immunity and deny immunity for commercial activities.[7] Of course, uncertainty remained over what

---

[4]   *Id.* at 145–46.

[5]   *E.g.,* Berizzi Bros. Co. v. S.S. Pesaro, 271 U.S. 562 (1926).

[6]   Compania Espanola De Navegacion Maritima, S.A. v. The Navemar, 303 U.S. 68, 74 (1938).

[7]   Letter from Jack B. Tate, Acting Legal Adviser, U.S. Dep't of State, to Philip B. Perlman, Acting Attorney General, U.S. Dep't of Justice (May 19, 1952), reprinted in 26 DEP'T OF STATE BULLETIN 984 (1952).

constituted commercial activity and whether to resolve this question through the bureaucratic process or the judicial process. It was only with the passage of the FSIA in 1976 that the basic uncertainty over the scope of the immunity and the procedure for determining it were definitively resolved. The Act established federal policy through the action of both of the political branches of government: Congress in passing the legislation and the President in signing it into law. Although it took several decades to reach fruition, this process exemplified the contribution that the political branches can make in resolving problems of foreign relations that come up in international civil litigation.

The structure of the FSIA establishes immunity as the general rule in American law, subject to enumerated exceptions.[8] As noted in the previous chapter, the immunity is framed in jurisdictional terms, although it operates also as a defense on the merits.[9] It also operates as an immunity of the foreign sovereign's assets from attachment and execution.[10] Because the FSIA has this structure, most cases come down to the crucial issue of the application of one or another exception found in the statute. Under the restrictive theory of sovereign immunity, the most important of these is the exception for commercial activity, which appears both in the provisions on immunity from litigation and on immunity of property from attachment and execution.[11] Related exceptions provide for waivers of immunity and for agreements to arbitrate, which frequently appear in contracts made by foreign sovereigns,[12] and to admiralty claims arising from commercial activity.[13]

Because it is central to the statute, the exception for commercial activity deserves close inspection. It has two features: the nature of the activity and its relationship to the United States. The term "commercial activity" itself has a special definition in the FSIA. Unfortunately, it is circular:

> A "commercial activity" means either a regular course of commercial conduct or a particular commercial transaction or act. The commercial character of an activity shall be determined by reference to the nature of the course of conduct or particular transaction or act, rather than by reference to its purpose.[14]

---

[8]   FSIA, 28 U.S.C. §§ 1604–05.

[9]   *Id.* §§ 1330, 1606.

[10] *Id.* §§ 1609, 1611, again subject to specified exceptions. *See id.* § 1610.

[11] *Id.* §§ 1605(a)(2); 1610(a)(2), (b)(2).

[12] *Id.* §§ 1605(a)(1), (6); 1610(a)(1), (6); (b)(1).

[13] *Id.* § 1605(b), (c), (d).

[14] *Id.* § 1603(d).

The first sentence in this definition defines "commercial activity" in terms of "commercial conduct" or "commercial transaction or act," leaving the word "commercial" without any special definition. The second sentence seems to make "purpose" irrelevant to the definition of "commercial activity," but it cannot be taken literally to exclude all evidence of intent. No one engages in commercial activity by accident; therefore, some element of intent infuses all forms of commercial activity. What the second sentence addresses is the further purpose of any course of action: whether a sovereign engages in commercial activity with governmental ends in view or whether it engages in other sovereign acts with commercial ends in view. These further purposes do not count; only the purpose inherent in the activity itself do.

The Supreme Court addressed the scope of the commercial exception in *Republic of Argentina v. Weltover, Inc.*[15] That case arose from Argentina's default on bonds issued as part of a plan to stabilize its currency. The plaintiffs argued that the issuance of the bonds, and the default on them, constituted commercial activity, no different from what a private individual or firm would do in incurring and then defaulting on debt obligations. Argentina argued that its actions were pursuant to the sovereign governmental objective of stabilizing its currency by obtaining funds denominated in American dollars that could be exchanged for Argentine pesos. The Court rejected this argument, reasoning that "the question is not whether the foreign government is acting with a profit motive or instead with the aim of fulfilling uniquely sovereign objectives. Rather, the issue is whether the particular actions that the foreign state performs (whatever the motive behind them) are the *type* of actions by which a private party engages in 'trade or commerce.' "[16] The bonds were "in almost all respects garden-variety debt instruments."[17]

The Court also found the geographical component of the commercial exception to be met. The bonds in question specified New York as one place where creditors could demand payment, and Argentina had made payments there before it defaulted on the bonds. Consequently, the default had "a direct effect in the United States" as required by the FSIA.[18] Moreover, this effect satisfied any constitutional requirements for application of American law, although the Court reserved the question whether a foreign sovereign was a "person" entitled to the protection of due process. Even if Argentina was a person for this purpose, the issuance of the bonds and the default on them had sufficient contacts with the

---

[15]   504 U.S. 607 (1992).

[16]   *Id.* at 614 (citation omitted).

[17]   *Id.* at 615.

[18]   FSIA, 28 U.S.C. § 1605(a).

United States.[19] The reappearance of contacts analysis, both under
the statute and under the Constitution, demonstrates how far the
significance of contacts goes beyond issues of personal jurisdiction.
Contacts determine when American law can affect the immunity of
foreign nations. If payments on the bonds could only have been made
in London, for instance, the question of immunity would have come
out entirely differently. The commercial exception in the FSIA would
not have applied at all. Contacts also figured in the ability of the
plaintiffs to obtain satisfaction of any judgment against Argentina,
since the FSIA allows attachment or execution only on "property in
the United States."[20] To the extent that Argentina kept its property
outside the United States and immune from execution here, it could
frustrate attempts to satisfy any judgment against it, as events
subsequently showed it did.[21]

Contacts figure even more prominently in the tort exception,
which is limited to "personal injury or death, or damage to or loss of
property, occurring in the United States."[22] Presence of property in
the United States constitutes a still more rigid requirement for
claims of expropriation of property in violation of international law:
the property itself or property exchanged for it must be in the United
States, or such property must be owned by an agency or an
instrumentality that engages in commercial activity in the United
States.[23] In *Argentine Republic v. Amerada Hess Shipping Corp.*,[24]
the Supreme Court took up these exceptions. The case arose from the
bombing of an oil tanker during the war between the United Kingdom
and Argentina over the Falkland-Malvinas Islands. Although
notified that the vessel's location was well outside the war zone, the
Argentine armed forces bombed the tanker, causing its eventual total
loss. The plaintiffs, two Liberian corporations, brought claims in
admiralty and under the Alien Tort Statute, alleging that the
bombing of neutral shipping was both unjustified and in violation of
the law of nations. The former allegations sounded in tort, but the
Supreme Court held that the tort exception did not apply because the
incident occurred thousands of miles from the territorial waters of
the United States.[25] The latter allegations also failed to trigger the
only applicable exception for violations of international law, which
was limited to expropriation of property. The FSIA, the Court held,

---

[19] *Weltover*, 504 U.S. at 619.

[20] FSIA, 28 U.S.C. § 1610(a), (b).

[21] NML Capital, Ltd. v. Republic of Argentina, 727 F.3d 230 (2d Cir. 2013).

[22] FSIA, 28 U.S.C. § 1605(a)(5).

[23] *Id.* § 1605(a)(3). The same is true of disputes over real property acquired by
succession or gift. It must be in the United States. *Id.* § 1605(a)(4).

[24] 488 U.S. 428 (1989).

[25] *Id.* at 441.

did not support any implied exception for violations of international law under the Alien Tort Statute.[26]

Another case, *Saudi Arabia v. Nelson*,[27] illustrates how the exceptions for torts and for violations of international law relate to the exception for commercial activity. They have a narrower scope that cannot be circumvented by relationship to commercial activity in this country. The plaintiff in this case alleged that he had been wrongfully arrested and tortured when he reported hazardous conditions at a hospital in Saudi Arabia where he worked. The hospital was wholly owned by the Saudi government, as was the corporation that had recruited the plaintiff in the United States to work in Saudi Arabia. Both of these entities qualified as an "agency or instrumentality" of the Saudi government and shared in its immunity from suit under FSIA. Although the complaint contained several separate counts alleging wrongdoing in Saudi Arabia and in the United States, Justice Souter concluded for a majority of the Court that none of the alleged conduct could be characterized as commercial: "The conduct boils down to abuse of the power of its police by the Saudi Government, and however monstrous such abuse undoubtedly may be, a foreign state's exercise of the power of its police has long been understood for purposes of the restrictive theory as peculiarly sovereign in nature."[28] Several separate opinions took issue with this characterization. Justice White took the position that running a hospital was a commercial activity, although in this case, one without sufficient contacts with the United States. Justice Kennedy, Justice Blackmun, and Justice Stevens all dissented on the ground that the process of recruiting the plaintiff in the United States involved commercial torts that did have sufficient contact with the United States.

All of the opinions in *Saudi Arabia v. Nelson* relied only on the commercial exception. The tort exception actually excludes commercial torts, and as *Amerada Hess* reveals, the tort exception has a stronger test for contacts than does the commercial exception.[29] The loss resulting from the tort must have occurred within the United States. In his majority opinion, Justice Souter resisted re-characterization of the plaintiff's claims as sounding in tort, partly to avoid the argument that they involved commercial activity in the United States. In any event, the immediate losses in this case to the plaintiff all occurred in Saudi Arabia, taking his claim out of the tort exception for that reason. The human rights dimensions of the plaintiff's claim did not come into play for another reason discussed

---

[26] *Id.* at 442.

[27] 507 U.S. 349 (1993).

[28] *Id.* at 361.

[29] *Amerada Hess*, 488 U.S. at 439–41.

in *Amerada Hess*: the exception for violations of international law only covered expropriation, not unlawful detention or torture.[30] As Justice Souter emphasized in his opinion, abusive though the alleged actions of the Saudi government were, they constituted "sovereign or public acts (jure imperii)," not "those that are private or commercial in character (jure gestionis)."[31] These might have violated international law, but they did not support a remedy under the restrictive theory of sovereign immunity embodied in the FSIA. The force of international law instead made itself felt in arguments, such as those adopted by the separate opinions, to extend the arguably applicable terms of the commercial exception.

In a subsequent decision, the Court has resisted arguments to extend the commercial exception on facts sympathetic to the plaintiff. In *OBB Personenverkehr AG v. Sachs*,[32] the Court refused to recharacterize a tort claim arising out of an accident in boarding a train in Austria into a contract claim arising within the United States based on the sale of a ticket here. As in *Nelson*, the plaintiff's claim sounded overwhelmingly in tort and could not be transformed into a claim from commercial activity in this country.[33]

The international law exception figured more prominently, if still indirectly, in another decision, *Republic of Austria v. Altmann*,[34] which held that the FSIA applied retroactively to the expropriation of art works, first by the Nazis immediately after the annexation of Austria in 1938, and then by the Republic of Austria after World War II in 1948. The plaintiff was the descendant of the Jewish owner of the expropriated paintings and sought to invoke the international law exception on the ground that the Austrian Gallery, which held the paintings, was an instrumentality of the Austrian government with commercial dealings in the United States. The Supreme Court did not reach this question, but the Court was plainly influenced by the allegations of Nazi wrongdoing and the failure of the Austrian government to restore the paintings to their rightful owner. The Court, for instance, noted that the paintings had been taken by an official with the inauspicious name of "Dr. Fuhrer," who donated one of them to the gallery in a letter signed "Heil Hitler."[35] The Court's actual reasoning relied upon the FSIA as a comprehensive codification of the restrictive theory of sovereign immunity.[36] The dissenting opinion, although acknowledging that the case was

---

[30] *Id.*

[31] 507 U.S. at 360.

[32] 136 S.Ct. 390 (2015).

[33] *Id.* at 395–97.

[34] 541 U.S. 677 (2004).

[35] *Id.* at 684.

[36] *Id.* at 691.

"difficult," could not accept that rationale for applying the FSIA to events that occurred decades before its enactment.[37] According to the dissent, the normal presumption against retroactivity instead should have limited the statute's coverage.

The opinions in *Altmann*, as much as those in *Amerada Hess* and *Saudi Arabia v. Nelson*, really stand for the intermittent coverage of human rights claims by the FSIA. Congress framed the statute with a focus on the commercial exception, with little attention paid to human rights as a distinct category of claims. That changed, but only to a limited degree, with the addition of the terrorism exception to the FSIA, and, soon thereafter, the passage of a corresponding cause of action, both of which now appear in § 1605A of the statute. The FSIA does not generally provide for causes of action, but only for immunity to claims that arise under some other source of law, whether federal of state. Section 1605A represents the sole exception to this principle. Congress framed it in extraordinarily narrow terms. The foreign state must be "state sponsor of terrorism," so designated by the Secretary of State; the plaintiff must be a national of the United States, a member of the armed forces, or otherwise working for the United States; and if the case arose in the foreign nation, the plaintiff must have exhausted remedies available by arbitration. Only three countries currently are on the list of state sponsors of terrorism: Iran, Sudan, and Syria.[38] This short list illustrates both the narrow scope of § 1605A and the control that the executive branch exercises over it. In effect, § 1605A selectively targets only a few claims, which in recent years have been brought mainly against Iran, for special treatment. Separate provisions create further exceptions to the general restrictions on attachment and execution of judgments against foreign sovereigns.[39]

Liability under § 1605A also extends to individual government officers acting in their official capacity. Other statutes create narrowly defined remedies against individuals, but not against foreign sovereigns. Among these are the Torture Victim Protection Act of 1991,[40] which creates a remedy for torture and extra-judicial killing, and the Anti-Terrorism Act of 1990,[41] which does the same for victims of terrorism. These statutes, like § 1605A, provide a remedy for citizens analogous to the remedy for aliens under the Alien Tort Statute, discussed in the previous chapter. Taken together, all of this legislation illustrates the patchwork nature of the existing remedies for human rights violations. They remain qualified

---

[37] *Id.* at 715, 717 (Kennedy, J., dissenting).

[38] DEP'T OF STATE, COUNTRY REPORTS ON TERRORISM 19–23 (2014).

[39] FSIA, 28 U.S.C. § 1610(a)(7), (b)(3), (f).

[40] Pub. L. No. 102–256, 106 Stat. 73 (codified at 28 U.S.C. § 1350, note).

[41] 18 U.S.C. §§ 2333–34, 2337 (2012).

along several dimensions: who can sue, for what wrongs, against which defendants, and subject to which kinds of immunity. The next section of this chapter takes up the last of these issues.

B. Agencies, Instrumentalities, and Officers of Foreign Sovereigns

The FSIA defines a "foreign state" to include its political subdivisions, agencies, or instrumentalities.[42] Certain provisions distinguish between the foreign state itself and its agencies or instrumentalities, primarily in limiting liability for punitive damages and in determining which assets can be seized to satisfy any resulting judgment.[43] "Agency or instrumentality" receives a separate definition, which requires the agency or instrumentality to have both separate status as a legal person and either be used as an organ of a foreign state or be majority owned by a foreign state. The agency or instrumentality must also be an entity other than one recognized as a citizen of the United States for purposes of diversity jurisdiction and other than one created under the laws of any third country.[44] The intricacy of this definition comes as no surprise, since plaintiffs seek out any potential defendant who might be liable and who has assets from a judgment that can be satisfied. For the same reason, not all the nuances of these definitions have been firmly settled by decisions under the FSIA. The main outlines, however, have been settled, with the notable exception of the treatment of individual officers of a foreign state. The FSIA does not address this issue at all, so courts have had to figure out the dimensions of individual immunity on their own.

The Supreme Court addressed the question of separate legal status of an instrumentality in *First National City Bank v. Banco Para El Comercio Exterior De Cuba.*[45] The decision takes the form of an exception that proves the rule. In most cases, "government instrumentalities established as juridical entities distinct and independent from their sovereign should normally be treated as such."[46] That principle tacitly accepts the law of the foreign sovereign as presumptively determinative, but the Court framed the issue of separate legal status as one of federal common law, "which in these circumstances is necessarily informed both by international law principles and by articulated congressional policies."[47] Federal common law led to an exception that supported a set-off in liability

---

[42] FSIA, 28 U.S.C. § 1603(a).

[43] *Id.* §§ 1606, 1610(b).

[44] *Id.* § 1610(b).

[45] 462 U.S. 611 (1983).

[46] *Id.* 626–27.

[47] *Id.* at 623.

because of the expropriation of City Bank's branches in Cuba by the Cuban government. The nominal plaintiff, Banco Para, sued City Bank on a letter of credit for delivery of sugar to the United States. City Bank sought a set-off, not for the conduct of Banco Para, but for the conduct of the Cuban government in expropriating Banco Para's bank branches. While the litigation was pending, the Cuban government merged the relevant assets and operations of Banco Para into its Ministry of Foreign Trade, making the government itself the direct beneficiary of the litigation. In those circumstances, the Court held, the government also had to accept liability for the set-off, as provided in § 1607 of the FSIA. The Court "pierced the corporate veil" in order to subject the nominal plaintiff, Banco Para, to a set-off based on the conduct of the real party in interest, Cuba.[48] The typical case, however, would simply follow the law of the foreign sovereign, as recognized by international law and federal common law, to determine the separate status of an agency or instrumentality.

The ownership stake of a foreign sovereign in a separate entity raises other questions about how the ownership stake is measured—in terms of direct or indirect control—and at what point in time—when the claim arose or when suit was filed. The Supreme Court resolved both of these issues in *Dole Food Co. v. Patrickson*,[49] which involved claims against two Israeli companies (among other defendants). The state of Israel held a controlling interest in each company, but only through intermediate companies, giving it indirect rather than direct ownership of each company. Adopting a clear-cut rule to define instrumentality status, the Court held that this test best reflected the statutory language, which refers to "a majority of whose shares or other ownership interest is owned by a foreign state or political subdivision thereof."[50] The Court took the phrase "other ownership interest" to apply only to entities that did not issue shares of stock and whose ownership was determined by other means.[51] On the issue of timing, the Court also adopted the simpler rule, looking to ownership at the time suit was filed. Sovereign immunity was designed only to relieve foreign sovereigns of the burden of defending actions in American courts, but if the sovereigns had already divested majority ownership in an instrumentality, a suit against the instrumentality would not impose a significant burden on them.[52]

---

[48] *Id.*

[49] 538 U.S. 468 (2003).

[50] FSIA, 28 U.S.C. § 1603(b)(2).

[51] *Dole Food Co.,* 538 U.S. at 476.

[52] *Id.* Curiously, the recent decision in OBB Personenverkehr AG v. Sachs, 136 S.Ct. 390 (2015), upheld the sovereign immunity of an indirect subsidiary of the Austrian government, apparently because the parties stipulated that it was an instrumentality of that government. The Court therefore did not address this issue. *Id.* at 293–94

Between them, *First National City Bank* and *Dole Food* did not resolve all the questions that arise over the definition of a foreign state. The decisions leave open, for instance, the distinction between a "subdivision" of a foreign state and an "agency or instrumentality." This distinction becomes significant when the sovereign proper is treated differently from separate entities that it controls, for instance, on questions of liability, punitive damages, and attachment and execution of judgments. Apart from cases like *First National City Bank*, an instrumentality's liability cannot be attributed to the foreign government and vice versa. As noted earlier, this principle also limits punitive damages, which cannot be recovered against the foreign government, and the assets from which a judgment can be collected.[53] In other contexts, these distinctions do not matter, as in claims against state sponsors of terrorism. Where the strict conditions of § 1605A have been met, foreign sovereigns are subject to broad liability, including punitive damages, and their assets within the United States are generally subject to attachment and execution.[54]

Among its several unique features, § 1605A also addresses individual liability, imposing it upon "any official, employee or agent of that foreign state while acting within the scope of his or her office."[55] The FSIA does not itself provide for any form of immunity for individuals, which must be resolved as a matter of federal common law.[56] The literal terms of § 1605A appear to abrogate individual immunity by directly imposing liability upon officers. Nevertheless, a network of rules developed from customary international law and treaties of the United States insulates foreign officials from personal liability. Heads of state and foreign diplomats have immunity by virtue of their office (immunity rationae personae) from any exercise of jurisdiction by domestic courts, while other foreign officials have immunity for their official acts (immunity *ratione materiae*) which extends to acts under color of foreign law. As a practical matter, American courts almost always defer to the State Department in deciding issues of foreign official immunity. Whether they would do so in interpretation of statutes like § 1605A, which explicitly impose liability upon foreign officials for their acts in their official capacity, remains doubtful. That question concerns interpretation of a statute rather than assessment of situation of a particular foreign official. Moreover, under § 1605A, the State

---

[53] FSIA, 28 U.S.C. §§ 1606, 1610(b).

[54] *Id.* §§ 1605A(c), 1610(a)(7), (b)(3), (f).

[55] *Id.* § 1605A(c).

[56] Samantar v. Yousef, 560 U.S. 305, 326 (2010).

Department already plays a decisive role in identifying the few nations that are designated as "state sponsors of terrorism."[57]

Claims under other statutes raise more difficult questions. In *Samantar v. Yousef*, the plaintiff sued a former official of the government of Somalia under the Alien Tort Statute and Torture Victim Protection Act. Neither statute addresses questions of immunity, although both impose liability upon individuals, and insofar as they impose liability upon foreign states, both are subject to the provisions of the FSIA. The Supreme Court unanimously held that the definition of a "foreign state" in the FSIA does not extend to individuals.[58] The Court therefore held that the federal district court had jurisdiction over the plaintiff's claims, but left open the question whether the defendant could assert immunity as a defense to such claims as a matter of federal common law. Some such immunity must be available in theory, although on the facts of this case, the State Department denied any official immunity to the defendant and the district court accepted this decision on remand from the Supreme Court.[59]

Three arguments counsel in favor of recognizing official immunity. The first, based on international law, accepts immunity as a recognized practice in dealings between one sovereign and the diplomats and other officials of another sovereign, particularly when they enter into the first sovereign's territory. The second, based on the practical need for comity, in the sense of respect for the actions of foreign sovereigns, goes back to the original rationale for foreign sovereign immunity in *The Schooner Exchange*. National sovereigns must have means of dealing with one another in a peaceful fashion that does not subject them, or their officials, to liability.[60] And the third reason rests upon the need to harmonize the immunity of foreign sovereigns with the immunity of their officials. The FSIA would have accomplished little if it allowed plaintiffs to transform every suit against a foreign sovereign into one against its officials. The immunity of both has to be coextensive to a large degree. A foreign state, and its agencies and instrumentalities, only act through individual officials who must therefore partake to some degree in the state's own immunity.

The question of how to shape individual immunity has become a more pressing question as more claims for violation of human rights

---

[57] FSIA, 28 U.S.C. § 1605A(2).

[58] *Samantar*, 560 U.S. at 326.

[59] Yousuf v. Samantar, No. 1:04cv1360, 2011 WL 7445583 (E.D. Va. Feb. 15, 2011).

[60] Underhill v. Hernandez, 168 U.S. 250, 254 (1897) (immunity conferred on individual because "the acts of the defendant were the acts of the government of Venezuela"); Schooner Exchange, 11 U.S. at 116–17.

have made their way to court. Decisions in domestic civil rights law have worked out the scope of individual immunity in that sphere, but it has developed against a different background than foreign sovereign immunity. The immunity of state officers under the general civil rights statute, § 1983,[61] usually takes a qualified form, to make up for the absence of a damage remedy against the state itself under the Eleventh Amendment. In many cases, the plaintiff can recover damages only against an individual officer. The restrictive theory of sovereign immunity, with its multiple exceptions for claims directly against foreign nations, dispenses with the need for a damage action against individual officers. Nevertheless, plaintiffs bring claims against individual officers, as in *Yousef v. Samantar*.

Another such case, *Kadic v. Karadzic*,[62] illustrates the intricacies of determining individual liability. The plaintiffs there sued for injury and death from atrocities allegedly committed by the self-proclaimed Bosnian-Serbian Republic of "Srpska." They sued Radovan Karadzic, the president of the three-person executive council of the republic, and served him with legal process while he was visiting New York to attend the United Nations. Service occurred outside the boundaries of immunity from service agreed to by the United States and the United Nations.[63] The defendant could claim no further immunity because, as it turned out, he was not the leader of any nation recognized by the United States.

The defendant tried to turn his failure to hold any official position in his favor, arguing that the claims against him applied only to individuals acting on behalf of a state. The court rejected that argument also. The plaintiff's claims under the Alien Tort Statute (ATS) and under the Torture Victim Protection Act (TVPA) applied to acts on behalf of unrecognized as well as recognized states, and in any event, the plaintiffs also alleged that the defendant acted on behalf of the recognized state of the former Yugoslavia. The court also suggested that some violations of human rights do not require any state action at all. The limits on claims under the ATS have to be sought in decisions restricting its scope, such as *Sosa v. Alvarez-Machain*[64] and *Kiobel v. Royal Dutch Petroleum*[65] discussed in Chapter 2. The limits on the TVPA derive from its literal terms,

---

[61] 42 U.S.C. § 1983 (2012).

[62] 70 F.3d 232 (2d Cir. 1995), *cert. denied*, 518 U.S. 1005 (1996).

[63] Agreement Regarding the Headquarters of the United Nations, U.S.-U.N., June 26, 1957, reprinted at 22 U.S.C. § 287 note.

[64] 542 U.S. 692 (2004).

[65] 133 S.Ct. 1659 (2013).

which impose a state action requirement and cover only individuals, as opposed to corporations and other entities.[66]

International law, however, does cut both ways in human rights cases. It protects basic human rights, but it also limits the remedies available under national law for violations that occur in other countries. Congress nevertheless has acted to expand remedies in both the broad sense of liability and in the narrow sense of assets subject to execution. An example, recently upheld by the Supreme Court, subjected the assets of the Iranian central bank, otherwise immune from seizure, to execution in satisfaction of existing judgments under § 1605A against Iran.[67] Critics of the TVPA and of § 1605A have pointed out that the reach of both statutes extends into the territory of other nations, contrary to the traditional principle of international law that each nation bears principal responsibility for protecting human rights within its own borders.[68] That principle of international law, in turn, triggers the canon of construction under *The Charming Betsy* that "an act of Congress ought never to be construed to violate the law of nations if any other possible construction remains."[69] The Supreme Court accepted this approach to the ATS in *Kiobel* to narrow the territorial coverage of the Act so that it did not apply to conduct within the boundaries of another nation; however, both the TVPA and § 1605A apply to acts of terrorism regardless of where they occur. The specific limitations in both statutes contain no geographical restrictions. In the terms used in *The Charming Betsy*, no "other possible construction remains."

American law apparently applies regardless of international law. That position has prompted retaliatory legislation by other nations, particularly those listed as "state sponsors of terrorism" subject to § 1605A. Retaliation by Iran might not seem to make much difference, although it could well complicate diplomatic initiatives to improve relations with other countries. To avoid such problems, the State Department could delete these nations from the list of state sponsors of terrorism, as Cuba was deleted as part of the process of normalizing relations with that country, and Libya was deleted after prolonged negotiations over a period of decades after the terrorist attack on an airliner in Lockerbie, Scotland. The executive branch cannot tailor the scope of the TVPA to diplomatic exigencies in such

---

[66] 57 Pub. L. No. 102–256, 106 Stat. 73, § 2(a) (1991) (codified at 28 U.S.C. § 1350 note); *see also* Mohamad v. Palestinian Authority, 132 S.Ct. 1702, 1706 (2012) (holding that the Act does not apply to non-sovereign organizations).

[67] Bank Markazi v. Peterson, 136 S.Ct. 1310 (2016) (holding that 22 U.S.C. § 8772 was not impermissibly retroactive, special legislation).

[68] CURTIS A. BRADLEY & JACK L. GOLDSMITH, FOREIGN RELATIONS LAW: CASES AND MATERIALS 424–25, 464–66 (5th ed. 2014); ANDREW CLAPHAM, BRIERLY'S LAW OF NATIONS 249–50 (7th ed. 2012).

[69] Murray v. The Schooner Charming Betsy, 6 U.S. (2 Cranch) 64, 118 (1804).

a straightforward fashion. The legislation might still be defended on grounds of "universal jurisdiction" over acts that violate mandatory norms of international law (*jus cogens*).[70] Other nations have recognized such jurisdiction, as in the prosecution of former President Pinochet for torture while he was in office in Chile.[71] Virtually all these cases, like the Pinochet case, involved criminal prosecutions, under the inherent control of government officials with executive and investigatory discretion. They do not involve civil actions initiated by private parties, who are largely outside government control.

The pressure for universal recognition of human rights still generates arguments for universal methods of enforcement. International tribunals constituted by multilateral treaties provide a partial response to such arguments, but again, mainly by way of authorizing criminal prosecutions. The International Criminal Court (ICC) exemplifies this trend, although it has predecessors with more limited jurisdiction going back to the Nuremburg Tribunal after World War II. By the same token, the response of the United States to the ICC exemplifies the doubts generated by any such tribunal, and in particular, the risk that it might be used against American officials and members of the armed forces who undertake missions overseas. The Clinton Administration signed the treaty creating the ICC, but only during its last days in office and with significant reservations. The Bush Administration subsequently expressed greater reservations and refused to send the treaty to the Senate for ratification.

The incremental process of expanding remedies through civil litigation does not pose the risk that suddenly American courts will recognize human rights claims on the scale of domestic tort or civil rights law. Both the courts and Congress have proceeded in piecemeal fashion to develop the remedies recognized today, with caution in both branches of government to target them on the worst abuses that most need redress. Over the short term, the law has slowly augmented the ability of victims to recover for violation of their human rights. Yet these rights have multiplied in the decades since World War II, transforming international law from a field concerned only with relations among sovereigns to also protecting individuals from the misuse of sovereign power. Over the long term, the remedies available to individuals might multiply as well. Here, as elsewhere in international civil litigation, a snapshot of the law as it exists today must take account of the trends that will, in all

---

[70] RESTATEMENT (THIRD) OF FOREIGN RELATIONS LAW § 404 (1987).

[71] Regina v. Bow Street Metropolitan Stipendiary Magistrate and Others (ex parte Pinochet Ugarte), [2000] 1 A.C. 147 (1999) (allowing extradition for prosecution in Spain).

likelihood, make it change in the future. Concern with international human rights, like the globalization of international commerce, shows no signs of diminishing.

C. The Act of State Doctrine

The act of state doctrine collides directly with protection of human rights. The doctrine accepts the validity of official acts of a sovereign within its own territory even if those acts violate international law. In this respect, it operates much like foreign sovereign immunity, and the two doctrines often are invoked together. Sovereign immunity, however, protects certain kinds of defendants and purports to do so in jurisdictional terms. The court cannot decide claims against sovereigns as defined in the FSIA unless specifically exempted by the Act itself. The act of state doctrine removes from the courts the power to question certain sovereign acts, regardless of the identity of the parties. Moreover, the doctrine goes to the merits of the dispute, so that it yields a binding resolution in favor of the validity and legal force of an act of state. It does so whether or not the act of state conforms to international law.

The act of state doctrine grew out of decisions also concerned with immunity, in particular, *Underhill v. Hernandez*,[72] a case against the commander of revolutionary forces in Venezuela, which eventually succeeded in toppling the existing regime and took power in a government recognized by the United States. On the issue of individual immunity, the Supreme Court held that the acts of the commander were the acts of the subsequently recognized government of Venezuela. As such, they could not be questioned in an American court because of the mutually exclusive sovereignty of each nation within its own territory. As the Court reasoned, "every sovereign State is bound to respect the independence of every other sovereign State, and the courts of one country will not sit in judgment on the acts of the government of another done within its own territory."[73] Cast in these terms, the act of state doctrine establishes an irrebuttable choice-of-law rule: the validity of official acts of another nation within its own territory must be assessed according to its own law. Despite the categorical command to apply the law of the foreign state, the conditions for applying the act of state doctrine impose important qualifications upon its scope.

The leading modern decision on the act of state doctrine, *Banco Nacional De Cuba v. Sabbatino*,[74] framed it in deliberately narrow terms, deciding only "that the Judicial Branch will not examine the

---

[72] 168 U.S. 250 (1897).

[73] *Id.* at 252.

[74] 376 U.S. 398 (1964).

validity of a taking of property within its own territory by a foreign sovereign government, extant and recognized by this country at the time of suit, in the absence of a treaty or other unambiguous agreement regarding controlling legal principle, even if the complaint alleged that the taking violates customary international law."[75] The holding addressed only the facts before the Court: the seizure of a shipment of sugar, bound for the United States, but expropriated while the vessel carrying the sugar was still in Cuban waters. If the expropriation had been attempted while the vessel was on the high seas, the Court would have faced a different question since Cuba would have acted outside its territorial boundaries. So, too, if the violation of international law did not involve a taking of property but some other violation of individual rights. The Court did not mention other violations of international law. Moreover, the Court left open the possibility that the political branches of government could alter the scope of the doctrine. As it turned out, a response was not long in coming, although in the form of legislation rather a treaty: the Second Hickenlooper Amendment abrogated the doctrine on the facts of the case, leading to an eventual decision against the Banco Nacional de Cuba.[76]

These subsequent developments anticipate the fate of the act of state doctrine, to be discussed shortly, but the source of the doctrine elicited most of the commentary on *Sabbatino*. The Court specifically refused to follow state law, despite the fact that the plaintiff's claim for the sugar was otherwise governed by state law. The Court found the principle of *Erie Railroad v. Tompkins*[77] inapplicable to an issue so deeply intertwined with foreign relations and the power of the federal government over foreign affairs.[78] Since no federal statute or treaty dealt with the act of state doctrine at the time, the Court was left with the only realistic alternative of applying federal common law. It devised its own approach to foreign relations, based only partly on the Constitution, insofar as it gave control over foreign relations to the political branches of government, and partly on international law, insofar as it counseled in favor of deferring to the acts of foreign sovereigns within their own territory. Of course, neither the Constitution nor international law dictated the result in *Sabbatino*. The constitutional principles of separation of powers gave great latitude to the Court to decide what the consequences were of assigning power over foreign relations to other branches of government. International law, the Court assumed, did not allow the

---

[75]   *Id.* at 428.

[76]   22 U.S.C. § 2370(e)(2) (2012); Banco Nacional de Cuba v. Farr, 383 F.2d 166 (2d Cir. 1967).

[77]   304 U.S. 64 (1938).

[78]   *Sabbatino*, 376 U.S. at 425–26.

expropriation of the disputed sugar, so that Cuba violated a specific rule of international law. At a more abstract level, however, international law authorized the territorial division of power among nations, so that actions of Cuba within its own borders had all the attributes of sovereignty.

The decision in *Sabbatino* excited interest among scholars because it left these questions in the hands of the federal judiciary, opening the door to judicial adoption of customary international law as federal common law. That practice dated back to an admiralty case at the turn of the twentieth century, *The Paquete Habana*,[79] which famously stated:

> International law is part of our law, and must be ascertained and administered by the courts of justice of appropriate jurisdiction, as often as questions of right depending upon it are duly presented for their determination. For this purpose, where there is no treaty, and no controlling executive or legislative act or judicial decision, resort must be had to the customs and usages of civilized nations. . . .[80]

As Justice White emphasized in his dissent in *Sabbatino*, international law cut both ways in that case, both in favor of and against taking the Cuban expropriation to finally decide title to the property.[81] But he agreed that what federal common law required in light of the Constitution and international law was a matter for the courts.[82] Justice Harlan, in his opinion for the Court, relied more heavily on the desirability of disentangling the judiciary from foreign policy issues assigned to the other branches of government. "Piecemeal dispositions of this sort involving the probability of affront to another state could seriously interfere with negotiations being carried on by the Executive Branch and might prevent or render less favorable the terms of an agreement that could otherwise be reached."[83]

This effort by the Supreme Court to extricate itself from controversies over foreign relations proved to be unavailing. Relations with Cuba had reached a low point in 1964, when the Court handed down *Sabbatino*. Expropriation of American assets in Cuba was only the first salvo in retaliatory actions that culminated in the Cuban Missile Crisis in 1962. In response to the decision, Congress passed the Second Hickenlooper Amendment, effectively barring the

---

[79]   175 U.S. 677 (1900).

[80]   *Id.* at 700.

[81]   *Sabbatino*, 376 U.S. at 454–55 (White, J., dissenting).

[82]   *Id.* at 441.

[83]   *Id.* at 432 (Harlan, J., majority opinion).

act of state doctrine as a defense to expropriation of property in violation of international law. The amendment contained an exception to protect certain letters of credit and another for case-by-case determinations by the President that the doctrine should apply. Yet the amendment as a whole sent a clear message that the Court should reconsider the scope of the act of state doctrine. In subsequent decisions, the Court has largely taken this course. Some might decry this step as surrendering to political pressure, but it follows directly from the nature of the Court's holding as a matter of federal common law. A statute, just as much as a treaty, can alter the terms on which international norms are received into American law. This is particularly true of customary international law which, by definition, has no definitive source in treaties or other international agreements.

The Court's retreat from the act of state doctrine began in *First National City Bank v. Banco Nacional de Cuba*,[84] an equivocal decision that both rejected the application of the doctrine and refused to give decisive weight to a State Department opinion on this issue. A majority of justices found the doctrine inapplicable, either by deference to the State Department or because it did not fit the facts of the case, which involved a set-off sought by City Bank based on the expropriation of its branches in Cuba. A different majority rejected any decisive role to the State Department letter, for reasons similar to those that eventually led Congress to abandon a similar practice in the FSIA. If the letter, in this context called a "Bernstein letter," resolved the act of state issue, it took over an essentially judicial function from the judicial branch of government. As Justice Douglas memorably said in a separate opinion, the Court should not become "a mere errand boy for the Executive Branch which may choose to prick some people's chestnuts from the fire, but not others."[85] Even on his view, courts could still ask for the views of the State Department without being bound by them. Despite the fractured opinion in *First National City Bank*, the Court ultimately went along with the State Department and denied application of the act of state doctrine.

Another decision that followed the signals sent from the political branches, but without strictly being bound by them, is *Alfred Dunhill of London, Inc. v. Republic of Cuba*.[86] As a result of another expropriation by Cuba, the former owners of seized tobacco companies sought money from importers for shipments to the American market. The Cuban government demanded return of this money, effectively repudiating its obligation to pay the money to the

---

[84] 406 U.S. 759 (1972).

[85] *Id.* at 773 (Douglas, J., concurring in the result).

[86] 425 U.S. 682 (1976).

importers who, in turn, would pay it to the former owners. The Court found this action to be a commercial rather than a political act and therefore outside the scope of the act of state doctrine. The Court relied by analogy on the restrictive theory of sovereign immunity and the FSIA, which was then under consideration by Congress. In any event, the Court could not have relied directly upon the FSIA even if it had been passed, since sovereign immunity and the act of state doctrine are technically distinct issues. The Court nevertheless took care to bring its view of the act of state doctrine into agreement with the emerging consensus that the commercial acts of a foreign nation do not deserve the same degree of deference as its sovereign acts. A more cynical interpretation of the decision might attribute it to a sense of which way the political winds were blowing on the treatment of foreign sovereigns. Yet such a pessimistic view of the decision again neglects the distinctive function of federal common law: not to make law independent of the other sources of federal law, a role disowned by the Supreme Court in *Erie*, but to fill in gaps left by federal statutes, treaties, and the Constitution, in a manner consistent with the principles underlying these undisputed sources of federal law.

If any doubt about the limited scope of the act of state doctrine remained, the Supreme Court put it to rest in *W.S. Kirkpatrick & Co v. Environmental Tectonics Corp. International.*[87] The plaintiffs there alleged that they had been denied a contract with the Nigerian government because of bribes paid by the defendant. The defendant characterized those payments as a "commission," authorized as an act of state by the Nigerian government. The Court rejected this contention, confining the act of state doctrine to the validity of official acts undertaken by a foreign government. The defendant could point to no source in Nigerian law that legitimated these payments, and in fact, if they were bribes, they were expressly prohibited by Nigerian law. The United States, appearing as amicus curiae, disagreed with the Court's strict approach, although not with the result in the case. The United States would have introduced a degree of flexibility in the doctrine, based on the principle from *Sabbatino* foregoing litigation when "alleged corruption in the award of contracts or other commercially oriented activities of foreign governments could sufficiently touch on 'national nerves' that the act of state doctrine or related principles of abstention would appropriately be found to bar suit."[88]

The Court disowned this discretionary view of the doctrine oriented to abstention from deciding a case. The Court took the act of

---

[87]   493 U.S. 400 (1990).

[88]   *Id.* at 408 (citation omitted) (internal quotation marks omitted).

state doctrine to be both narrower and more powerful. It applied only to official acts of a foreign nation, but when it did, it resulted in a decision on the merits, confirming the validity of that nation's acts within its own borders.[89] The abstention doctrine takes a very different form. As we will see in Chapter 6, it usually results in deferral of proceedings in one court in favor of those in a different court. Dismissal on abstention grounds does not result in a decision on the merits, and it often depends upon the exercise of judicial discretion. The act of state doctrine has neither of these characteristics. Nevertheless, some lower federal courts continue to appeal to the doctrine to avoid cases that they seemingly would prefer not to decide, such as claims that the international oil cartel sponsored by the Organization of Petroleum Exporting Countries violates the American antitrust laws.[90] A court's reluctance to bring the full force of American law to bear upon foreign sovereigns, some of which are crucial allies of the United States, certainly responds to foreign policy concerns. Yet it risks transforming the act of state doctrine into an opportunity for American courts to pick and choose among the cases implicating the actions of the foreign nations that they want to hear. To the extent such cases involve foreign sovereigns, or their agents and instrumentalities, the FSIA offers a better and more definite means of handling them: better because its terms have been approved by Congress, more definite because it defines the exceptions to sovereign immunity with some precision. Alternatively, courts can re-examine the application of American law in the first place to conduct that occurs largely overseas. The presumption against the extraterritoriality of federal statutes offers another means of restricting the scope of American law and therefore the power of American courts. The act of state doctrine does the same, but only in a narrow range of cases that the Supreme Court, taking cognizance of the views of the political branches, has allowed to it.

---

[89] *Id.* at 409–10.

[90] Spectrum Stores, Inc. v. Citgo Petroleum Corp., 632 F.3d 938 (5th Cir.), *cert. denied*, 132 S.Ct. 366, 367 (2011) (act of state doctrine and political question doctrine barred antitrust suits against petroleum producing companies, many owned by foreign governments).

Chapter V

SERVICE OF PROCESS, DISCOVERY, AND BLOCKING STATUTES

Legal process that reaches into another country raises especially formal and sensitive issues of sovereignty—formal because process is issued in the name of a sovereign, sensitive because it is backed by the threat of legal sanctions. Questions about legal process come up at the beginning of litigation with the service of process upon the defendant, in the middle of proceedings with discovery and blocking statutes, and at the end with the enforcement of judgments. This chapter takes up the earlier stages of litigation, and Chapter 7 takes up the last stage after judgment. The issues at each stage involve intricate questions of procedure, governed by interlocking rules and treaties. Service of process must be accomplished in exactly the right way, with little leeway for mistakes. Discovery overseas must be done with the proper foundation, prepared to counter objections based on confidentiality and on the burdens of disclosure. In both spheres, the outcome depends upon the relationship of detailed provisions in the Federal Rules of Civil Procedure and upon international conventions. The complexity of these issues both reflects and embodies the tensions inherent in the threatened exercise of force by one nation inside the boundaries of another. Nations cede their control over the use of force within their territory only grudgingly and by agreement.

Service of process represents the least controversial of these methods of threatening the use of force. The need to give effective notice to the defendant at the outset of the action constitutes a basic principle of procedural fairness, embodied in American law in the Due Process Clauses of the Fifth and Fourteenth Amendments. As the Supreme Court said in the foundational decision on this issue, *Mullane v. Central Hanover Bank & Trust Co.*, "when notice is a person's due, process which is a mere gesture is not due process."[1] No nation wants to deny the individuals and firms within its border notice of foreign proceedings against them, if only to allow them to protest against the exercise of jurisdiction by a foreign court. And virtually all nations refuse to recognize judgments in actions initiated by inadequate service of process. Consequently, treaties and international practice have promoted effective means for service of process overseas.

Discovery from an opposing party in another country rests on no such consensus, and for that reason, raises many more contentious

---

[1]   339 U.S. 306, 315 (1950).

issues. The United States stands out as the country that allows the widest scope for private civil actions and for discovery in aid of such actions, including interrogatories, requests for production of documents, and depositions. Other nations with much narrower discovery often bridle at the enforcement of American discovery orders within their boundaries. Some have reacted by adopting "blocking statutes" that prevent the compelled disclosure of information to American litigants. These statutes also extend beyond discovery to other laws protecting privacy, for instance extending to bank secrecy laws that inhibit tax collection and enforcement of other laws by public authorities. Hence these statutes receive separate consideration in the last section of this chapter. As with service of process overseas, overly broad discovery can result in refusal to enforce discovery orders and any resulting judgment in a foreign country.

A. Service of Process

Federal Rule of Civil Procedure 4 contains the basic requirements for service of process to initiate an action in federal court. It divides permissible means of service into two kinds: mailed service of a request for waiver of formal service and formal service itself. The first kind is designed to provide a less expensive alternative to the second kind, which itself is broken down into several different categories based on the identity and location of the defendant. In particular, formal service of process on a defendant overseas is treated differently from service in the United States. Both identity and location of the defendant also matter for waiver of formal service, often restricting its availability.

A request for waiver of formal service is accomplished by mail and so could be regarded as an informal kind of service, but it still must meet the specific and detailed requirements enumerated in Rule 4(d). These include mailing "a copy of the complaint, two copies of a waiver form, and a prepaid means for returning the form."[2] A defendant outside the United States has at least sixty days to return the waiver, and if the defendant signs and returns the waiver, proof of service is not required.[3] Notwithstanding the terminology of "waiver," the waiver of service "does not waive any objection to personal jurisdiction or to venue."[4] By its terms, Rule 4(d) applies to individuals and private firms found overseas,[5] but it does not apply to service on a minor or an incompetent person.[6] It also does not apply

---

[2]   FED. R. CIV. P. 4(d)(1)(C).

[3]   FED. R. CIV. P. 4(d)(1)(F).

[4]   FED. R. CIV. P. 4(d)(5).

[5]   FED. R. CIV. P. 4(d)(1), (f), (h)(2).

[6]   FED. R. CIV. P. 4(g).

to service on a "foreign state or its political subdivision, agency, or instrumentality," which must be served according to the terms of the Foreign Sovereign Immunities Act.[7] Foreign states, just like the United States,[8] receive special treatment, partly out of the practical need to assure service upon the correct subdivision of the state and partly out of respect for the state's sovereign status.

Despite limits on mailed service of process in foreign countries, to be discussed shortly, mailed requests for waiver of service do not raise any issues of compliance with international law or the law of the state of destination.[9] Undoubtedly this is because, with respect to foreign defendants, a request for waiver of service is not at all coercive. Unlike a domestic defendant, a foreign defendant who refuses to waive formal service cannot be held liable for the costs of formal service if the failure to waive was unjustified.[10] The request for waiver carries no implicit threat of government sanctions, unlike ordinary service of process, which carries the threat of entry of a default judgment. From the perspective of a foreign country, the request for waiver appears to be no different from any other unsolicited and uncoerced offer received through the mail.

Formal service of process raises many more issues, partly because the mechanics of giving formal notice in a foreign country are more complicated and partly because of the need to comply both with international law and with the law of the destination state. Translation of the summons and the complaint into a foreign language, for instance, might be necessary to give adequate notice to the foreign defendant and to comply with international and foreign legal requirements. Just determining what those requirements are can be costly in and of itself because it requires specialized legal advice. Compliance with the applicable requirements imposes additional costs. For plaintiffs, this makes the prospect of waiver of formal service more attractive. But since foreign defendants suffer no adverse effects from unjustified refusal to waive formal service, they can easily force plaintiffs to bear the cost of formal service.

Formal service can be made in a variety of different ways, under multiple provisions of Rule 4(f) and the international agreements and foreign law to which it refers. The rule begins by requiring that all forms of service be "reasonably calculated to give notice," in accord with the Due Process Clauses as interpreted in *Mullane*.[11] Rule

---

[7]   FED. R. CIV. P. 4(j); 28 U.S.C. § 1608 (2012).

[8]   FED. R. CIV. P. 4(i).

[9]   4B CHARLES ALAN WRIGHT, ARTHUR R. MILLER & ADAM N. STEINMAN, FEDERAL PRACTICE AND PROCEDURE 259 (4th ed. 2015).

[10]   *See* Rule 4(d)(2) (shifting costs only for "a defendant located within the United States").

[11]   FED. R. CIV. P. 4(f); *Mullane*, 339 U.S. at 314.

4(f)(1) then identifies the Hague Service Convention on the Service Abroad of Judicial and Extrajudicial Documents as the main vehicle for formal service of process.[12] The Hague Service Convention requires every signatory state to organize a "Central Authority" for service of process, either through the authority's own actions or those of "an appropriate agency."[13] Service itself is accomplished by two methods within a foreign state, either as "prescribed by its internal law for the service of documents in domestic actions upon persons who are within its territory" or as requested by the applicant "unless such a method is incompatible with the law of the State addressed."[14] As these provisions illustrate, the law of the foreign state takes a leading role in defining the permissible means of service.

The alternative methods of service specified in Rule 4 give the same priority to the law of the foreign state, with one significant exception. Rule 4(f)(3) provides for a residual means of service "as the court orders" and if "not prohibited by international agreement."[15] This form of service assures compliance with federal law since it requires a court order, but it runs the risk of being inconsistent with the law of the destination state, in which case that state might not give effect to any resulting judgment. The pressure to conform to that state's law reflects both the practical problem of executing the judgment and the foreign relations problem of detracting from the foreign state's sovereign control over service of process within its boundaries. A brief survey of the other means of service demonstrates how pervasive such deference to sovereign territorial interests is.

Rule 4(f) authorizes service in a variety of forms, including "by any internationally agreed means of service," in addition to the Hague Service Convention; "as prescribed by the foreign country's law for service in that country in an action in its courts of general jurisdiction"; "as the foreign authority directs in response to a letter rogatory or letter of request"; and by personal service or mail with return receipt "unless prohibited by the foreign country's law."[16] All of these means of service presuppose acquiescence by the foreign state either by international agreement, by its own law, or through its officials. The most traditional of these means of service is by "a letter rogatory or a letter of request," which formerly was transmitted

---

[12] FED. R. CIV. P. 4(f)(1) itself applies only to individuals who are not minors or incompetents, but its provisions extend to corporations, partnerships, and associations by a cross-reference in FED. R. CIV. P. 4(h)(2).

[13] Hague Convention on the Service Abroad of Judicial and Extrajudicial Documents in Civil and Commercial Matters arts. 2, 5, Nov. 15, 1965, 20 U.S.T. 361, 658 U.N.T.S. 163 [hereinafter Hague Convention].

[14] *Id.* art. 5.

[15] FED. R. CIV. P. 4(f)(3).

[16] FED. R. CIV. P. 4(f).

through diplomatic channels in the State Department.[17] These can now also be transmitted directly from a federal court to a foreign court.[18] This form of service also depends upon an agreement with the foreign state and foreign law identifying the "foreign authority" which can effectuate service of process.

The Hague Service Convention recognizes a similar range of alternative methods of service, although it also reserves to the destination state the right to object to particular means of service.[19] Moreover, even if the Hague Service Convention authorizes service, the foreign state may refuse to comply "if it deems that compliance would infringe its sovereignty or security."[20] The alternative means of service, like those in Rule 4(f), involve agreements between states, service through consular and diplomatic channels, and direct requests to "judicial officers, officials or other competent persons."[21] The foreign state can also allow service according to its internal law without reference to the Hague Service Convention,[22] reinforcing the degree of control that the foreign state exercises over service within its borders.

The Hague Service Convention adds to the Federal Rules of Civil Procedure along another dimension as well, by addressing the consequences of failure of service and of failure to respond to service. The Federal Rules themselves impose no definite time limit for effective service on defendants overseas,[23] although a failure to pursue service diligently can result in a dismissal for failure to prosecute under Rule 41(b).[24] The Hague Service Convention provides for notice to the plaintiff when service has, or has not, been effected.[25] If service has been effected and the defendant has not made a timely response within 90 days under Rule 12(A)(ii), the court enters a notice of default under Rule 55(a). Unless set aside, the default is followed by a default judgment under Rule 55(b), but such a judgment can be entered only after six months and is subject to the other conditions of Article 15 of the Hague Service Convention. That article provides for entry of a default judgment even if no certification has been returned by the foreign state if "every reasonable effort has been made to obtain it through the competent authorities of the State

---

[17] FED. R. CIV. P. 4(f)(2)(B).

[18] 28 U.S.C. § 1781; WRIGHT, MILLER & STEINMAN, *supra* note 9, at 261–62.

[19] Hague Convention, *supra* note 13, arts. 8, 10.

[20] *Id.* art. 13.

[21] *Id.* arts. 8–11.

[22] *Id.* art. 19.

[23] FED. R. CIV. P. 4(m).

[24] WRIGHT, MILLER & STEINMAN, *supra* note 9, at 392–94.

[25] Hague Convention, *supra* note 13, art. 6.

addressed."[26] Article 16 then goes on to flesh out the conditions, analogous to those under Rule 60(b), for setting aside a default judgment. Taken together, these provisions express an understandable concern with service of process that has gone awry for one reason or another, leaving the defendant vulnerable to the entry of a default judgment.

The interlocking provisions of the Federal Rules and the Hague Service Convention give rise to many questions, of which two stand out: First, when do the Federal Rules apply regardless of the Hague Service Convention? And second, when is mailed service, or equally inexpensive forms of service under the Federal Rules, consistent with the Hague Service Convention? Both questions become more complicated to the extent that they involve reference to the law of domestic American states and to foreign law. Both Rule 4 of the Federal Rules and the Hague Service Convention make several references to the law of other states, either domestic or foreign, causing these sources of law to remain relevant and often to become decisive regarding the validity of service of process.

On the first question, the Hague Service Convention declares that it "shall apply in all cases, in civil or commercial matters, where there is occasion to transmit a judicial or extrajudicial document for service abroad."[27] As a treaty ratified by the United States, it therefore constitutes the "supreme Law of the Land" under the Article VI of the Constitution, and it overrides inconsistent state law as well as inconsistent provisions of the Federal Rules.[28] As we have seen, whenever the convention does apply, it leaves considerable latitude for the operation of forum law and the law of the state of service. The Convention, however, does not apply to all cases requiring service overseas. The Supreme Court considered one such case in *Volkswagenwerk Aktiengesellschaft v. Schlunk*.[29] The plaintiffs there served process on the defendant's wholly owned subsidiary in the United States, which then transmitted process to the parent corporation in Germany. Illinois authorized service of process on the parent corporation in this manner. The plaintiffs sued in state court, but if they had filed in federal court, they could also have relied upon service of process by operation of Rule 4(h)(1), which authorizes service as allowed by the state in which the district court sits.[30]

---

[26] *Id.* art. 15.

[27] Hague Convention, *supra* note 13, art. 1.

[28] U.S. CONST. art. VI, cl. 2.

[29] 486 U.S. 694 (1988).

[30] FED. R. CIV. P. 4(h)(1) (cross-referencing to FED. R. CIV. P. 4(e)(1), which refers to state law).

From a distance, the case looks like an attempt under state law to circumvent the requirements of the Hague Service Convention for service on a foreign defendant. However, this perspective does not quite capture the relationship between the Convention and national law, which depends upon the law of both the sending and receiving states at several crucial points. This perspective also reveals the essentially territorial definition of the limits on valid service of process. The Supreme Court recognized that the conference that adopted the Hague Service Convention wanted to eliminate *notification au parquet*: substituted service on an official of the forum state followed by notice to the actual defendant without complying with the actual terms of the Convention. Whether the convention succeeded in eliminating this form of service remains somewhat uncertain, but the Court in any event distinguished service upon a subsidiary of a foreign corporation from other forms of service on foreign corporations. That form of service did not require any judicial process to be transmitted overseas, but was complete upon receipt of the papers by the subsidiary in the United States. Accordingly, the Hague Service Convention did not apply. As a practical matter, the decision left open to plaintiffs the more familiar and less expensive procedures in the chosen forum rather than the intricate requirements of the Convention and its references to foreign law, which can easily be misapplied.

The same tendency to prefer simpler and cheaper methods of service informs another line of decisions under the Hague Service Convention. These concern Article 10(a), which preserves, absent an objection from a signatory state, "the freedom to send judicial documents, by postal channels, directly to persons abroad."[31] The use of the word "send" in subsection (a) contrasts with the phrase "to effect service" in subsections (b) and (c) of Article 10, leading to the inference that the Article 10(a) does not cover service of process.[32] Federal circuit courts are split on this issue,[33] although the weight of international authority supports mailed service under this provision. The leading decision internationally was rendered by the European Court of Justice and held that Article 10(a) "allows service by post."[34] Purely textual arguments might cut the other way, since "send" under subsection (a) seems to be so much broader than "effect service" under subsections (b) and (c). However, the breadth of subsection (a) could just as easily be taken to subsume the narrower provisions of

---

[31]   Hague Convention, *supra* note 13, art. 10(a).

[32]   *Id*. art. 10(b)-(c).

[33]   *See* Brockmeyer v. May, 383 F.3d 798 (9th Cir. 2004) (service of process covered); Bankston v. Toyota Motor Corp., 889 F.2d 172 (8th Cir. 1989) (service of process not covered).

[34]   Case C-412/97, E.D. Srl. v. Italo Fenocchio, 1999 E.C.R. I-3845, C.M.L.R. 855 (2000).

subsections (b) and (c), leaving states the choice of objecting only to (a) and accepting (b) and (c), with all their inherent limits. Although other nations have expressed qualms about service by mail, the trend in recent cases has been to endorse more efficient forms of notice, progressing from physical mail to electronic means of communication. In the end, the trend towards less rigid and more effective forms of service gradually seems to be displacing traditional and cumbersome methods, so long as the state of service has no objections.

The connection between service of process and personal jurisdiction has been a long and intimate one. In the United States, it is reinforced by the sufficiency of personal service within a domestic state's boundaries as a sufficient means of acquiring personal jurisdiction over individual defendants.[35] As we have seen in the discussion of both of these subjects, territorial conceptions of sovereignty exercise a profound influence on the contours of legal doctrine. With respect to personal jurisdiction, they determine the adequacy of the defendant's connection with the forum. With respect to service of process, they result in a labyrinth of requirements, some simple and some complex, that determine whether process has been successfully served. On such matters, the parties and their attorneys would do well to heed Justice Holmes's advice that they "must turn square corners when they deal with the Government."[36] Compliance with the technical details of service process, because it invokes the sovereign power of the state, must be complete and exact. The same lesson holds true for discovery, although in much more contentious terms.

B. International Discovery

The Federal Rules of Civil Procedure transformed American litigation by greatly expanding the scope of discovery—the process of judicially assisted investigation of a case after it has progressed beyond preliminary motions to dismiss. The prominence of discovery in America has displaced almost all subsequent stages of litigation, leaving summary judgment and settlement as the principal means of disposition, with trial relegated to resolving a tiny fraction of cases. After the parties obtain the information available in discovery, whether favorable or unfavorable, they place themselves in a position to bring the case to a conclusion if either they settle or the judge decides that "there is no genuine dispute as to any material fact and the movant is entitled to judgment as a matter of law."[37] The Federal Rules transformed and extended discovery from a limited procedure

---

[35] Burnham v. Sup. Ct. of Cal., 495 U.S. 604 (1990).

[36] Rock Island, A. & L. R. Co. v. United States, 254 U.S. 141, 143 (1920).

[37] FED. R. CIV. P. 56(a).

for investigation in equity practice to the centerpiece of American litigation over all kinds of claims. To the consternation of courts in other countries, broad discovery falls mainly under the control of private parties in American courts, and it greatly assists private plaintiffs in bringing actions for damages, allowed under American law on a scale not recognized in other countries. Despite repeated attempts to limits the scope of discovery, effective judicial control depends primarily upon the initiative of trial judges and magistrates in wading into intricate and often bitter disputes over the evidence that must be disclosed.

The rest of the world has not followed this dramatic innovation, especially in giving the parties control over discovery, with only intermittent judicial supervision. Other common law countries have never extended discovery this broadly, and civil law countries have maintained a system of close judicial control over pretrial investigation. This divergence in approach has made American discovery an unwelcome intruder in foreign legal systems, generating suspicion of the motives that lead parties to seeking broad discovery and concern over the threats to confidentiality of information held overseas. The tendency of other nations to view control over pretrial investigations as a sovereign prerogative has only heightened their opposition to discovery initiated by parties to American litigation. Judicial control over discovery by American judges comes too late in the process, with too little deference to foreign interests. Decisions in this country have tried to alleviate the burdens of discovery on parties and witnesses overseas but more by moderating sanctions and orders than by abandoning the basic principles of party control and broad discovery.

Recent amendments to the Federal Rules have taken a similar approach, seeking to avoid the excesses of overly broad discovery and the tendency to use discovery to impose costs upon the opposing party. Thus, Rule 26(b)(1) now limits the overall scope of discovery, in the absence of a court order, to "any nonprivileged matter that is relevant to any party's claim or defense."[38] Other provisions limit the amount of discovery, both by numerical limits on the number of interrogatories and on the length of depositions and by a general prohibition against discovery that is "unreasonably cumulative or duplicative, or can be obtained from some other source that is more convenient, less burdensome, or less expensive."[39] Whether these provisions have had the desired effect or whether they have further complicated the process of discovery remains a matter of debate. In the same way, the flexible limits upon discovery open the door to

---

[38] FED. R. CIV. P. 26(b)(1).

[39] FED. R. CIV. P. 26(b)(2)(C)(i), 30(d)(1), 33(a)(1).

accommodating the interests of other countries, but they also complicate the process of formulating rules that actually restrain discovery.

The extraterritorial scope of discovery results primarily from its effects on parties, who are subject to discovery requests and sanctions without any geographical limits under the Federal Rules. Just being named as a party, without a finding of personal jurisdiction, can result in discovery that goes to the issue of jurisdiction.[40] Discovery against nonparties, by contrast, is hedged about with numerous restrictions. Subpoenas directed to a nonparty overseas can be served only upon "a United States national or resident,"[41] in conformity with the requirements for service of process overseas, and upon tendering the expenses of travel. By statute, the court must also find "that it is not possible to obtain his testimony in admissible form without his personal appearance or to obtain the production of the document or other thing in any other manner."[42] Discovery against a party is subject to no such restrictions and makes a finding of personal jurisdiction particularly consequential, subjecting the party to broad discovery on the merits which can, in theory, take place anywhere in the world.

Most of the disputes over international discovery concern the production of documents, which now appear as frequently in electronic form as they do in hard copy. Parties must supply these documents in response to a request for production under Rule 34. The request can extend to all documents "in the responding party's possession, custody, or control," including documents in the possession of a nonparty controlled by a party.[43] A foreign corporation sued in the United States can be forced by these means to produce documents under the control of its agents in a foreign country. Like all discovery, requests for production can be met by objections based on privilege, work product, and the disproportionate burden of disclosure. These grounds might overlap, as when a party had a privileged conversation with an attorney in anticipation of litigation or when production of documents might result in disclosure of information that already comes under a recognized privilege, like the one that protects confidential communications between attorney and client. These objections do not vary in principle between domestic and international litigation, but as the next section of this chapter discusses, blocking statutes enacted by foreign countries create a kind of privilege against disclosure. So, too, the relative inaccessibility of documents in foreign countries, or the threat of

---

[40] Ins. Corp. of Ir. v. Compagnie Des Bauxites De Guinee, 456 U.S. 694 (1982).

[41] FED. R. CIV. P. 45(b)(3).

[42] 28 U.S.C. § 1783 (2012).

[43] FED. R. CIV. P. 34(a)(1).

foreign sanctions if they are disclosed, increase the practical burden of complying with a request for production. If the parties cannot resolve such objections or if they fail to do so, and the court orders production of the documents, the refusal to produce can result in sanctions, ranging from admission of the issues to which the documents are relevant to contempt or entry of judgment on the merits against the refusing party.[44] The threat of sanctions poses a real risk to a party who fails to produce documents within the territory of another nation, creating an obvious source of friction with any nation anxious to preserve its territorial sovereignty.

In the absence of a blocking statute, American decisions tend to enforce requests for production based only on the assertion of power over the party from whom discovery is sought, so long as the terms of the Federal Rules are met. Questions might arise over the party's control of documents in the hands of an agent or subsidiary, or over the scope and burden of discovery, but the location of the documents makes no difference. As the well-known decision in *In re Uranium Antitrust Litigation*[45] describes: "Once personal jurisdiction over the person and control over the documents by the person are present, a United States court has power to order production of the documents." The analysis proceeds quite differently if discovery is sought from a nonparty. The terms of Rule 45 and the accompanying statute require more exacting preliminary findings, which generally incline American courts against ordering discovery from nonparties overseas. The nonparty must instead generally be found in some federal judicial district where a court (not necessarily the court hearing the case) can issue the subpoena.[46] Artful attempts to use this power to defeat the limits on subpoenas directed to nonparties overseas, such as by serving some company related to the nonparty, typically fail.[47]

Attempts to depose parties or nonparties overseas encounter similar obstacles. Since a deposition resembles a miniature version of a trial, foreign countries do not allow this form of discovery lightly, absent consent of the person deposed and compliance with their own procedures. Finding the person to be deposed within the United States, or securing their presence here, promises to be a more effective strategy. This is, again, easier for depositions of parties rather than nonparties. Parties can be summoned to a deposition simply through the receipt of reasonable written notice. A nonparty must receive a subpoena under Rule 45, with all the attendant

---

[44] FED. R. CIV. P. 37.

[45] 480 F. Supp. 1138, 1145 (N.D. Ill. 1979).

[46] FED. R. CIV. P. 45(b)(2)(A).

[47] Laker Airways, Ltd. v. Pan Am. World Airways, 607 F. Supp. 324 (S.D.N.Y. 1985).

complications of service overseas.[48] Likewise, a party may be sanctioned simply for failure to attend its own deposition without issuance of a subpoena.[49] A corollary of these provisions allows a party to notice the deposition of a corporate party and require the corporation to designate individuals who can testify to the matters set out in the notice.[50] The same can be done for a nonparty organization, but it raises problems of service overseas if the organization and its relevant agents can only be found there. For a corporate party, notice of the deposition in the United States can require it to produce an individual from another country as the person to testify on its behalf. Taken together, all of these provisions ease the way to depositions of parties and their representatives, while leaving depositions of nonparties dependent on their presence within the United States, their consent to a deposition, or more problematically, issuing legal process against them abroad.

The last alternative becomes especially problematic if the foreign country does not consent to the form of legal process used. American courts seldom issue such orders unilaterally, and when they do, foreign courts rarely enforce them.[51] Litigants are thrown back upon traditional means of acquiring evidence through a letter rogatory or by a letter of request under the Hague Evidence Convention. The former alternative is cumbersome, just as it is when used for service of process. It requires an American court to contact a foreign court, usually through diplomatic channels in the State Department, often resulting in bureaucratic delays. The process also is unreliable, since the foreign court can refuse the request to take evidence. Even if the foreign court grants the request to take evidence, it will take it subject to its own procedures, which might severely limit the role of counsel. The United States proposed the Hague Evidence Convention as a remedy for these deficiencies, requiring signatory states to establish a "Central Authority," like the one for service of process under the convention on that subject, to which letters of request could be transmitted. The Central Authority would proceed to obtain the evidence requested and could not refuse to do so, unlike the procedure in response to a letter rogatory. Nevertheless, the Hague Evidence Convention suffers from a great drawback as a vehicle for conducting discovery. Signatory states can declare that it will not honor requests "for the purpose of obtaining pre-trial discovery of documents as known in Common Law

---

[48] FED. R. CIV. P. 30(a)(1), (b)(2).

[49] FED. R. CIV. P. 37(d)(1)(A)(i).

[50] FED. R. CIV. P. 30(b)(6). This provision also applies to other kinds of organizations that are parties.

[51] GARY B. BORN & PETER B. RUTLEDGE, INTERNATIONAL CIVIL LITIGATION IN UNITED STATES COURTS 971–72 (5th ed. 2011).

countries."[52] Many states have exercised this option, some to the extent of denying any pretrial discovery of documents. In those countries, documents can be obtained only according to the law of the foreign state or by separate agreement.[53]

Partly for this reason, the Supreme Court has held that the Hague Evidence Convention does not prevent resorting to independent means of discovery under the Federal Rules. In *Societe Nationale Industrielle Aerospatiale v. United States District Court*,[54] the Court held that the plaintiffs could obtain discovery under the Federal Rules from the defendants (French corporations that were instrumentalities of the French government) without resort to letters of request under the convention. Because of the permissive language of the Convention, providing that a court of one contracting state "may" send a letter of request to another contracting state,[55] the Court held that the Convention did not displace the discovery devices available under the Federal Rules. Nor did the Court require the discovering party to exhaust remedies under the Convention by making a prior letter of request.

All these aspects of the decision make good sense. The Court also recognized the principles of international cooperation underlying the convention in the form of a case-by-case consideration of comity, which does not support a specific rule but rather "a more particularized analysis of the respective interests of the foreign nation and the requesting nation."[56] Some courts have interpreted the decision to put the burden of proof upon the party or witness who is insisting upon resort to the Hague Evidence Convention.[57] That approach tends to give decisive weight to the burdens of foreign discovery and the likely effectiveness of a request under the convention. It also tends to discount the sovereign interests of foreign countries insofar as they conflict with broad discovery under the Federal Rules. An interpretation of *Aerospatiale* along these lines, although not uniformly adopted, has the advantage of orienting analysis towards the practical problems of discovery, rather than theoretical conflict of laws. Just the mechanics of gaining access to information in a foreign country increases the cost of discovery, through the expense of travel, translation, and the use of unfamiliar sources. The risk that discovery will fail also increases, especially if

---

[52] Hague Service Convention on the Taking of Evidence Abroad in Civil or Commercial Matters art. 23, *opened for signature* Mar. 18, 1970, 23 U.S.T. 2555, 847 U.N.T.S. 241 [hereinafter Evidence Convention].

[53] *Id.* arts. 27, 28.

[54] 482 U.S. 522 (1987).

[55] Evidence Convention, *supra* note 52, art. 1.

[56] *Aerospatiale*, 482 U.S. at 543–44.

[57] Valois of Am., Inc. v. Risdon Corp., 183 F.R.D. 344, 346 (D. Conn. 1997).

the foreign country is hostile to disclosure of any kind. Foreign interests, to that extent, inevitably figure into any realistic assessment of how to resolve transnational discovery disputes. District courts certainly have discretion to consider such indirect effects of foreign law in managing discovery.[58]

Direct consideration of foreign interests, however, introduces a discordant element that invites courts to balance American interests against those of a foreign state.[59] The American Law Institute takes this approach in the Restatement (Third) of Foreign Relations Law. The provisions in the Restatement (Third) might do no more than reflect the pressures that courts inevitably feel in international cases, but if it invites them to become the arbiters of national interests, it goes too far with too few rules. Judge Easterbrook memorably expressed his reluctance "to accept an approach that calls on the district judge to throw a heap of factors on a table and then slice and dice to taste. Although it is easy to identify many relevant considerations, as the ALI's *Restatement* does, a court's job is to reach judgments on the basis of rules of law rather than to use a different recipe for each meal."[60]

Direct conflicts between American law and foreign law can be handled by other means, as discussed in the next section of this chapter. A party or witness who cannot comply with a discovery order because of foreign law deserves some relief from the sanctions ordinarily imposed for discovery abuse. It does not follow that a court must anticipate that its discovery orders will be violated and must disregard domestic law for that reason. Any court order might be violated, but that risk does not justify departure from the ordinary rules of litigation. Nor does the risk of conflict with foreign law require a court to remake American law to avoid the conflict. Any such ad hoc accommodations threaten the stability of the rules that otherwise govern international litigation. The invitation to make them, to the extent it can be found in *Aerospatiale*, should be resisted because of uncertainties they create for the parties and the vicissitudes they create in judicial decisions.

Deference to the requirements of foreign law can properly play a much larger role in cases in which discovery runs in the opposite direction: when a person with a stake in litigation overseas seeks the assistance of an American court in obtaining discovery. Section 1782 of the Judicial Code authorizes such discovery in broad terms:

---

[58] FED. R. CIV. P. 26(b)(2), (c).

[59] *Aerospatiale*, 482 U.S. at 544 n.28, citing what became the Restatement (Third) of Foreign Relations Law of the United States § 442.

[60] Reinsurance Co. of Am., Inc. v. Administratia Asigurarilor de Stat, 902 F.2d 1275, 1283 (7th Cir. 1990) (Easterbrook, J., concurring).

The district court of the district in which a person resides or is found may order him to give his testimony or statement or to produce a document or other thing for use in a proceeding in a foreign on international tribunal, including criminal investigations conducted before formal accusation.[61]

Limitations derived from evidentiary privileges and from the Federal Rules limit the scope of such assistance, but the Supreme Court has broadly interpreted the statute, leaving most issues of implementation to the discretion of the district court.[62] The foreign or international proceedings need not themselves be judicial; it is sufficient if they are "administrative" or "quasi-judicial."[63] The person seeking discovery need not be a formal party to those proceedings, but simply may play a significant role in them, for instance, as a complainant.[64] The proceedings themselves need not be pending, but only "within reasonable contemplation."[65] And the information sought need not be discoverable under the law of the relevant tribunal, or, apart from privileges, discoverable under federal law.[66] Within these broad limits, the district court can tailor discovery to the role of the person from whom discovery is sought, the nature of the tribunal and proceedings underway, and whether the tribunal would likely accept assistance with discovery.[67] This degree of discretion, and the generally more permissive attitude toward discovery in American law, minimizes the risk of conflict with foreign law. Moreover, to the extent that cooperation with foreign courts in assisting in discovery in foreign cases induces them to assist in discovery in American cases, the statute tends to alleviate conflicts over transnational discovery disputes. Discretion remains with the district court in responding to incoming discovery requests, as it does with respect to outgoing requests, but the liberal policy sanctioned by statute accords with the approach taken in the Federal Rules. The risk of conflict with foreign law is slight—in dramatic contrast to the subject taken up next in this chapter.

C. Blocking Statutes

Foreign countries enacted blocking statutes in response to criminal prosecutions and regulatory litigation by the United States. Blocking statutes do not uniquely concern issues of civil discovery. If

---

[61] 28 U.S.C. § 1782 (2012).

[62] Intel Corp. v. Advanced Micro Devices, Inc., 542 U.S. 241 (2004).

[63] *Id.* at 257–58.

[64] *Id.* at 256–57.

[65] *Id.* at 258–59.

[66] *Id.* at 259–63.

[67] *Id.* at 264–66.

anything, by opposing enforcement actions by the federal government, they show how adamant other nations have been in protecting information within their borders. Blocking statutes generally prohibit foreign citizens and foreign corporations from complying with court orders requiring disclosure of information. They began with the extraterritorial enforcement of American antitrust and securities laws. Expanded coverage as a matter of substance led to expanded coverage of the procedures needed for enforcement. The "effects test" for coverage of the antitrust laws reached foreign firms in international cartels that sought to fix prices in the American market. Discovery necessarily had to reach those foreign firms as well, whether it was by a subpoena issued in connection with proceedings before a grand jury or by an order for production of documents in civil litigation.

The United Kingdom, in particular, took exception to the extended reach of American antitrust law, mainly because it took a much narrower view of the anticompetitive practices that should be prohibited. The Protection of Trading Interests Act accordingly authorizes the British Secretary of State to prohibit compliance with any foreign discovery order that "infringes the jurisdiction of the United Kingdom or is otherwise prejudicial to the sovereignty of the United Kingdom" or to its "security."[68] In another provision, the Act also prohibits enforcement of any judgment for "an amount arrived at by doubling, trebling or otherwise multiplying a sum assessed as compensation."[69] It takes aim specifically at American antitrust judgments for treble, and in a further provision, allows a defendant who has had to pay noncompensatory damages in another country, to bring an action to recover those damages in the United Kingdom.[70] Some nations, notably Switzerland, had adopted bank secrecy laws decades earlier and then expanded them to protect any "secret relating to a manufacturing process or a business."[71] Other blocking statutes, like the original bank secrecy laws, protect only information from particular industries, almost always as a reaction to discovery orders in American litigation.[72]

The prevalence of these statutes is matched only by the direct conflict that they pose with American law. Where an American court order or subpoena requires production of documents or information, these blocking laws forbid it. The paradigm case of such a conflict came before the Supreme Court in *Societe Interantionale Pour*

---

[68]   The Protection of Trading Interests Act, 1980, c. 11 §§ 1–4.

[69]   *Id.* § 5.

[70]   *Id.* § 6.

[71]   SCHWEIZERISCHES STRAFGESETZBUCH [STGB] [CRIMINAL CODE], art. 273.

[72]   BORN & RUTLEDGE, *supra* note 51, at 972–73.

Participations v. Rogers.[73] The plaintiff, a Swiss corporation, had filed a claim to recover assets seized under the Trading with the Enemy Act during World War II. The United States as defendant sought production of documents on the issue of whether the plaintiff was under the control of German interests. The district court duly ordered production of the documents, but the plaintiff sought to have the order lifted on the ground that compliance with it would violate Swiss law. After continued negotiations and disclosure of some, but not all, of the requested documents, the district court eventually ordered that the plaintiff's claim be dismissed with prejudice.

The Supreme Court held that an order to this effect could not be entered "when it has been established that failure to comply has been due to inability, and not willfulness, bad faith, or any fault of petitioner."[74] The Federal Rule on discovery sanctions, Rule 37(b), had to be read in light of the Due Process Clause to relieve the plaintiff of penalties for actions beyond its control. The Court nevertheless left open the possibility of lesser sanctions on remand, and in any event, left the burden of proof on the merits on the plaintiff. Its failure to disclose the documents in question could defeat its efforts to regain the assets in dispute. The Court also left open the possibility that the United States could again challenge the plaintiff's good faith in relying upon its fear of prosecution under Swiss law. The opinion sent the unmistakable message that a party who fails to comply with a discovery order because of foreign law, even though it might escape the most severe sanctions, still cannot "profit through its inability to tender the records called for."[75]

The opinion in *Rogers* emphasizes fault and due process, rather than comity and respect for foreign law. The latter issues, of course, bear upon the former, but as with analysis of discovery orders, so too with the sanctions for noncompliance: Foreign law has mainly an indirect impact. The Court in *Rogers*, and then again in *Aerospatiale*, upheld the underlying discovery orders over the objection that they required violation of foreign law. The plaintiff in *Rogers* argued that Swiss law had effectively taken the requested documents out of its control, thereby defeating one of the prerequisites for production under Rule 34. The Court rejected this argument and held that the district court, considering the importance of the documents to the central issues in the case, had properly ordered production. The Court rejected the foreign blocking statute in *Aerospatiale* in more categorical terms, reasoning that applying the statute would give it extraterritorial effect to impede proceedings in this country.[76] The

---

[73]   357 U.S. 197 (1958).

[74]   *Id.* at 212.

[75]   *Id.*

[76]   *Aerospatiale*, 482 U.S. at 544 n.29.

lesson of comity, according to the Court, was "that neither the discovery order nor the blocking statute can have the same omnipresent effect that it would have in a world of only one sovereign."[77] In a world of multiple sovereigns, an American court can issue a discovery order without expecting it automatically to be obeyed in a foreign country.

Both *Rogers* and *Aerospatiale* presented distinctive facts, but not so much that no general lessons can be distilled from them. The plaintiff in the first case sought recovery from the United States, even though it also resisted compliance with the discovery order. The presence of the United States as a party facilitated negotiations with Switzerland to overcome the effect of the blocking statute. Similarly, in the second case, the plaintiff sued an instrumentality of the French government, which also prompted its participation in the litigation. The presence of government parties in both cases increased the likelihood of a settlement of the discovery dispute, and the opinions in both cases hold out the possibility of such a resolution. Of course, how settlement negotiations proceed depends upon what happens if they fail and how the parties bargain in the shadow of the law.

Subsequent decisions have generally put the burden of proof on the party seeking to avoid sanctions. That burden has several elements: proof of the existence of a blocking statute and the actual threat that it poses to the objecting party; establishing good faith efforts to try to avoid or to lessen the effect of the statute; and otherwise full compliance with the discovery order.[78] Failure to establish any of these elements justifies the imposition of sanctions. The party resisting discovery falls under a longer shadow of the law, and for that reason, has additional incentives to seek relief from foreign blocking statutes. These incentives come into play whether or not the foreign country has taken an active role in the litigation. Foreign countries determined to enforce their blocking statutes can make their intentions known to the court easily enough, and often their failure to do so indicates that an objecting party faces no real risk of punishment.

The limited weight accorded to foreign blocking statutes does not presume the superiority of American discovery rules—only the priority that American procedures have for American courts. The discovery provisions of the Federal Rules have been subject to repeated criticism and amendment, which, as noted earlier, has narrowed the scope of discovery and increased the discretion of federal judges to limit discovery's most burdensome aspects. Having

---

[77] *Id.*

[78] Richmark Corp. v. Timber Falling Consultants, 959 F.2d 1468, 1474 (9th Cir. 1992); In re Marc Rich & Co., A.G., 736 F.2d 864, 866 (2d Cir. 1984).

set itself apart from discovery practices elsewhere, American law has incrementally imposed a degree of restraint on what parties can obtain and what courts should order. These trends inherent in recent procedural reforms offer enough flexibility to the courts to resolve most transnational discovery disputes. If they are resolved by way of settlement, that does as much to foster international cooperation as direct consideration of the interests underlying foreign law.

The same also holds true for specific treaties governing the production of evidence on particular subjects. Treaties and other international agreements cover criminal and tax investigations, displacing the previous default rule in which countries refused to assist in prosecuting crimes or collecting taxes under another country's laws.[79] Bank secrecy laws, to take a notable example, have gradually given way before the exceptions established by such agreements, exemplified in a recent case by the agreement between the United States and Switzerland over disclosure of evidence of tax evasion aided and abetted by the United Bank of Switzerland.[80] Such secrecy laws still pose significant obstacles to disclosure, but as direct cooperation between public authorities has become more common in some areas, it has given collateral support to methods of international discovery in other areas. Agreements between sovereign states remain the foundation of international law, and in the field of discovery as elsewhere, international agreements provide the model for reconciling discordant national laws. Judges need not take the leading role in making ad hoc adjustments to the procedures that they normally employ in wholly domestic cases. The parties and witnesses in the litigation, along with the governments which represent their interests, can make progress by negotiations within the structures recognized and enforced by the courts. These actors are in a far better position than the courts by themselves to strike the compromises necessary for achieving cooperation with other nations.

---

[79] *See* Pasquantino v. United States, 544 U.S. 349, 361 (2005).

[80] Agreement Between the United States of America and the Swiss Confederation, U.S.-Switz., Aug. 19, 2009.

Chapter VI

COMPETING CASES IN DIFFERENT COUNTRIES

This chapter takes up several different procedural devices all dealing with the prospect of multiple proceedings in different courts on the same claims. Motions to dismiss for *forum non conveniens* presuppose the possibility that the plaintiff could have sued elsewhere, while motions to stay a case in favor of a related case or, on the contrary, to enjoin proceedings in a related case, presuppose that someone has already filed a second action. These motions fit into the category of dilatory motions, both in the historical sense in that they address issues apart from the merits and in the ordinary sense in that they often delay the proceedings at hand. In the guise of finding the most efficient forum for deciding the case, these motions themselves can be the source of inefficiency, multiplying proceedings not directly addressed to the merits. Partly for that reason, these motions are disfavored. Another reason goes to the mandatory quality of exercising jurisdiction. Once a plaintiff properly invokes the subject-matter jurisdiction of a court and gains personal jurisdiction over the defendant, the court usually has a duty to decide the claim presented by the plaintiff. The party making the motion—usually the defendant in the proceeding to be dismissed, stayed, or enjoined—therefore bears the burden of proof and must make a strong showing to satisfy it.

Nevertheless, if granted, these motions can have dramatic consequences for the outcome of litigation, bringing a case effectively to a close or tilting the outcome in favor of one side or the other. The stakes on these motions increase in international litigation as the differences between a domestic and a foreign forum become greater, along with the differences between domestic and foreign forum law. Taken literally, the motions address purely procedural issues, but just beneath the surface, they engage issues, such as choice of law, that go to the merits. Which court will resolve a dispute, and under which law, often determines the ultimate outcome, no matter how much courts try to keep such questions separate and reserve ruling on them. These motions thus often serve as a vehicle for pursuing the merits by other means.

These motions also bear a systematic relationship to the topics taken up in other chapters. The doctrine of *forum non conveniens* looks back to restrictions on the choice of a proper court. Technically, it is part of the law of venue, which is closely related to personal jurisdiction in identifying a proper court in which the action can go forward. *Forum non conveniens* also depends indirectly, if still significantly, on choice of law. A court might well be reluctant to deny a motion to dismiss on this ground and then be faced with the task of deciphering the intricacies of unfamiliar foreign law. Stays and abstention come into play only when issues of jurisdiction and venue have been resolved, and these devices figure prominently in the law of preclusion and arbitration. The rules of preclusion give priority to the first case to reach final judgment in resolving the conflict between judgments in competing litigation. A stay therefore takes a case out of the running to be the first to reach final judgment. Stays of litigation also function as a means of enforcing arbitration agreements. Disputes subject to arbitration cannot be taken to court, and litigation over those disputes routinely is stayed pending arbitration. So too, injunctions against competing proceedings most often are granted to protect the jurisdiction of the court or to effectuate its judgment. And an injunction, once issued, seeks to prevent a related case from going forward to final judgment. If given preclusive effect by a court entertaining a competing case, the injunction shuts down the proceedings before that forum. Because the injunction purports to dictate the result in a related case, it constitutes the most intrusive means of deciding which of two competing cases can go forward. This chapter begins at the opposite end of the spectrum, with motions to dismiss for *forum non conveniens*, in which a court effectively defers in favor of proceedings that could be brought elsewhere.

A. *Forum Non Conveniens*

Venue occupies an uneasy position in the array of rules that govern the selection of the proper court for litigating a dispute. Venue supposedly focuses upon efficiency, without regard to the issues of sovereignty that inform personal and subject-matter jurisdiction. Yet in pursuing that goal, the law of venue has recourse to the same considerations as jurisdictional determinations: first, the contacts of the parties and the case with the forum, and second, the applicability of forum law. These considerations yield a range of factors that should enter into selection of an efficient forum, including the residence of the parties, the location of the evidence, the local interest in the dispute, the need to assure that the plaintiff can sue in some feasible forum, and the defendant's ability to mount a vigorous defense.

Unfortunately, distilling these factors into workable rules has proved to be very difficult, resulting in progressively liberalized provisions on venue. The general federal venue statute illustrates this tendency. In its current form, § 1391 of the Judicial Code provides for venue based on the residence of the defendants, the district "in which a substantial part of the events or omissions giving rise to the claim occurred," or if there is no other venue, where "any defendant is subject to the court's personal jurisdiction with respect to such action."[1] The statute then broadly defines residence of artificial persons, such as corporations, to include "any judicial district in which any defendant is subject to the court's personal jurisdiction with respect to such action," It also provides that "a defendant not resident in the United States may be sued in any judicial district."[2] The last two of these provisions makes it very easy to acquire venue over aliens not resident in the United States and over foreign corporations—two kinds of parties likely to be sued in international civil litigation. Nonresident aliens simply cannot object to venue and do not count at all in determining proper venue with respect to other parties.[3] Defendant corporations, and other artificial entities, are residents of any state in which they are subject to personal jurisdiction, and if there is no such state, then they are treated like nonresident aliens.[4]

All of these provisions, taken together, give plaintiffs a wide range of choice among permissible venues, most of them framed in terms that would also support personal jurisdiction. The provisions themselves, and others in § 1391, add further complexity to the statute, but in the end, they do not add much to personal jurisdiction as a limit on selecting a proper forum. The liberality of the venue rules enlarges the role played by the doctrine of *forum non conveniens*, first, by opening the door wider to the plaintiff's initial choice of forum, and second, by substituting a case-by-case analysis of convenience for a rule-bound determination of venue. A similar analysis of convenience takes place under transfer statutes,[5] but since these only apply to transfer between forums in the United States, they play a limited role in international litigation.

The leading decision on *forum non conveniens, Piper Aircraft Co. v. Reyno*, illustrates these points.[6] The case arose from an airplane accident in Scotland in which everyone aboard the aircraft was killed. The next-of-kin of the passengers sued in the United Kingdom, naming the owner, the operator, and the pilot's estate as defendants. They also sued the manufacturer of the aircraft and the manufacturer of the propeller in California state court, apparently to take advantage of the more generous tort law and more generous juries there. The defendants removed the case to federal district

---

[1]   28 U.S.C. § 1391(b)–(c) (2012).

[2]   *Id.* § 1391(c).

[3]   *Id.* § 1391(c)(3).

[4]   *Id.* § 1391(c)(2), (3).

[5]   *Id.* §§ 1404, 1407.

[6]   454 U.S. 235 (1981).

court, based on diversity of citizenship. The federal court then transferred the case from the Central District of California to the Middle District of Pennsylvania, where the aircraft was manufactured. At that point, the defendants moved to dismiss for *forum non conveniens* in favor of consolidating the case with the action pending against them in the United Kingdom. The district court granted the motion, and its ruling was eventually affirmed by the Supreme Court.

The Court's decision endorsed the pre-existing standards for dismissal for *forum non conveniens*, which contained several different elements. First, "there is ordinarily a strong presumption in favor of the plaintiff's choice of forum," which is strongest when the plaintiff is a resident of the forum.[7] Second, a trial court's decision on *forum non conveniens* "may be reversed only when there has been a clear abuse of discretion."[8] And third, both public and private factors go into the trial court's decision. The Court framed these factors as follows, describing and quoting from its prior decision in *Gulf Oil Corp. v. Gilbert*:[9]

> The factors pertaining to the private interests of the litigants included the "relative ease of access to sources of proof; availability of compulsory process for attendance of unwilling, and the cost of obtaining attendance of willing, witnesses; possibility of view of premises, if view would be appropriate to the action; and all other practical problems that make trial of a case easy, expeditious and inexpensive." The public factors bearing on the question included the administrative difficulties flowing from court congestion; the "local interest in having localized controversies decided at home"; the interest in having the trial of a diversity case in a forum that is at home with the law that must govern the action; the avoidance of unnecessary problems in conflict of laws, or in the application of foreign law; and the unfairness of burdening citizens in an unrelated forum with jury duty.[10]

The Court elaborated on each of the elements of this analysis in its earlier decision in *Gilbert*, but the most important was the presumption in favor of the plaintiff's choice of forum.

That presumption was eroded in *Piper Aircraft* itself because all of the next-of-kin were British and because the case was brought initially in California only by using the device of appointing the

---

[7]   *Id.* at 255.

[8]   *Id.* at 257.

[9]   330 U.S. 501, 508–09 (1947).

[10]   *Piper Aircraft*, 454 U.S. at 241 n.6 (quoting *Gilbert*, 330 U.S. at 508–09).

secretary for the plaintiff's lawyer as administrator of the estates of the deceased. The plaintiff sought to reinforce the presumption in favor of her choice of forum—artificial though it was—by arguing that Scottish law would be less favorable to her than either the law of California or Pennsylvania. The Third Circuit had accepted this argument, but the Supreme Court interpreted *Gilbert* to hold that "dismissal may be warranted where a plaintiff chooses a particular forum, not because it is convenient, but solely in order to harass the defendant or take advantage of favorable law."[11] Change in the applicable law entered into the analysis to determine if any remedy was available in the alternative forum.[12] It also figured indirectly as a complicating factor if the court retained the case but was forced to apply foreign law.[13] Neither of these factors operated against granting a dismissal on the facts of *Piper Aircraft* itself. With respect to the presumption in favor of the plaintiff's choice of forum, the case was the exception that proved the rule.

The other elements of the analysis of *forum non conveniens* confirmed the soundness of dismissing the case. Since the district court had ordered dismissal, the court of appeals could reverse only if it found "a clear abuse of discretion."[14] Such a lenient standard acknowledged the district court's closer acquaintance with the issues in the case, as well as the risk that continued litigation over an issue that is supposed to improve overall efficiency would be self-defeating. The timing of appeals through the final judgment rule has much the same effect. In cases in which the court denies the motion to dismiss, an appeal must ordinarily await a final judgment on the merits. By the time that happens, the argument for dismissing the case has lost most of the force that it might have had. A new trial in a foreign court usually does not outweigh the value of a disposition of the plaintiff's claims by the district court. Quite the opposite occurs. Combined with the lenient standard of review, the final judgment rule leaves a defendant moving to dismiss for *forum non conveniens* with only one real shot at getting the motion granted—before the district court. If the court denies the motion, the case then goes forward, with only a very limited chance for an interlocutory appeal and only a limited chance for reversal after final judgment.

The last element of the analysis of *forum non conveniens*, balancing the multiple public and private factors, also favored dismissal in *Piper Aircraft*. Litigation already was pending in the United Kingdom; most of the witnesses and the physical evidence of the wreckage were there. Resolving all the claims and cross-claims in

---

[11] *Id.* at 249 n.15.

[12] *Id.* at 254–55.

[13] *Id.* at 260.

[14] *Id.* at 257.

a single proceeding eliminated the risk of inconsistent judgments. And finally, the United Kingdom had a greater interest than the United States in resolving the claims of its citizens arising from the death of other citizens within its own territory. The only factor that favored keeping the case in this country was the presence of evidence relating to the manufacture of the aircraft and the propeller, but most of this evidence could be brought to the United Kingdom.

Strictly speaking, the weighing of public and private factors does not involve a delicate balance. In the district court, the factors must "clearly point towards trial in the alternative forum."[15] And on appeal, those same factors must lead the court to find "a clear abuse of discretion."[16] Moreover, the private factors must be restricted according to the interests of the parties. Only the defendant's interests in litigating in the alternative forum support dismissal. The plaintiff's interests in litigating there have already been discounted by her choice to litigate in the original forum. And conversely, only the plaintiff's interests in keeping the case in the original forum should count. By making the motion to dismiss, the defendant has discounted his or her interest in continuing to litigate there. Narrowing the consideration of public and private factors along these lines assures a degree of objectivity, which reduces the risk that rulings on *forum non conveniens* might become subjective exercises of discretion that vary from one judge to the next.

Only a narrow range of circumstances makes it likely that a court will grant a motion to dismiss for *forum non conveniens*. The motion presupposes that the requirements of personal jurisdiction have already been met but that the defendant's contacts with the forum do not tip the balance of convenience decisively in favor of keeping the case there. This situation occurs most frequently if the court has general jurisdiction over the defendant and the defendant's contacts with the forum are largely divorced from the events that gave rise to the plaintiff's claim. That might have been true in *Piper Aircraft* because Piper had a major plant in Pennsylvania; moreover, Piper also was subject to specific jurisdiction because the plane was designed, tested, and manufactured there.[17] The other defendant, Hartzell, manufactured the propeller in Ohio, but apparently had a long-term contract to supply propellers to Piper in Pennsylvania.[18] The contacts of both defendants with Pennsylvania, however, did not outweigh the other contacts in the case with Scotland. Only a configuration of facts along these lines explains how personal

---

[15] *Id.* at 256.

[16] *Id.* at 257.

[17] *Id.* at 239.

[18] *Id.*

jurisdiction could exist and yet the case could still be dismissed for *forum non conveniens*.

Under conditions like these, the plaintiff's residence or citizenship often assumes decisive significance. It strengthens the presumption in favor of the plaintiff's choice of forum, as the Court emphasized in *Piper Aircraft*. It also strengthens the forum's interest in retaining control over the case. The choice between dismissing or retaining the case becomes particularly stark for claims of personal injury and wrongful death, where the disparity between domestic and foreign law can make the difference between a viable claim and one not worth pursuing. A dismissal ostensibly in favor of a foreign forum might effectively sound the death knell of the claim.[19] When an American plaintiff sues, the reality of a greatly reduced or nonexistent recovery overseas weighs heavily against dismissal.

An illuminating case is *Guidi v. Inter-Continental Hotels Corp.*, which arose out of a terrorist attack on a hotel in Cairo, Egypt, where two Americans were killed and one was injured.[20] Three other foreign guests were also victims of the attack. The American plaintiffs brought an action against the corporation that managed the hotel in federal district court in New York, where the corporation had its headquarters. That court granted a motion to dismiss for *forum non conveniens*, on the ground that most of the evidence was in Egypt and that other claims arising from the terrorist attack had already been brought there. The district court reached this conclusion despite the fact that the plaintiffs were American citizens and resided in states near New York. The court of appeals, however, reversed because the plaintiffs had decided to sue in what amounted to their home forum and because they had a well-founded fear of further terrorist attacks if they returned to Egypt. Their counsel made the powerful point that litigation in Egypt would require them to stay in a hotel just like the one where the terrorist attack had occurred.

Apart from this fact-bound feature of the case, the decision stands for the renewed force of the presumption in favor of the plaintiff's choice of forum when the plaintiff chooses his or her home forum. As the Supreme Court framed the presumption in the first case that recognized it, *Koster v. Lumbermens Mutual Casualty Co.*, the plaintiff "should not be deprived of the presumed advantages of his home jurisdiction except upon a clear showing of facts" that establish either oppression or vexatiousness toward the defendant or compromise the forum court's own administrative or legal interests.[21]

---

[19] *See* David Robertson, *Forum Non Conveniens* in America and England: "A Rather Fantastic Fiction", 103 L.Q. REV. 398, 418–19 (1987) (finding that only 4% of cases dismissed for *forum non conveniens* go to trial in a foreign court).

[20]   224 F.3d 142 (2d Cir. 2000).

[21]   330 U.S. 518, 524 (1947).

Koster figured prominently in *Piper Aircraft*, yet the two cases are distinct. Indeed, the presumed advantages of a home forum were not available to the plaintiff in *Piper Aircraft*, who had no real interest in the case as an administrator appointed solely to bring the claims for wrongful death in California. The affirmance of a dismissal for *forum non conveniens* in *Piper Aircraft* stands in marked contrast with the reversal of a dismissal in *Guidi*. Foreign plaintiffs face a much larger risk of dismissal for *forum non conveniens* than American plaintiffs, at least if the latter take care to sue in a forum that can be characterized as their "home."

The contrast between foreign and domestic plaintiffs raises the specter of unequal treatment, even if it does not rise to the level of a colorable constitutional claim. Distinctions between citizens and aliens, or more precisely between residents of this country and residents elsewhere, are drawn all the time. The statutes on diversity jurisdiction and on venue draw precisely those distinctions and have not been questioned for this reason. Nevertheless, treaties might require equal treatment of foreigners and citizens, and, as a matter of policy, it remains unsettling that litigants who otherwise are identical can be treated so differently.[22] An American resident has access to an American court, but a foreign plaintiff injured in the same incident does not. For better or for worse, Americans have preferential access to American justice.

Foreign plaintiffs advanced arguments to this effect in *In re Union Carbide Gas Plant Disaster*, but the court found them to be unpersuasive.[23] The case arose from a gas leak in Bhopal, India, at a plant operated by the wholly owned subsidiary of an American chemical company. The leak resulted in thousands of deaths and serious injuries, and the plaintiffs, including the government of India, brought suit against the parent corporation in federal court in New York. Almost all of the victims of the tragedy were from India, which was also the location of most of the witnesses and evidence. The government of India, as indicated by its participation in the lawsuit, had a compelling interest in the lawsuit and had, in fact, heavily regulated the operations of the subsidiary in Bhopal.[24] The argument that the Indian courts could not handle the case and that the federals courts here were much more experienced with mass tort cases fell short of establishing that the Indian courts did not provide an effective alternative forum.

---

[22]   Pollux Holding Ltd. v. Chase Manhattan Bank, 329 F.3d 64 (2d Cir. 2003), *cert. denied*, 540 U.S. 1149, 1150 (2004).

[23]   809 F.2d 195 (2d Cir. 1987), *cert. denied*, 484 U.S. 871 (1987).

[24]   *Id.* at 202–03.

The conditions imposed by the district court on dismissal were another matter. Some were standard, like the defendant's waiver of objections based on personal jurisdiction and the defense of the statute of limitations, but one was not: that the defendant agree to enforcement in this country of any judgment against it and to discovery against it in India under the Federal Rules of Civil Procedure. Waiver of personal jurisdiction or statute of limitations just assures that the foreign court is a genuine alternative forum. The other conditions imposed by the district court in *Union Carbide* were another matter. On review of the district court's decision, the court of appeals held that consent to enforcement of the judgment was superfluous, given the New York law on the enforcement of foreign judgments, and that the consent to federal discovery was an unwarranted shift in the playing field against the defendant. The district court had given the plaintiffs broad discovery under the Federal Rules, while limiting the defendant's discovery to the narrower devices under Indian procedure. Implicit in the court of appeals rejection of this condition was a concern over interference with Indian procedure and Indian sovereignty. Just like the courts of the United States, the courts of India remain free to structure their proceedings as they believe to be best. Hence any agreement for disclosure of evidence by both sides had to be subject to the requirements of Indian law, and, if needed, the approval of the Indian courts.[25] In an interesting twist, the defendant argued for continuing supervision of the Indian proceedings by the federal district court to avoid prejudice against it as a foreign corporation, but the court of appeals rejected this proposed condition on dismissal for the same reason: The Indian courts only needed to provide an adequate forum for the plaintiff's claim, not one subject to American oversight.[26] A dismissal for *forum non conveniens* presupposes that a case can be brought in a foreign court. A court can condition dismissal on waiver of personal jurisdiction and the statute of limitations, but it cannot condition dismissal on continuing control over the proceedings in a foreign court.

The doctrine of *forum non conveniens* also raises complicated issues about exactly whose law determines the standard for dismissal. Under *Erie Railroad v. Tompkins*,[27] federal courts must usually follow state law on issues that are governed by judge-made law and that are likely to be "outcome determinative."[28] *Forum non conveniens* fits this description perfectly, yet the dominant approach

---

[25] *Id.* at 203–06.

[26] *Id.* at 205.

[27] 304 U.S. 64 (1938).

[28] Guaranty Trust Co. v. York, 326 U.S. 99 (1945).

of federal courts is to apply federal judge-made law.[29] To be sure, they rarely need to make this choice, because most states have a version of *forum non conveniens* that closely resembles federal law. Yet some do not, and some do not allow any dismissal in favor of proceedings in another jurisdiction.[30] For transfers between federal courts within the United States, these restrictive state laws pose no problem, because the federal statute authorizing transfers takes priority over state law under the Supremacy Clause.[31] Dismissals for *forum non conveniens* could be treated similarly, as in accord with the federal statutory policy in favor of locating litigation in a more convenient forum. In that case, the dismissal would not be a matter of wholly judge-made law but would reflect a judgment ultimately made by Congress. That line of reasoning would support existing law that, in any event, shows little tendency to take state law to be decisive on issues of federal venue, which are largely governed by statute. Rulings on *forum non conveniens* could be treated the same way.

State law nevertheless plays a persistent role throughout international civil litigation. State courts have the power to hear cases with international dimensions, and in the absence of federal subject-matter jurisdiction, they are the only American courts that have jurisdiction. Enforcement of forum selection clauses, for instance, often depends on principles of state contract law, as discussed in Chapter 1. State courts can merge those principles with their own procedural rules to determine whether to enforce a forum selection clause. When a plaintiff sues in federal court, however, state law and federal law on enforcement of these clauses might diverge. Forum selection clauses bear upon issues of *forum non conveniens* in two different ways. First, a contractual clause that allows or requires suit to be brought in another forum gives some indication of the parties' assessment of the relative convenience of litigating in an American or a foreign court. Second, the Supreme Court has held that in purely domestic cases, a forum selection clause should be enforced by a motion to transfer.[32] By analogy, in international cases, a clause selecting a foreign forum should be enforced by a motion to dismiss for *forum non conveniens*, as some lower courts have held.[33] This line of cases, like those on *forum non conveniens*, reveals that the role of state law can be circumscribed by federal law, and often is for claims

---

[29]   *See* In re Air Crash Disaster near New Orleans, 821 F.2d 1147 (5th Cir. 1987) (en banc), *vacated and remanded on other grounds*, 490 U.S. 1032 (1987), *reinstated in relevant part*, 883 F.2d 17 (5th Cir. 1989) (en banc).

[30]   Stewart Org., Inc. v. Ricoh Corp., 487 U.S. 22, 29 (1988).

[31]   *Id.* at 31.

[32]   Atlantic Marine Constr. Co., Inc. v. U. S. Dist. Court for the Western Dist. of Tex., 134 S.Ct. 568 (2013).

[33]   *E.g.,* In re Lloyd's Register N. Am., Inc., 780 F.3d 283, 293 (5th Cir.), *cert. denied*, 136 S.Ct. 64 (2015).

in federal court. But it cannot be entirely ignored, since it applies of its own force in state proceedings in the absence of federal preemption. Likewise, in the absence of federal subject-matter jurisdiction, litigation must be brought in state court, and even when it could be brought in federal court, federal subject-matter jurisdiction is often concurrent with the jurisdiction of the state courts.

B. Stays and Abstention

The Latin term "*lis alibi pendens*" covers stays and abstention on the ground that competing litigation is pending or possible elsewhere. Stays or abstention on this ground bear a striking similarity to dismissals for *forum non conveniens*. Most fundamentally, both kinds of motions presuppose the existence of an alternative forum superior to the one initially chosen by the plaintiff. Both motions seek to move the litigation to a forum where it can be resolved more efficiently. *Lis alibi pendens* operates in much the same way as *forum non conveniens*. Outside of a few well-defined areas, motions to stay or abstain on this ground trigger a presumption in favor of the plaintiff's choice of forum. The cost of duplicative litigation, while substantial, must be balanced against the cost of granting a stay, with the possibility always present that the litigation in the initially chosen forum will be reactivated. In general, the benefits of finding a more efficient forum might be outweighed by the cost and uncertainty of determining whether there is such a forum and whether a motion for a stay or abstention should be granted. The parties' own self-interest in avoiding duplicative litigation might serve as a better deterrent than judicial interference with their choices.

Parallel litigation within the same court system, such as litigation in two different federal courts, presents fewer problems than parallel litigation in different systems, such as litigation divided between federal and state courts or between American and foreign courts. Within the same system, the existence of overlapping or identical lawsuits creates issues of judicial administration: whether devoting twice the resources to the litigation makes sense for the parties and for the court, when the courts within the same system are themselves essentially the same. The Supreme Court has characterized this issue as one of "wise judicial administration" to be resolved in the discretion of the district court.[34] Courts have usually exercised this discretion to favor the first of the cases filed, leaving the burden of proof on the party favoring the second case to

---

[34] Kerotest Mfg. Co. v. C-O-Two Fire Equipment Co., 342 U.S. 180, 183 (1952).

demonstrate why that case should go forward instead.[35] If the first forum truly is inconvenient, a motion to transfer can bring the entire litigation to the second forum. Without resort to *lis alibi pendens*, motions to transfer can handle all the legitimate concerns over the first forum. If the case should not be transferred, the residual reasons that might have motivated a party to prefer the second forum then look too much like simple dissatisfaction with the first judge assigned to the case. It follows that a stay or abstention should be denied in this situation.

The stakes get higher when the two cases are in different judicial systems. One system might offer a different perspective on the case or apply different law to it, with a likely effect on the ultimate outcome. In domestic cases, these issues come up in the choice between federal and state courts, and, as with cases in the same judicial system, other procedural devices can handle most of the routine problems. Thus a defendant dissatisfied with the plaintiff's choice of state court can usually have the case removed to federal court, if it could have been filed there initially.[36] Conversely, the plaintiff can structure the case so that it can be brought initially in federal court, or alternatively, so that it cannot—for instance, by adding a nondiverse party to a claim based on state law. In deciding what claims to bring and what parties to sue, the plaintiff can get the case into federal court or keep it from going there. The instances of duplicative state and federal litigation therefore arise most frequently when the defendant in state court goes to federal court to sue, in effect taking on the role of a plaintiff and creating competing state and federal actions. The strong presumption in that situation favors both parties' choice of forum and the maintenance of parallel litigation. As the Supreme Court framed the rule in *Colorado River Water Conservation District v. United States*, this presumption "stems from the virtually unflagging obligation of the federal courts to exercise the jurisdiction given them," and "[o]nly the clearest of justifications will warrant dismissal."[37]

Ironically enough, however, the Supreme Court held that this obligation did flag in *Colorado River Water* itself. The decision, like *Piper Aircraft*, occupies the paradoxical position of the exception that proves the rule. The United States had brought suit in federal court to determine its rights to water from the Colorado River in one of the water districts administered by the state of Colorado. Shortly thereafter, interested parties brought an action before the state court that determined the division of water among all the users in that

---

[35] *E.g.*, Semmes Motors, Inc. v. Ford Motor Co., 429 F.2d 1197, 1203 (2d Cir. 1970).

[36] 28 U.S.C. § 1441 (2012).

[37] 424 U.S. 800, 817, 819 (1976).

district. The Supreme Court held that the federal court had jurisdiction, but that it had properly abstained in favor of the state proceedings. The state case resembled one for the adjudication of rights to specific pieces of property, in which the risk of inconsistent adjudication in separate cases threatened the finality of any resulting judgment.[38] Abstention for that reason plays a prominent role in both domestic and international litigation, by centralizing judicial control over a particular asset and adjudicating competing claims to it. Proceedings as different as bankruptcy,[39] interpleader,[40] and certain mandatory class actions[41] have mechanisms for shutting down competing litigation over claims to a single asset. We will return to this subject in the next section of this chapter.

Other forms of federal abstention in favor of state proceedings involve deference to state determination of questions of state law and state criminal proceedings.[42] None of these varieties of abstention have exact analogues in international litigation. Deference to foreign determination of questions of foreign law, as we have seen, figures indirectly in resolution of motions to dismiss for *forum non conveniens*. If, however, such a motion cannot be granted, American courts do not shy away from deciding difficult questions of foreign law. So, too, they do not shy away from difficult questions of American law even though those questions might be mooted or otherwise avoided if the case came before a foreign tribunal. Yet a well-known form of abstention by federal courts in favor of state proceedings hinges on the ability of state courts to resolve uncertain questions of state law that must first be resolved before reaching a question of federal constitutional law.[43] American courts also do not interfere with foreign criminal prosecutions in the same way that a federal court might enjoin enforcement of an unconstitutional state law. The occasion for abstention in favor of foreign prosecutions does not arise at all because there is no practice of interfering with foreign law enforcement.

That leaves abstention based on the control over property in a foreign court, analogous to the situation in *Colorado River Water*, as the most promising ground for abstention by the courts in this country in favor of foreign proceedings. The reasons offered for abstention in *Colorado River Water* have as much force, if not more, in international cases as they do in domestic cases. The need for a single, consistent adjudication of property rights has as much

---

[38] *Id.* at 817.

[39] 11 U.S.C. §§ 362(a), 541(a)(1) (2012).

[40] 28 U.S.C. §§ 1335, 2361 (2012).

[41] FED. R. CIV. P. 23(b)(1)(B).

[42] *Colorado River Water*, 424 U.S. at 814–17.

[43] Railroad Comm'n of Tex. v. Pullman Co., 312 U.S. 496 (1941).

urgency for property in foreign countries as in this country, particularly when a matter might cross national boundaries or concern parties from different countries. Yet the terms of *Colorado River Water* open the door to a variety of further considerations, none of which is dispositive: the inconvenience of the federal forum, the desirability of avoiding piecemeal litigation, and the order in which the cases were filed.[44] As with the dismissals for *forum non conveniens*, hard-and-fast rules cannot easily be distilled from the cases. In fact, the resemblance to *forum non conveniens* goes further, since the relative convenience of the competing forums figures into the decision to stay or dismiss.[45] The main difference in the analysis of the two motions concerns "the order in which jurisdiction was obtained by the concurrent forums."[46] Where the court defers to litigation pending elsewhere, the decisive factor often appears to be how far along the foreign proceedings have gone towards final judgment.

The reason to emphasize this factor looks forward to issues of preclusion at the end of litigation rather than backward to issues of jurisdiction at the beginning. If an American court would recognize a final judgment of a foreign court when it issued one and that court was well along to doing so, then a stay or dismissal of the American case would just anticipate recognition of the foreign judgment.[47] *Ingersoll Milling Machine Co. v. Granger* illustrates the close connection between the two issues.[48] The case arose out of parallel proceedings between Ingersoll Mining and its former employee, Granger, who worked for the company in Illinois and later in Belgium. When Granger was discharged from his position in Belgium, he sued the company in a labor court there. While that action was pending, Ingersoll Milling sued Granger in Illinois state court. Ingersoll Mining sought the return of funds advanced to Granger, a declaration that it owed him nothing more, and an injunction against the Belgian proceedings. Granger removed the case to federal court and moved to dismiss on grounds both of *forum non conveniens* and of the pendency of the proceedings in Belgium. The federal court denied these motions, but Granger renewed them after the Belgian case resulted in a judgment in his favor. The federal court then stayed its proceedings pending the outcome of an appeal in Belgium, and when that, too, resulted in a judgment for Granger, the federal court gave it preclusive effect.

---

[44] *Colorado River Water*, 424 U.S. at 818.

[45] *Id.*

[46] *Id.*

[47] *See* GARY B. BORN & PETER B. RUTLEDGE, INTERNATIONAL CIVIL LITIGATION IN UNITED STATES COURTS, 535–37 (4th ed. 2007).

[48] 833 F.2d 680 (7th Cir. 1987).

The Seventh Circuit affirmed the federal district court's judgment, holding that the stay entered after the initial judgment in Granger's favor constituted a measured response to problems posed by parallel proceedings.[49] While a stay often has the same practical effect as a dismissal,[50] on the facts of this case, it made the difference between deferring to a foreign judgment that might be overturned on appeal and waiting for one that had become final in all respects. More generally, a court can issue a stay in any kind of action, but a dismissal on grounds of abstention can be granted only in an action in equity or when the plaintiff seeks some other form of discretionary relief.[51] In an action at law for damages, the court has no similar discretion to exercise in determining the appropriate remedy. And in federal court, the plaintiff could have exercised the right to a jury trial under the Seventh Amendment.

By the time the federal district court issued the stay in *Ingersoll Mining*, the foreign proceedings were far enough along to yield a judgment that likely would be given preclusive effect, making further proceedings on the merits entirely superfluous and a matter of needless expense. The likelihood of preclusion amplified the inconvenience of duplicative proceedings. Conversely, if the Belgian case had not yet come close to a final judgment, the federal court would have been subject to a strong presumption in favor of exercising jurisdiction. Competing proceedings alone do not make out the clear justification required by *Colorado River Water*. The presumption could still be overcome by the multiple factors that courts have invoked in favor of a stay. A representative list appears in *Finova Capital v. Ryan Helicopters*:

> (1) the identity of the court that first assumed jurisdiction over the property; (2) the relative inconvenience of the federal forum; (3) the need to avoid piecemeal litigation; (4) the order in which the respective proceedings were filed; (5) whether federal or foreign law provides the rule of decision; (6) whether the foreign action protects the federal plaintiff's rights; (7) the relative progress of the federal and foreign proceedings; and (8) the vexatious or contrived nature of the federal claim.[52]

To the extent that these factors look beyond the possibility of preclusion, they look back towards the analysis of *forum non conveniens*. As the prospect of preclusion by a foreign judgment diminishes, the foreign court just becomes an alternative forum that

---

[49] *Id.* at 685.

[50] Moses H. Cone Mem'l Hosp. v. Mercury Constr. Corp., 460 U.S. 1, 28 (1983).

[51] Quackenbush v. Allstate Ins. Co., 517 U.S. 706, 721–22 (1996).

[52] 180 F.3d 896, 898–99 (7th Cir. 1999).

might be more convenient for litigating the case than the one in this country.

As the last of the factors indicates, the cases also look behind objective factors of efficiency to the subjective bad faith of a party seeking to maintain parallel proceedings. Because the presumption is against a stay or dismissal, the costs and strategic maneuvering must go beyond what ordinarily occurs in duplicative proceedings.[53] As the facts of *Ingersoll Mining* suggest, interference with foreign proceedings most often tips the balance in favor of a stay. Thus, litigation here that might interfere with a foreign bankruptcy proceeding often justifies a stay,[54] as does competing litigation over rights to property.[55] Comity, in the sense of general respect for the integrity of proceedings in foreign courts, does not alone justify a stay or dismissal of proceedings here. The principle is better stated the other way around: Litigation here must show an inherent lack of respect for the proceedings in foreign courts. The next section of this chapter takes up the sharpest form of such a conflict.

C. Countersuit Injunctions

As with the topics previously discussed in this chapter, domestic decisions offer the best guide to understanding countersuit injunctions in international cases. But as with those topics, domestic decisions supply only a starting point, after which one must take account of the different legal framework in which international litigation takes place. Competing international litigation always takes place in different legal systems with no superior law or supreme tribunal that can make rulings binding on the courts in both systems. These differences make countersuit injunctions particularly volatile as a source of international conflict. The presumption in favor of the plaintiff's choice of forum, even if it results in parallel litigation, takes on even greater force with respect to countersuit injunctions. Such injunctions are rarely issued, and with stays and abstention, done mainly in order to protect the integrity of any resulting judgment on the merits. As a matter of formal deference to foreign courts and foreign judges, the countersuit injunction only runs against the parties to competing litigation, not against the court itself. Even so, the injunction effectively shuts down the foreign proceedings and amounts to a command to the foreign court as if it were inferior to the court in this country. Rarely would a foreign

---

[53] *E.g.*, Royal & Sun Alliance Ins. Co. of Can. v. Century Int'l Arms, Inc., 466 F.3d 88, 95 (2d Cir. 2006).

[54] *See, e.g.*, JP Morgan Chase Bank v. Altos Hornos de Mex., S.A. de C.V., 412 F.3d 418, 424 (2d Cir. 2005).

[55] *Finova Capital*, 180 F.3d at 899.

court, or in the converse situation, an American court, acquiesce in its presumed inferiority.

In domestic cases, well-defined rules govern countersuit injunctions between state and federal courts. State courts cannot issue injunctions against federal proceedings, based on reasoning that relies ultimately on the Supremacy Clause. Because federal law is supreme over state law, a state court cannot take away the federal forum provided by a federal statute.[56] A federal statute imposes a similar obligation on federal courts, generally prohibiting injunctions against state proceedings. The governing statute, however, recognizes three exceptions: for injunctions "expressly authorized by Act of Congress, or where necessary in aid of its jurisdiction, or to protect or effectuate its judgments."[57] The last two exceptions have clear analogues in international civil litigation, and they are augmented by the power, generally asserted by federal courts, to enjoin foreign proceedings. Nevertheless, a majority of circuits impose strict standards for issuing countersuit injunctions, so that the rule in international cases looks much like the statutory rule governing injunctions against state proceedings. Courts rarely issue countersuit injunctions outside a narrow range of standard cases where they need to do so to protect the integrity of their own proceedings or their own judgments. International comity does not create a hard-and-fast rule against countersuit injunctions, but it does discourage the issuance of such injunctions in all but a handful of cases.

The dominant approach returns to the presumption in favor of allowing parallel litigation. A leading decision, *Quaak v. Klynveld Peat Marwick Goerdeler Bedrijfsrevisoren*, frames the standard as "whether the foreign action either imperils the jurisdiction of the forum court or threatens some strong national policy."[58] As a preliminary matter, the foreign litigation must involve the same parties and issues.[59] It must be genuinely duplicative of the litigation here. If so, the presumption in favor of parallel litigation can be overcome by reliance on a variety of factors, resembling those for stays or abstention, but again focused upon preserving the integrity of the proceedings before the court. In *Quaak*, these were threatened by a lawsuit in Belgium seeking to prevent discovery in a securities fraud action in federal court. The plaintiff sought to obtain copies of the work papers of the defendant, an accounting firm that was subject to a related criminal prosecution in Belgium. The defendant objected that the work papers were confidential client material under

---

[56] *See, e.g.*, Donovan v. Dallas, 377 U.S. 408, 412–13 (1964).

[57] 28 U.S.C. § 2283 (2012).

[58] 361 F.3d 11, 17 (1st Cir. 2004).

[59] *Id.* at 18.

Belgian law and filed a claim to that effect in the Belgian court, seeking an injunction against the plaintiffs' discovery request in the federal court. The federal court, in turn, enjoined the Belgian proceedings, and the First Circuit affirmed, although only after it had conducted its own "independent review of the justification for the issuance of an international antisuit injunction."[60] The court reasoned that it was the defendant, not the plaintiff, who "set the stage for a crisis of comity."[61] The defendant could have exhausted its remedies in the federal judicial system or asked the Belgian court to clarify the scope of protected client confidences under Belgian law. Although the conflict came up as a dispute over discovery, the defendant essentially contested the continued exercise of jurisdiction in the American proceedings by seeking to bring discovery there to a halt. The decision in *Quaak* therefore falls into the line of cases in which the court issues an injunction "in aid of its jurisdiction," to use the terminology from § 2283. The decision upholds the injunction, but on narrowly defined grounds.

A competing line of decisions, represented by *Kaepa, Inc. v. Achilles Corp.*, takes a more relaxed view of countersuit injunctions.[62] The Fifth Circuit there upheld a countersuit injunction under an abuse of discretion standard, reasoning that the district court did not need to "genuflect before a vague and omnipotent notion of comity every time that it must decide whether to enjoin a foreign action."[63] The district court could instead rely upon a variety of factors to decide whether the foreign action "would entail 'an absurd duplication of effort' and would result in unwarranted inconvenience, expense, and vexation."[64] In *Kaepa*, the court emphasized the presence of a forum selection clause that allowed the defendant to be sued in Texas, where the action was brought, and the fact that the defendant's action in Japan was the mirror image of the plaintiff's action in the United States. The defendant had simply switched sides to sue as a plaintiff in Japan. While worth considering, these factors would hardly satisfy a stricter standard for issuing a countersuit injunction, as the dissent in *Kaepa* made clear.[65] The forum selection clause was not mandatory; it did not require the action to be brought in Texas. And parallel litigation, as noted earlier, always involves duplication of expense and effort. Instead of relying on these considerations, the majority panel for the Fifth Circuit appeared to be impressed by the defendant's investment and strategic maneuvering in the action in

---

[60]   *Id.* at 16.

[61]   *Id.* at 20.

[62]   76 F.3d 624 (5th Cir.), *cert. denied*, 519 U.S. 821 (1996).

[63]   *Id.* at 627.

[64]   *Id.*

[65]   *Id.* at 633–34 (Garza, J., dissenting).

Texas. The defendant had been sued initially in state court but removed the action to federal court, where it engaged in comprehensive discovery. Only then did the defendant file its own action in Japan, apparently because it was dissatisfied with the prospects of success in the Texas litigation. The defendant seemed to be engaged in after-the-fact forum shopping for a more favorable result, or at least to drive up the cost of a victory for the plaintiff. The subjective factor of vexatious litigation seemed to take precedence over objective factors of comity and efficiency.

That said, the Fifth Circuit correctly noted that the principles of comity do not constitute a set of determinate rules. Even courts that take a stricter view of countersuit injunctions leave some discretion to the district court to adapt its rulings to the complicated setting in which international litigation often takes place. The question cannot escape being one of degree, especially when competing cases are pending in more than one jurisdiction. Resolving the stand-off between potentially conflicting decisions requires more than a set of simple rules. A rule, for instance, against any countersuit injunctions would invite harassing behavior by litigants disappointed by the forum initially chosen, without any possibility of a remedy if the alternative forum refused to stay its proceedings. Within a single judicial system, a supreme court can eventually resolve the conflict between competing proceedings, as the European Union does by forbidding countersuit injunctions between courts within its system and by maintaining a strong rule in favor of stays of the later-filed litigation.[66] Even so, the latter rule had to be modified to prevent parties from pre-emptively filing suit in Italy, under a strategy called "the Italian torpedo," in order to prevent litigation elsewhere within the European Union. The notorious delays in the Italian legal system allowed prospective defendants, by this means, to postpone any judgment of liability against them. The EU regulations now accord priority to the court designated by a mandatory forum selection clause.[67] These rules, no matter how simple or intricate, presuppose enforcement by review in the Court of Justice of the European Union.

In cases that span different judicial systems, no such court with the ultimate power of review exists. This creates the risk, realized in a few cases, such as *Quaak*, of countersuit injunctions flying between courts of different countries, each escalating the dispute with the other. At the extreme, a total breakdown of comity can generate

---

[66] Gregory Paul Turner v. Felix Fareed Ismail Grovit & Others, Case C-159/02, 2004 E.CR.R. I-03565 (Court of Justice of the European Communities); Council Regulation (EC) 44/2001 on Jurisdiction and the Recognition and Enforcement of Judgments in Civil and Commercial Matters § 9, Art. 27.

[67] Regulation (EU) 1215/2012 of the European Parliament and of the Council of 12 December 2012 Art. 31, ¶¶ 2, 3.

international disputes that can only be resolved by diplomatic means. This course of events played out in the celebrated case of *Laker Airways Ltd. v. Sabena, Belgian World Airlines*.[68] Laker Airways brought an antitrust action against various competing airlines, including British Airways, alleging that they had conspired to drive it out of business on the transatlantic passenger routes that all the airlines served. British Airways responded by bringing suit in the United Kingdom, seeking to enjoin the American proceedings. The British trial court granted the injunction, although it was eventually reversed on appeal to the House of Lords. In the meantime, the federal district court enjoined the British proceedings, in a ruling eventually affirmed by the D.C. Circuit. Also at the same time, the Department of Justice had launched a criminal investigation into antitrust violations. Before an indictment could be issued however, Prime Minister Thatcher prevailed upon President Reagan to have the criminal proceedings dropped. She also worked to have the civil antitrust action settled.[69]

Just as in *Quaak*, the issuance of the countersuit injunction was affirmed under the stricter standard for such injunctions endorsed by most of the federal circuits. The judges on the D.C. Circuit nevertheless disagreed over whether an injunction could be issued on the facts of the case. Judge Wilkey, writing for the majority, upheld the injunction on the ground that the British proceedings threatened "the strong public policies of the forum" as evidenced by the antitrust laws.[70] He recognized the desirability of comity to further international cooperation, but he found limits on it to the extent that it would require judges to subordinate the policies of their own country to those of a foreign country. Judge Starr dissented primarily on the ground that a private antitrust action did not, by itself, implicate the strong public policies of the forum necessary to disregard the actions of a foreign court.[71] He weighed more heavily the interests of the British government, manifested in its position supporting British Airways under an act specifically authorizing the government to protect British interests. He also expressed skepticism, similar to that of the British government, about the extraterritorial application of American antitrust law.[72]

The conflicting approaches of the two opinions, not to mention the conflict between the stricter and more lenient approaches in different circuits, raise questions at two different levels of analysis:

---

[68]   731 F.2d 909 (D.C. Cir. 1984).

[69]   ANDREAS F. LOWENFELD, INTERNATIONAL LITIGATION AND ARBITRATION 139–45 (3d ed. 1993).

[70]   *Laker Airways*, 731 F.2d at 937.

[71]   *Id.* at 956 (Starr, J., dissenting).

[72]   *Id.* at 956–57, 958–59.

How broadly to construe American interests? And what role should judges take in this process? The first question cannot be examined anew every time a court confronts a request for a countersuit injunction. The only variables that change from one case to another are the circumstances that affiliate the case more or less closely with the United States. In *Laker Airways*, no one could question the interest of the United States in regulating competition on transatlantic airline routes. Hence the second question properly took on a prominent role in Judge Wilkey's majority opinion. As he wrote: "Despite the real obligation of courts to apply international law and foster comity, domestic courts do not sit as internationally constituted tribunals. Domestic courts are created by national constitutions and statutes to enforce primarily national laws."[73] He particularly opposed balancing a wide range of factors to determine the comity to be accorded to foreign law and foreign proceedings, rather than simply following the duty to apply American law.[74] Even so, he acknowledged the legitimacy of taking comity into account, but found it wanting, primarily because it was the British court that first sought to interfere with American proceedings.[75]

More determinate rules must await a superstructure of international law and international legal institutions that can adjust and resolve disputes over parallel litigation. A good example of an effort along these lines is the Hague Choice of Court Convention.[76] Like the EU regulation, this convention would give priority to the court selected by a choice-of-forum clause and would require all other courts to "dismiss or suspend" all actions brought before them, subject to narrow exceptions.[77] The convention has not yet entered into force, and its scope is limited to cases governed by mandatory forum selection clauses. It also contains a public policy exception in cases in which "giving effect to the agreement would lead to a manifest injustice or would be manifestly contrary to the public policy" of the forum.[78] This provision, like the litigation in *Laker Airways*, leaves room for the forum to give priority to its own local policies. In this respect, it represents a seemingly necessary compromise to preserve the sovereign interests of the forum, just like the discretion that a court must exercise in deciding whether to issue a countersuit injunction. The interests of competing sovereigns must be adjusted, either in a case-by-case fashion or by international agreements. The sovereigns themselves are the parties to

---

[73] *Id.* at 951.

[74] *Id.* at 948–53.

[75] *Id.* at 939–40.

[76] Convention of 30 June 2005 on Choice of Court Agreements, 44 I.L.M. 1294.

[77] *Id.* arts. 5, 6.

[78] *Id.* art. 6

international treaties like the Hague Choice of Court Convention, and they cannot reasonably be expected to forsake their national interests without qualification. Countersuit injunctions remain one means by which they can protect those interests through their own courts.

Chapter VII

RECOGNITION AND ENFORCEMENT
OF JUDGMENTS

By the time a case reaches final judgment, much of the uncertainty that ordinarily surrounds litigation has been dispelled. The court has resolved the issues disputed by the parties, identified others as irrelevant, and determined what, if any, relief should be granted to the plaintiff. The law on recognition of judgment (sometimes generally called *res judicata*) takes on the same determinate form. Balancing tests, weighing of interests, and assessment of contacts—typical of choice of law and personal jurisdiction—give way to more precise tests for the preclusive effect of a judgment. The outcome, too, takes a more definite form: either the judgment is given preclusive effect or it is not. This chapter therefore has a very different tone from the preceding chapters, such as those on personal jurisdiction and choice of law. Where flexibility and discretion played a dominant role in those chapters, rules and exceptions play the dominant role in enforcement and recognition of judgments.

The law of preclusion rests primarily on the need to give finality and repose to the parties, so that they can go forward with their affairs with a degree of certainty about their rights and obligations. This interest holds for both parties, but more for the prevailing party, whether plaintiff or defendant, who naturally wants to take advantage of the judgment in its favor. A prevailing plaintiff wants to obtain satisfaction of the judgment. If the losing defendant's assets cannot be found in the forum that rendered the judgment (which we can call F1), the plaintiff must seek enforcement in another forum (which we can call F2). A prevailing defendant also has an interest in invoking the judgment of F1 in case of renewed litigation, either in F1 or some other forum, F2. Losing parties often contest judgments through various means of collateral attack, which will be discussed in detail in this chapter. They nevertheless have a residual interest in the certainty obtained by a judgment, and for that reason, might not contest its validity. They might, on balance, prefer the newly established relations they have with the prevailing party over the prospect of continued litigation, which might disrupt business or personal relations.

Even more so than in previous chapters, the treatment of preclusion in international civil litigation derives from its treatment in domestic cases, discussed in the first section of this chapter. In the

United States, the Full Faith and Credit Clause in the Constitution,[1] along with implementing legislation, prescribes the preclusive effect that one state must give to the judgment of a sister state. With only a few exceptions, the rule is that F2 must give the same effect to the judgment of F1 that F1 would. In other words, the courts of the enforcing or recognizing state must give the judgment the same effect as the courts of the rendering state would. This nearly absolute rule of preclusion in domestic cases has deeply influenced the practice of American courts in international cases. A wider range of exceptions allows American courts to disregard foreign judgments, but the courts rarely take up the invitation offered by the formal terms of the statutes and precedents governing foreign judgments. Foreign judgments receive less than full faith and credit in theory, but almost as much in practice.

The foundational decision on recognition of foreign judgments, *Hilton v. Guyot*,[2] establishes the baseline from which the American principles on this subject subsequently evolved. Those principles take the same general approach of comity towards foreign courts as *Hilton* does, while at the same time departing from the exact contours of the decision in several respects. It therefore gives an ambivalent signal about the current state of the law: in the abstract, in accord with the decision, but in concrete cases, different in crucial details. The second section of this chapter analyzes *Hilton* and its uncertain legacy, derived partly from its genesis in the era of federal common law before *Erie Railroad v. Tompkins*.[3] This section takes up that issue as well, examining the federal power to prescribe rules of preclusion. In international cases, this power has its strongest basis in legislation under the Commerce Clause and in the exercise of the Treaty Power. The latter, in particular, authorizes treaties like the Hague Convention on Choice of Court Agreements, which also prescribes the effect of judgments resulting from such agreements.[4]

Despite *Hilton*, state law governs almost all issues of enforcement and recognition of foreign judgments. It does so through uniform legislation, which has generated a surprisingly strong consensus on the treatment of foreign judgments, subject only to occasional state variations. Almost all states follow one or another version of the Uniform Foreign-Country Money Judgments Act, which prescribes when a foreign judgment must be recognized, when it may not be recognized, and when it must not be recognized. These

---

[1]   U.S. Const. art. IV, § 1.

[2]   159 U.S. 113 (1895).

[3]   304 U.S. 64 (1938).

[4]   Hague Convention on Private International Law, Convention on Choice of Court Agreements art. 1, June 30, 2005, 44 I.L.M. 1294 [hereinafter Hague Convention].

circumstances coincide with issues of fair procedure, personal subject-matter jurisdiction, and public policy, all of which have figured in earlier chapters. The terms and interaction of these provisions become quite complicated—a tendency aggravated by the incentives of a losing party in F1 to challenge the judgment on a variety of grounds in F2. Nevertheless, as noted earlier, the strong tendency of American courts is toward recognition and enforcement of judgments within the scope of the Uniform Act.

The Act, as its name implies, extends only to money judgments. And even certain money judgments—for example, taxes, penalties, and judgments in divorce cases—fall outside its scope. A final section examines the treatment of these judgments and the treatment of injunctions, neither of which routinely receive recognition. These exceptions to the general rule of recognition and enforcement return to basic principles of sovereignty and the power that nations typically reserve to themselves to engage in law enforcement within their own borders. That power can, of course, be delegated or limited by international agreements, which typically address narrowly defined issues, such as tax collection and extradition of suspected criminals. Sovereignty, as elsewhere emphasized in this book, provides the starting point for analysis of international obligations, even as the acts of sovereign nations themselves have gradually generated common international law.

A. Full Faith and Credit

Interstate and international recognition of judgments takes place against the backdrop of the principles of preclusion that apply within a single judicial system. Those principles have four elements, only two of which play a prominent role in international litigation. The four elements are claim preclusion, issue preclusion, privity among the parties to both actions, and due process, including jurisdiction and notice and opportunity to be heard. Only the first and last issues appear with any regularity in international cases. Claim preclusion (sometimes known as *res judicata* in the narrow sense) determines whether entire claims can be barred and whether a judgment favorable to the plaintiff can be enforced. Most international cases take up preclusion in this all-or-nothing fashion, either barring further litigation on the claim adjudicated in the foreign court and enforcing any judgment for the plaintiff; or allowing further litigation to go forward and relieving a losing defendant of the burden of paying off any unfavorable judgment. The principal obstacle to giving preclusive effect to a foreign judgment usually turns on whether the court rendering the judgment had jurisdiction over the losing party and gave that party a fair opportunity to be heard. Personal jurisdiction, and to a lesser extent, subject-matter jurisdiction, combine with some minimal conception of due process—often called "international due process"—to determine the effect of a foreign judgment.

The scope of issue preclusion and the existence of privity between the parties have been controversial issues in domestic cases, and these issues could also arise in international cases, but they seldom do so. The reason for this has to do with the basic character of the inquiry into preclusion when a foreign judgment comes before an American court. Usually, the question is whether to recognize the foreign judgment at all. In contrast, in domestic cases, the nearly absolute rule of full faith and credit assures that the judgments of sister states must be recognized, leaving the case to turn on how much recognition they should receive. Thus, issue preclusion (or "collateral estoppel," as it is also known) has been extended by many states and by the federal courts to "non-mutual" cases: those in which the party asserting issue preclusion is not in privity with any party in the original action.[5] Privity itself has also been much litigated, as prevailing parties have sought to extend the scope of judgments in their favor.[6] International cases do not usually get into these subtleties, because it would take the analysis too far away from the central issue of recognition and also because it would require an inquiry into how foreign courts would treat these intricacies of preclusion. Both sorts of issues lend themselves to easier treatment in the more familiar context of wholly domestic cases.

The rule of faith and credit in domestic cases comes from the Full Faith and Credit Clause in the Constitution, which has two parts, the first requiring that "Full Faith and Credit shall be given in each State to the . . . judicial Proceedings in every other State," and the second authorizing Congress to prescribe "the Manner in which such . . . Proceedings shall be proved and the Effect thereof."[7] Congress has acted under this second part to pass implementing legislation that extends full faith and credit to state judgments in federal court and provides for the effect of judgments in certain kinds of cases, like child custody.[8] The constitutional clause, however, does not address the preclusive effect of foreign judgments in American courts. The constitutional and statutory rule of full faith and credit stops at the water's edge. It does not reach foreign judgments, whose effect is determined mainly by state law.

The rule of full faith and credit in domestic cases admits of a few narrow exceptions and qualifications, foreshadowing the more

---

5   Parklane Hosiery Co. v. Shore, 439 U.S. 322 (1979).

6   Taylor v. Sturgell, 553 U.S. 880 (2008).

7   U.S. CONST. Art. IV, § 1.

8   28 U.S.C. §§ 1738, 1738A (2012).

flexible treatment accorded to foreign judgments. The best known exception concerns defects of personal jurisdiction. A default judgment entered without personal jurisdiction does not bind the defendant, who can collaterally attack it in separate proceedings.[9] A default judgment in F1 is not binding in F2 in the absence of personal jurisdiction. However, if the defendant appears in F1, the defendant is bound by the judgment, either because the defendant litigated the issue of personal jurisdiction and lost, or because the defendant waived any objection to personal jurisdiction by not raising it in a timely fashion.[10] Either way, the defendant has had a full opportunity to raise the issue in F1. An exception for lack of subject-matter jurisdiction in F1 has similar dimensions, but these have not been clearly set forth in the precedents. As we will see, the corresponding exceptions to recognition of foreign judgments have broader scope.

The domestic rule of full faith and credit also does not apply to penal judgments or to tax judgments, and it applies in a more qualified form in domestic relations cases and to injunctions.[11] The contours of these exceptions can be altered by agreement between states, as the exception for tax collection has been, but the precise contours of these qualifications need not be pursued here. They bear upon the treatment of foreign judgments only because they correspond to broader and more firmly established exceptions to recognition in international cases. These all derive from the hesitancy of one sovereign to concede its essential sovereign powers within its own territory to a foreign sovereign acting through the judgment of a foreign court. The same hesitancy seems to be at work in domestic cases, but it has not crystallized into such clear-cut limits on recognition of judgments. An enforcing court in F2, might accept the desirability of giving effect to an ordinary civil judgment from a foreign court in F1, but not cede to F1 determinations that have automatic effect within its territory with respect to penal and tax matters. Domestic relations cases and injunctions involve similar issues of the direct and coercive effect of court orders, in domestic cases by changing the parties' marital status and custodial rights, and in injunctions by enforcement through the threat of contempt.

The principles of full faith and credit establish a structure of rules favoring recognition of domestic judgments with limited exceptions. The domestic principles indirectly affect recognition of foreign judgments by setting the tone and creating a practice in favor of recognition, but with the greater flexibility inherent in the concept

---

[9] Pennoyer v. Neff, 95 U.S. 714 (1878).

[10] Baldwin v. Iowa State Traveling Men's Ass'n, 283 U.S. 522 (1931).

[11] Baker v. General Motors Corp., 522 U.S. 222 (1998); Williams v. North Carolina, 317 U.S. 287 (1942).

of comity. As with other topics in international civil litigation, the absence of a superstructure of binding international authority causes nations to fall back upon mutual respect and cooperation through comity, reserving to themselves the final decision over the effect of a foreign judgment. The leading decision in *Hilton* expounds upon the central role of comity, but it has been supplemented over more than a century by statutes and treaties that supply more definite standards for recognition. We start with *Hilton* itself.

B. *Hilton v. Guyot*

The full report of the arguments and opinions in *Hilton* takes up well over a hundred pages in U.S. Reports. The authority of the decision in *Hilton* rests partly on its comprehensive survey of decisions in the nineteenth century, both here and abroad, on recognition of judgments. Following the lead of Justice Story, in his Commentary on the Conflict of Laws, the Court defined comity as a duty "of imperfect obligation, like that of beneficence, humanity and charity. Every nation must be the final judge for itself, not only of the extent of the duty, but of the occasion on which its exercise may be justly demanded."[12] Applied to the facts of the case, comity allowed the Court to refuse to recognize the foreign judgments at issue. These had resulted from commercial litigation in France, in which the plaintiff prevailed and then sought enforcement in a federal court in the United States. The Court refused enforcement on grounds of reciprocity—because the French courts would not enforce a similar judgment from an American court. Four justices dissented, on the ground that a foreign judgment, rendered by a court with subject-matter and personal jurisdiction, supported a common law claim for enforcement, regardless of the practice in other nations.[13] For the majority, the flexible concept of comity under international law governed, rather than the rules of the common law, and this concept allowed the Court to disregard the French judgment because of lack of reciprocity. For the dissenters, the finality accorded to judgments in common law countries, such as the United States and the United Kingdom, proved to be decisive. The fact that some civil law countries, like France, did not recognize foreign judgments did not displace the principle of finality of foreign judgments under the common law.

The majority in *Hilton* devoted most of its opinion to an exact account of past American and British decisions on recognition of judgments, leading to the conclusion that a foreign money judgment

---

[12] *Hilton*, 159 U.S. at 165.

[13] *Id.* at 231–33 (Fuller, J., dissenting).

usually had prima facie effect. The Court elaborated on the principle in these terms:

> When an action is brought in a court of this country, by a citizen of a foreign country against one of our own citizens, to recover a sum of money adjudged by a court of that country to be due from the defendant to the plaintiff, and the foreign judgment appears to have been rendered by a competent court, having jurisdiction of the cause and of the parties, and upon due allegations and proofs, and opportunity to defend against them, and its proceedings are according to the course of a civilized jurisprudence, and are stated in a clear and formal record, the judgment is prima facie evidence, at least, of the truth of the matter adjudged; and it should be held conclusive upon the merits tried in the foreign court, unless some special ground is shown for impeaching the judgment, as by showing that it was affected by fraud or prejudice, or that by the principles of international law, and by the comity of our own country, it should not be given full credit and effect.[14]

The French judgment met all the prerequisites for recognition in terms of jurisdiction and fair procedure, although it might have been tainted by fraud, a question the Supreme Court did not reach. Instead, on an inspection of French law, the Court found that an American judgment would not be recognized by the French courts.[15] The Court found the French position to be anomalous, even among civil law countries, and adhered to Justice Story's position in favor of reciprocity.[16] Thus the holding of the case denies recognition, while most of the opinion supports recognition as "prima facie evidence" in the interest of comity. This prolonged dicta, ironically enough, has proved to be more durable than the holding, which has been widely rejected as a matter of state law.

The role of state law in recognition of foreign judgments leads to the other irony in the legacy of *Hilton.* The Supreme Court rendered the decision under the regime of federal general common law that was rejected, some decades later, by *Erie Railroad v. Tompkins.*[17] Hence it has no binding authority, outside of its possible application to the effect of foreign judgments on federal claims. It was rendered, as the majority goes to some pains to point out, without the benefit of a federal statute or treaty prescribing the effect of the judgment in

---

[14]   *Id.* at 205–06.

[15]   *Id.* at 210–17.

[16]   *Id.* at 227.

[17]   304 U.S. 64 (1938).

question.[18] And, as noted earlier, the Full Faith and Credit Clause does not apply to foreign judgments at all, leaving *Hilton* without any support in the usual sources of federal law after *Erie*. That makes the continuing influence of the decision all the more puzzling. It survives as dicta rather than holding, and as the product of a "way of looking at the law" that was subsequently discredited.[19] The persistence of the decision rests mainly on its incorporation of the views of Justice Story, expressed in Commentary on the Conflict of Laws.[20] Much like the jurisdictional holding in *Pennoyer v. Neff*,[21] the decision itself has been rejected, while the endorsement of Story's views of sovereignty has survived, albeit with modifications made over decades of subsequent developments.

Even before the decision in *Erie*, state courts asserted their independence from the Supreme Court and its holding in *Hilton*. The New York Court of Appeals led the way in *Johnston v. Compagnie Generale Transatlantique*.[22] The court reasoned, along the same lines as the dissenters in *Hilton*, that a foreign judgment between private parties did not implicate international relations, which lie within the exclusive province of the federal government. As the court said, "the question is one of private rather than public international law, of private right rather than public relations and our courts will recognize private rights acquired under foreign laws and the sufficiency of the evidence establishing such rights."[23] The judgment in question came from a French court and *Johnston* still gave it effect despite the absence of reciprocity, which was the basis for the decision in *Hilton*. On the facts of *Johnston*, the recognition of private rights under the foreign judgment was particularly compelling because it was the American plaintiff who had first sued in a French court and lost, and then sued again in a New York court. The American plaintiff had submitted to the jurisdiction of the French courts and then sought to re-litigate the same claim in an American court. The facts presented the strongest possible case for recognition, but *Johnston* stands more generally for the proposition that state courts need not follow federal common law, a proposition that then became entrenched after *Erie* declared that there is "no general federal common law."[24]

---

[18]   *Hilton*, 159 U.S. at 163.

[19]   Guaranty Trust Co. v. York, 326 U.S. 99 (1945).

[20]   JOSEPH STORY, COMMENTARY ON THE CONFLICT OF LAWS FOREIGN AND DOMESTIC (8th ed. 2007).

[21]   95 U.S. 714 (1877).

[22]   242 N.Y. 381 (1926).

[23]   *Id.* at 387.

[24]   *Erie Railroad*, 304 U.S. at 78.

The inconsistency of *Hilton* with *Erie* has implications that extend beyond the force of federal case law to the authority of Congress to enact general legislation on the effect of foreign judgments. The American Law Institute has proposed such a federal statute and offered the foreign commerce clause and control over foreign affairs as sources for federal legislative power.[25] This proposal originated as part of an effort to devise an international convention on recognition of judgments, and if signed and ratified by the United States, the proposed statute would have served as implementing legislation. Hence the statute, as originally conceived, rested on the Treaty Power,[26] as augmented by the Necessary and Proper Clause.[27] In the absence of any immediate prospect for adoption of the convention, the proposed statute would have to depend upon less certain sources of federal power. Foreign judgments have a significant effect on foreign commerce, certainly in financial and commercial matters, but not necessarily in other kinds of foreign litigation. So, too, the general powers of the federal government over foreign relations do not quite match the scope of a statute on recognition of foreign judgments. Other congressional powers, to enforce the Fourteenth Amendment and to control the federal courts,[28] could fill in the gaps in the argument for authority for a federal statute.

The appeal, however, to scattered clauses in the Constitution reveals the weaknesses of arguments based on sources other than the Treaty Power. Similar problems confront a much more narrowly tailored federal statute, the SPEECH Act, which prevents enforcement of foreign libel judgments that do not meet federal and state standards for protecting free speech.[29] The statute seeks to discourage "libel tourism" by suits overseas, mainly in the United Kingdom, followed by collection efforts in the United States in a not-so-subtle attempt to evade the protection of free speech under the First Amendment and under state law. Legislation against this practice has much to be said for it, but it need not be enacted at the federal level. No state court has looked kindly on foreign libel judgments that do not protect rights to free speech.[30] Likewise, no provision in the Constitution gives Congress general authority to

---

[25] LINDA J. SILBERMAN, THE NEED FOR A FEDERAL STATUTORY APPROACH TO THE RECOGNITION AND ENFORCEMENT OF FOREIGN COUNTRY JUDGMENTS, IN FOREIGN COURT JUDGMENTS AND THE UNITED STATES LEGAL SYSTEM 101, 116–17 (Paul Stephan, ed. 2014).

[26] U.S. CONST. art. II, § 2, ¶ 2.

[27] U.S. CONST. art. I, § 8, cl. 18.

[28] U.S. CONST. amend. XIV, § 5, art. I, § 8, cl. 9, art. III, § 1, § 2, ¶ 2.

[29] Securing the Protection of our Enduring and Established Constitutional Heritage (SPEECH) Act, Pub. L. No. 111–223, 124 Stat. 2380 (2010).

[30] *E.g.*, Telnikoff v. Matusevitch, 347 Md. 561, 702 A.2d 230 (1997).

enforce the First Amendment, which is famously framed as a restraint on Congress: that "Congress shall make no law" infringing the rights enumerated in the amendment.[31] The Hague Convention on Choice of Court Agreements offers an alternative approach to federal regulation, based directly on the Treaty Power.[32] Although the Convention has yet to come into force, it directly provides for the enforcement of judgments rendered in the exercise of personal jurisdiction under forum selection clauses within its scope.[33] This chapter does not take up the precise terms of the Convention, but its validity once it comes into force cannot be questioned. It is a self-enforcing treaty directly authorized by the Treaty Power.

The survival of *Hilton* rests on less definite but surprisingly durable foundations. It has been followed as persuasive rather than binding authority, which courts and legislatures are free to disregard as they see fit. Apart from the issue of reciprocity, however, the decision did a remarkable job of anticipating future developments. By endorsing comity and the prima facie effect of a foreign judgment, the decision established the trend toward recognition of foreign judgments. The decision also established the main exceptions to recognition, based on lack of personal and subject-matter jurisdiction, an absence of fair procedures, fraud in obtaining the judgment, and violations of public policy. State law has endorsed all of these features of the opinion and elaborated upon them in detailed statutory provisions.

C. The Uniform Foreign-Country Money Judgments Recognition Act

The predominant vehicle for framing state law on the recognition of foreign judgments has been uniform legislation, in the form of the Uniform Foreign-Country Money Judgments Recognition Act[34] and its predecessor, which had a similar name and similar terms.[35] A total of thirty-two states have adopted one version or another of this legislation. This legislation should be distinguished from the federal and state laws that provide for registration of judgments.[36] One of these goes by the name of the Uniform Enforcement of Foreign Judgments Act but applies only to enforcement in one American state of judgments from another American state. The 2005 and 1962 Uniform Acts and the judicial

---

[31] U.S. CONST. amend. I.

[32] Hague Convention, *supra* note 4.

[33] *Id.* arts. 8–15.

[34] Uniform Foreign-Country Money Judgments Recognition Act of 2005 § 4(b)(2), (3) [hereinafter 2005 Uniform Act].

[35] Uniform Foreign Money-Judgments Recognition Act of 1962 § 4.

[36] 28 U.S.C. § 1963 (2012).

decisions in the states that have not adopted these acts contain the only general rules on recognition of judgments from foreign countries.

The uniform acts incorporate the principle of full faith and credit from constitutional law, subject to a wider range of exceptions than in domestic cases. The 2005 Uniform Act makes a foreign judgment "conclusive between the parties to the same extent as the judgment of a sister-state entitled to full faith and credit in this state would be conclusive."[37] To the extent it is conclusive, a foreign judgment then is enforced according to the same procedures as judgments from the enforcing state.[38] In schematic terms, if F2 (the enforcing state) has enacted the 2005 Uniform Act, and no exception in the Act prevents recognition of a judgment from F1 (the rendering state), then F2 gives the judgment the same faith and credit that it would have received in F1. In short, a combination of the Uniform Act and the law of F1 determine whether the judgment from F1 is recognized in F2. If it is, then it can be enforced there according to the law of F2.

The exceptions to recognition constitute the heart of the 2005 Uniform Act. They fall into three categories: substantive exceptions, notably for judgments contrary to the public policy of F2; procedural exceptions, concerned with reliability and integrity of the judicial system in F1 and with the particular judgment rendered by F1; and jurisdictional objections focused upon absence of personal jurisdiction. All three categories seek to preserve the freedom of F2 to exercise its sovereign prerogative to refuse to recognize the judgment from F1. This is clearest in the first category of exceptions based on substantive policy, but these exceptions have seldom been successfully invoked. Far more commonly accepted are the second and third categories, for procedural and jurisdictional defects. These might be influenced by concerns over the substance of the judgment, but they are cast in terms internal to the processes of litigation. Procedural and jurisdictional exceptions also have a stronger basis in the domestic recognition of judgments from sister states. They also provide the only grounds on which a judgment from F1 must not be recognized. If applicable, the exceptions for absence of due process, lack of personal jurisdiction, and lack of subject-matter jurisdiction deprive the court in F2 of discretion to recognize the judgment from F1.[39] A detailed discussion of each kind of exception follows.

1.   Public Policy

The purely substantive exception for judgments "repugnant to the public policy of this state or of the United States" constitutes a

---

[37] 2005 Uniform Act, *supra* note 34, § 7(a).

[38] *Id.* § 7(b).

[39] *Id.* § 4(b).

ground on which the court in this country "need not recognize a foreign-country judgment."[40] It also has no correlative in the domestic law of full faith and credit. A state must recognize a judgment of a sister state even if it is contrary to the public policy of the enforcing state.[41] Perhaps because of the absence of any support in domestic law, the public policy exception has tended to receive a narrow interpretation. The terms of the exception itself require that the judgment be "repugnant," not just different from or inconsistent with the policy here. The classic statement comes from Judge Cardozo (then on the New York Court of Appeals) in a choice of law case, explaining, "[w]e are not so provincial as to say that every solution of a problem is wrong because we deal with it otherwise at home."[42] Despite the decidedly different context in which Judge Cardozo offered this observation, it has been prominently quoted in decisions narrowing the public policy exception.

A representative case is *Ohno v. Yasuna*,[43] which enforced a Japanese judgment over objections that the judgment violated public policy and denied constitutional rights. The plaintiff had brought an action in Japan against a church and its principal pastor, alleging that they had defrauded her by pressuring her to make contributions to the church amounting to half a million dollars. The Japanese court ordered judgment for that amount, and the plaintiff then brought an action to enforce it in a federal court in California, basing jurisdiction upon diversity of citizenship. The defendants objected on the ground that enforcement of the Japanese judgment would violate the religion clauses of the First Amendment and that it was, in any event, repugnant to the public policy of California and the United States. The first argument failed for lack of state action in enforcing the judgment, which amounted to no more than vindicating the private rights of the plaintiff. The second failed under the California version of the 2005 Uniform Act because, as the Ninth Circuit observed, "California courts have set a high bar for repugnancy under the Uniform Act."[44] The plaintiff's claim under Japanese law for intentional or negligent infringement of her rights resembled tort claims under California law for undue influence, fraud, negligent or intentional infliction of emotional distress, and undue enrichment.[45] Even though the defendants were a church and its pastor, they were not entitled to immunity based on their religious affiliation.[46] Neither

---

40   *Id.* § 4(c)(3).
41   Fauntleroy v. Lum, 210 U.S. 230 (1908).
42   Loucks v. Standard Oil Co., 224 N.Y. 99, 111 (1918).
43   723 F.3d 984 (9th Cir. 2013).
44   *Id.* at 1002.
45   *Id.* at 1006.
46   *Id.* at 1005–09.

California law nor the First Amendment created blanket immunity for religiously inspired action that was otherwise tortious. Nor did the Japanese judgment infringe religiously related speech, as opposed to coercive conduct, or infringe upon the defendants' core religious beliefs.[47]

Following the terms of the 2005 Uniform Act, the Ninth Circuit analyzed both the plaintiff's claim under foreign law and the plaintiff's foreign judgment under the public policy exception. This particular provision allows states to choose between analyzing the judgment, the claim, or both (as California did in *Ohno v. Yasuna*).[48] Although the claim normally merges in the final judgment, the difference between the two can become important if one is analyzed at a higher level of abstraction than the other. For instance, a claim for punitive damages might be repugnant to public policy because it exposes the defendant to unlimited liability, while a judgment for a definite amount might not be large enough to offend the public policy of F2. Conversely, a cause of action might be characterized in a way that makes it consistent with public policy, while the resulting judgment reveals that it is not. For instance, in *Southwest Livestock & Trucking Co., Inc. v. Ramon*,[49] the Fifth Circuit reached this conclusion under the Texas version of the 1962 Uniform Act, which referred only to the plaintiff's "cause of action." The court held that it was a simple claim for contract, routinely enforced by the Texas courts, although the judgment revealed that the contract was for a usurious interest rate in excess of that allowed by Texas law.[50] The Fifth Circuit manipulated the characterization of the claim to preserve the enforceability of the judgment, although its decision might be justified on the ground that Texas policy favored freedom of contract and that the defendant had waived the protection of the Texas usury statute by knowingly executing a distinctively Mexican contract, a "pagare," with a Mexican citizen. Judgment had then been entered on the contract against the defendant in Mexico.[51]

Such contractual dealings contrast with the judgments for defamation that have received the harshest treatment from American courts, culminating (as noted earlier) in the enactment of the SPEECH Act. Those decisions have the same foundation in the Constitution as the Ninth Circuit's decision in *Ohno*, but they reach the opposite result—refusing recognition of a foreign judgment. This contrast results from the heightened suspicion of libel claims in this

---

[47] *Id.* at 1010–13.

[48] 2005 Uniform Act, *supra* note 34, § 4(c)(3).

[49] 169 F.3d 317 (5th Cir. 1999).

[50] *Id.* at 320–21.

[51] *Id.* at 319.

country after *New York Times Co. v. Sullivan*.[52] By invoking principles of free speech in this decision and others, the Supreme Court has drawn American law ever further away from the common law roots of claims for defamation, opening more than a historical gap in the treatment of these claims. It has also opened a gap with the law of England, where many modern libel claims are brought. Hence state courts, like the Maryland Court of Appeals in *Telnikoff v. Matusevitch*,[53] have felt free to identify libel judgments inconsistent with American law as repugnant to the public policy embodied in the First Amendment and in state constitutions. The tendency to seek a basis in constitutional doctrine, evident in these cases, reveals how narrow the public policy exception is. Invoking the exception requires support in fundamental principles of American law. The resort to constitutional doctrine also resembles appeals to due process in the analysis of procedural and jurisdictional defects in foreign judgments, to be discussed shortly.

2. Procedural Defects

Defects in the proceedings in the foreign court can take a variety of forms that prevent enforcement of the judgment under the 2005 Uniform Act. The most extreme, which requires nonrecognition of the judgment, condemns the entire foreign judicial system on the ground that it "does not provide impartial tribunals or procedures compatible with the requirements of due process of law."[54] Other procedural defects in F1 allow the court in F2 to refuse to recognize the judgment, but do not require it to do so. These focus on the specific proceedings in F1 and revolve around the general principles of due process, or as it is sometimes called, "the international concept of due process." That is, procedures "that are fundamentally fair and do not offend against basic fairness."[55] The foreign procedures need not conform to all the specifics of American decisions on due process.[56] The statute articulates several specific rules of fairness, some of which simply repeat the requirements of due process and others which take it much further. The rules, in the order in which they appear in the statute, are the following: lack of notice, fraud on the court, conflict with another final judgment, selection of a forum contrary to a forum selection clause, selection of a seriously inconvenient forum, substantial doubt about the integrity of the foreign court, and whether the specific proceeding itself violated due

---

[52] 376 U.S. 254 (1964).

[53] 347 Md. 561 (1997).

[54] 2005 Uniform Act, *supra* note 34, § 4(b)(1).

[55] Society of Lloyd's v. Ashenden, 233 F.3d 473, 477 (7th Cir. 2000) (citation omitted).

[56] *Id.* at 478.

process.[57] The statute delineates these exceptions in detail, but they all retain sufficient flexibility to permit the court in F2 to exercise discretion in deciding whether an exception applies to the judgment from F1, and if it does, whether the judgment should be recognized anyway. The burden of proof in all cases is on the party seeking nonrecognition.[58]

The question underlying all of these exceptions, as with the concept of international due process, is how much they depart from conceptions of procedural fairness under the domestic law of F2. To take just the first exception, it applies if "the defendant in the proceeding in the foreign court did not receive notice of the proceeding in sufficient time to enable the defendant to defend."[59] The standard of "sufficient time" departs from the strict time limits for filing an answer in order to avoid entry of a default judgment.[60] Similarly, to determine when a "foreign country judgment conflicts with another final and conclusive judgment," the court must engage in a process of interpretation.[61] For judgments from sister states, the Full Faith and Credit Clause refers to the law of F1 to determine when a judgment is sufficiently final to receive preclusive effect. Whether a foreign judgment is "final and conclusive" under the terms of the 2005 Uniform Act requires the exercise of more discretion by the court in F2, as evidenced by the discretion the court has to invoke this exception at all. The court "need not recognize" the judgment of F1 if this exception applies.[62]

The concept of "international due process" brings the comparison between American and foreign procedures into sharp relief. An American court can hardly expect a foreign court to follow all the details of the American case law on due process. Yet it also cannot easily reach the conclusion that a procedure which denies due process in this country still remains fundamentally fair in another country. The solution to this dilemma appears to lie in the fit between a particular disputed procedure and the procedural system that surrounds it. Thus, Judge Posner, speaking for the Seventh Circuit in *Society of Lloyd's v. Ashenden*,[63] looks to the particular objections that the losing party had to the procedures in F1 and whether they detracted from the overall fairness of the proceedings there. In *Society of Lloyd's*, the defendants objected to clauses in their

---

[57] 2005 Uniform Act, *supra* note 34, § 4(c)(1)–(2), (4)–(8).

[58] *Id.* § 4(d).

[59] *Id.* § 4(c)(1).

[60] FED. R. CIV. P. 12(a) (twenty-one days for serving an answer for defendants, ninety days for defendants overseas).

[61] 2005 Uniform Act, *supra* note 34, § 4(c)(4).

[62] *Id.* § 4(c)(3).

[63] 233 F.3d 473, 479–80 (7th Cir. 2000).

reinsurance contracts that restricted their procedural rights, first, to pay an assessment that they owed under the contract before they sued, and second, to accept the plaintiff's power to set the amount of the assessment unilaterally, without discovery into how reasonable the assessment was. Contractual provisions such as these, particularly between commercial parties as in this case, might well be permissible in wholly domestic cases. Yet it would be difficult to require parties and courts in a foreign country to anticipate all of the objections that might be made to such clauses as a matter purely of American law. Judge Posner admitted that both clauses curtailed the defendants' rights. "But," he continued, "due process is not a fixed menu of procedural rights. How much process is due depends on the circumstances."[64] Because the contract as a whole was valid and enforceable, so too were the procedural terms that implemented it.[65]

The opinion in *Society of Lloyd's*, as it progresses, gradually moves from procedural issues of access to the court and discovery to substantive issues of contract law. As noted earlier, that feature of the decision is typical of the permeability of the distinction between procedure and substance, especially when it comes to recognition of foreign judgments. If the judgment appears to be basically sound as a matter of substantive law, then American courts typically exercise their discretion to enforce it over procedural objections, as most of the exceptions in the 2005 Uniform Act allow.[66] Courts in states that have not adopted the Act can reach the same result by appealing to the general standards of comity conducive to a climate of international cooperation.[67] Because of the narrowness of the public policy exception, courts often displace doubts about the substance of a judgment onto procedural and jurisdictional issues.[68] The next subsection offers several vivid illustrations of this tendency.

3.   Jurisdiction

Jurisdiction over the subject-matter of a dispute and personal jurisdiction over the defendant depend upon concepts of sovereignty directly connected to issues of comity. Both depend to a great extent on territorial power, no matter how flexible and indefinite it has become under modern theories of jurisdiction. Both forms of jurisdiction therefore presuppose the same territorial basis as the principle of comity: that the enforcing court in F2 has the sole power

---

[64]   *Id.* at 479.

[65]   *Id.* at 481.

[66]   2005 Uniform Act, *supra* note 34, § 4(c).

[67]   159 U.S. 113, 202–03 (stating presumption of recognition); RESTATEMENT (SECOND) OF CONFLICT OF LAWS §§ 92, 98 (1971).

[68]   *E.g.*, Int'l Transactions, Ltd. v. Embotelladora Agral Regiomontana, 347 F.3d 589, 594–96 (5th Cir. 2003) (finding lack of notice to support judgment confirming allegedly fraudulent assignment of arbitration award).

to recognize judgments within its territory, but does so only if the rendering court in F1 has acted within its authority. Both lack of subject-matter jurisdiction and lack of personal jurisdiction constitute mandatory grounds for refusing to recognize a judgment. A court in F2 cannot recognize a judgment from a court in F1 lacking these prerequisites of authority.[69] Lack of personal jurisdiction furnishes the most commonly litigated reason for refusing to recognize a foreign judgment, but a brief examination of subject-matter jurisdiction reveals its importance also.

A court that acts without subject-matter jurisdiction resembles a public official who acts *ultra vires*, outside the authority conferred upon him or her by law. Without authority, the public official exercises the coercive power of government beyond the constraints imposed by law. A court that does this calls into question its impartiality, its adherence to due process, and its integrity, along the lines of the exceptions to recognition discussed in the previous subsection. Lack of subject-matter jurisdiction nevertheless seldom furnishes the reason for refusing to recognize a judgment. The court in F1 must follow rules on subject-matter jurisdiction under the law of F1, which is less accessible to the court in F2 than to the court in F1, which can rely on its knowledge of its own law.[70] Without quite finding collateral estoppel based on the finding in F1 of subject-matter jurisdiction, the court in F2 ends up deferring to a degree to the finding in F1. Only blatant disregard of the law of F1 would trigger a different assessment by the court in F2. Another rare example of the absence of subject-matter jurisdiction occurs when the court in F1 goes too far in applying its law to a controversy that has no discernible connection to that forum.[71] Strictly speaking, this kind of case involves the absence of prescriptive jurisdiction—the power of F1 to apply its own law to the controversy—rather than subject-matter jurisdiction—the power of the courts of F1 to adjudicate the controversy. But as discussed in Chapter 2, the two types of jurisdiction are related to one another, in this way: the subject-matter jurisdiction of F1 based on the application of F1's substantive law depends on the existence of a reasonable argument for prescriptive jurisdiction that supports the application of F1's law to the case.

Lack of subject-matter jurisdiction has been invoked less frequently to defeat recognition of foreign judgments than lack of

---

[69] 2005 Uniform Act, *supra* note 34, § 4(b)(2), (3).

[70] S.C. Chimexim SA v. Velco Enters. Ltd., 36 F. Supp. 2d 206, 212 (S.D.N.Y. 1999) (federal court finds no basis to challenge subject-matter jurisdiction of Romanian court under Romanian law).

[71] Barry E. (Anonymous) v. Ingraham, 43 N.Y.2d 87, 92–93 (N.Y. 1977) (Mexican court lacks subject-matter jurisdiction over members of American family, all of whom resided in New York, in adoption dispute).

personal jurisdiction because the latter has proved to be more successful, with stronger roots in domestic law. At least since the decision in *Pennoyer v. Neff*,[72] a collateral attack upon a domestic judgment for lack of personal jurisdiction has been an established exception to the rule of full faith and credit within the United States. Although the strict territorial theory of *Pennoyer* has eroded over the last century, its holding on the permissible means of collateral attack remains good law. A defendant who takes a default judgment, by failing to appear in F1, can attack the judgment for lack of personal jurisdiction in a sister state, F2. That is not quite the law for collateral attack upon foreign judgments, but it represents a good first approximation.

The approximation comes in because the defendant can challenge personal jurisdiction in F1, lose on that issue, and then in limited circumstances renew the challenge in F2. The 2005 Uniform Act catalogues in some detail the conditions under which a defendant can—or more precisely, cannot—challenge personal jurisdiction in F2. The Act precludes a challenge under a nonexclusive list of conditions that conclusively establish personal jurisdiction in F1.[73] These catalogue several of the standard grounds sufficient for personal jurisdiction under American law, and for the most part under the law of other countries, beginning with personal service in the foreign country on the model of service in a sister state under *Burnham v. Superior Court*.[74] It is followed by appearance to defend upon the merits or consent to jurisdiction, as in the domestic law of waiver and consent.[75] General jurisdiction can be based on domicile for individuals and on incorporation or principal place of business for business organizations.[76] Specific jurisdiction can be based on claims arising from a business office in the foreign country and on claims arising from the operation of a motor vehicle or airplane there.[77] The most contentious cases in foreign litigation, as in domestic litigation, involve specific jurisdiction, although nations in the European Union do not recognize service within F1 as sufficient for personal jurisdiction to support recognition in F2.[78]

---

[72] 95 U.S. 714 (1877).

[73] 2005 Uniform Act, *supra* note 34, § 5(a).

[74] *Id.* § 5(a)(1); 495 U.S. 604 (1990).

[75] 2005 Uniform Act, *supra* note 34, § 5(a)(2), (3).

[76] *Id.* § 5(a)(4).

[77] *Id.* § 5(a)(5), (6).

[78] Council Regulation 44/2001 of 22 December 2000 on Jurisdiction and the Recognition and Enforcement of Judgments in Civil and Commercial Matters, arts. 3(2), 35(1), annex I, O.J. (L 12) 1, 4 (EC). For the pending changes in the regulation, *see* Regulation (EU) 1215/2012 of the European Parliament and of the Council of 12 December 2012 on jurisdiction and the recognition and enforcement of judgments in

Review of foreign judgments for defects of personal jurisdiction involves a re-examination of the basis for personal jurisdiction in F2, even if it has been determined in F1. This difference from collateral attack on sister state judgments also requires a determination of which law, that of F1 or F2, applies to the review of personal jurisdiction. Most American courts offer "both" as an answer, although American law might be discounted by "the international concept of due process," as it is in purely procedural cases. The motive behind double review in F2 even if it has already been found in F1 and according to the law of both F2 and F1, derives from the central role of personal jurisdiction in protecting the defendant from the unwanted assertion of power by a foreign court. Other doctrines, such as limits on choice of law and the public policy exception for recognition of foreign judgments, could prevent the oppressive application of foreign law by a foreign court, but personal jurisdiction has been deployed most frequently for this purpose. The extreme case of a defendant with "no contacts, ties, or relations" with F1[79] also makes the strongest case for protecting the defendant from the adverse effects of a foreign judgment. Some European nations have taken this principle to the opposite extreme and simply refused to recognize foreign judgments against their nationals, unless required to do so by treaty or by the law of the European Union.[80]

A recent case, *Evans Cabinet Corp. v. Kitchen International, Inc.*, both illustrates and surveys current American approaches.[81] The case arose from an ordinary contract claim brought in Quebec by a corporation based there (although it was incorporated in Louisiana) against a Georgia corporation. When the Georgia corporation failed to appear in the Quebec lawsuit, the Quebec court entered a default judgment against it. The Georgia corporation responded by suing in federal court in Massachusetts, bringing its own claim for breach of contract. That court entered summary judgment for the Quebec business based on res judicata, but the First Circuit reversed because of the inadequacy of the record on two issues: first, whether the Quebec court had personal jurisdiction under Quebec law; and second, whether it had jurisdiction under the Due Process Clause. Both conditions had to be satisfied to recognize the judgment under the Massachusetts version of the 2005 Uniform Act.

On the first issue, the court did not have to contend with a finding of the Quebec court that it had jurisdiction under Quebec law,

---

civil and commercial matters (recast). Official Journal, OJ 20 December 2012, L 351/1, arts. 4, 5, 6, 45(e).

[79] Int'l Shoe Co. v. Wash., 326 U.S. 310, 319 (1945).

[80] ANDREAS F. LOWENFELD, INTERNATIONAL LITIGATION AND ARBITRATION 531 (3d ed. 2006).

[81] 593 F.3d 135 (1st Cir. 2010).

since it had entered a default judgment without further proceedings. For that reason, the record was confused on exactly which provision of the Quebec Civil Code supported the exercise of personal jurisdiction. It might have been a catch-all provision for some form of jurisdiction by necessity because the suit could not have been brought elsewhere. Or it might have been because the contract was made in Quebec and was to be performed there. The former ground was implausible because the case involved two corporations from this country and could easily have been brought in Georgia, the state of incorporation of the original defendant. The latter ground depended upon resolving a conflict between the affidavits submitted by both parties, which raised an issue of credibility that could not be resolved on summary judgment. The analysis of Quebec law shows how seriously courts take issues of personal jurisdiction. It might well have been handled more summarily if the Quebec court had found personal jurisdiction, and indeed, under the ALI's proposed statute on recognition of foreign judgments, such a finding would have been binding on issues of fact and foreign law if litigated in the original forum.[82]

The second issue required the court to determine whether the Quebec court could have exercised jurisdiction consistent with Massachusetts law. Because Massachusetts extended its long-arm statute to the constitutional limits, this inquiry reduced to analysis under the Due Process Clause. That put the court in the peculiar position of applying the clause to proceedings overseas, raising the same doubts about the desirability of subjecting foreign courts to the nuances of American conceptions of due process. The "international concept of due process" might fit better with the retrospective nature of the court's inquiry—determining whether the Quebec proceedings met requirements of procedure of which the parties and the court should have been aware. In the end, however, any difference between Quebec law and the Due Process Clause had little effect on the actual decision, since the same ambiguities in the record that prevented entry of summary judgment on the issue of Quebec law also prevented entry of summary judgment on the constitutional issue. If the contract had actually been made or was to be performed in Quebec, it probably would have supported a finding of minimum contacts of the Georgia corporation with the forum.[83]

The First Circuit did note that the due process analysis encompassed a range of "Gestalt factors," such as the burden on the defendant of appearing in the forum, the forum's interest in

---

[82] AMERICAN LAW INSTITUTE, RECOGNITION AND ENFORCEMENT OF FOREIGN JUDGMENTS: ANALYSIS AND PROPOSED FEDERAL STATUTE § 4(b), (c) (2005) [hereinafter ALI].

[83] *Evans Cabinet Corp.*, 593 F.3d at 145.

adjudicating the dispute, and the various interests of different sovereigns in the case.[84] This turn towards discretionary consideration of broadly defined factors underlined the court's decision that the case needed to be reconsidered on remand, but like the consideration of Quebec law, it reveals how seriously courts in F2 take the existence of personal jurisdiction in F1. An open-ended, multi-factor inquiry invites the use of personal jurisdiction as a proxy for generalized concerns about the fairness of the foreign judgment. In the absence of few other grounds that can, as a practical matter, succeed in overcoming the presumption in favor of recognition, personal jurisdiction can serve as the vehicle for closely examining the foreign judgment. The case-by-case contours of modern tests for personal jurisdiction under the Due Process Clause make it a particularly good means of detecting and refusing to enforce aberrant foreign judgments.

The re-examination of personal jurisdiction has its limits, however. As noted earlier, under the ALI proposed federal statute, litigation of the issue in F1 precludes many of the grounds for raising the issue again in F2. Moreover, a defendant who steps over the line and litigates more than personal jurisdiction in F1 and proceeds to the merits waives the opportunity to re-litigate the issue in F2. The 2005 Uniform Act provides for such a waiver if "the defendant voluntarily appeared in the proceeding, other than for the purpose of protecting property seized or threatened with seizure in the proceeding or of contesting the jurisdiction over the defendant."[85] The leading decision on waiver of objections to personal jurisdiction in this way, and on all the complications that it entails, is *Somportex, Ltd. v. Philadelphia Chewing Gum Corp.*[86] The defendant there fell afoul of the intricate rules for making an objection to personal jurisdiction in the English courts by means of a "conditional appearance"—one which, under English law, does not constitute litigation on the merits. Because the defendant failed to adhere to these rules, it was bound by the judgment of the English court, even though such judgment was entered as a default judgment after the defendant had attempted to withdraw from the proceedings.[87] To the extent that the American court re-examined the judgment for compliance with the Due Process Clause, it held that it was bound by findings of the English court, entered after the defendant had attempted to withdraw, that established minimum contacts with the forum.[88] The details of English procedure need not be explored

---

[84] *Id.* at 146.

[85] 2005 Uniform Act, *supra* note 34, § 5(a)(2).

[86] 453 F.2d 435 (1st Cir. 1971), *cert. denied*, 405 U.S. 1017 (1972).

[87] *Id.* at 442.

[88] *Id.* at 444.

further, beyond noting that failure to adhere to acceptable procedures in F1 can forfeit jurisdictional objections in F2. The American court specifically held that "the English procedure comports with our standards of due process."[89] When F2 trusts the procedures of F1, it has little reason to upset them by allowing a challenge based on lack of personal jurisdiction there.

D. Foreign Recognition of American Judgments

Foreign courts also rely upon the public policy exception in determining the effect of American judgments. They have had particular problems with the award of punitive damages in private civil actions, finding them to resemble penal judgments that, as a matter of longstanding tradition, do not receive any recognition at all from courts in other countries. That, too, is the law in this country.[90] Foreign courts have worried about the nearly unlimited discretion that American courts have in making awards of punitive damages, so that their concerns over public policy have merged with concerns over procedure. In *Re the Enforcement of a U.S. Judgment*, the German Federal Supreme Court took this position, offering the following criticism of American law:

> In the U.S. "punitive damages" awarded by courts in their discretion without a fixed relationship to the injury suffered and sometimes awarded at an excessively high level have had the effect of contributing to a rapid increase in the burden of compensation in economic terms. . . .[91]

In the same case, however, the court allowed enforcement of damages for anxiety, pain, and suffering, probably because these were roughly proportional to medical expenses and were only half the amount of punitive damages. The combination of discretion and punishment, unrelated to actual loss, led the court to refuse to enforce the judgment to the extent that it awarded punitive damages.

In response to some American judgments, notoriously those for treble damages under the antitrust laws, a few foreign countries have enacted "clawback" statutes. The United Kingdom enacted such a law in response to aggressive use by American courts of the "effects test" to expand the scope of American antitrust laws.[92] These statutes authorize defendants subjected to such judgments to bring their own actions in their own courts to recover the amount of damages assessed against them. Trade disputes have also resulted in

---

[89] *Id.*

[90] 2005 Uniform Act, *supra* note 34, § 3(b)(2).

[91] Case IX ZR 149/91 (1992), *reprinted in* English in 5 Intern. Lit. Rep. 602 (1994).

[92] George A. Bermann, *Parallel Litigation: Is Convergence Possible?*, 13 YEARBOOK OF PRIVATE INT'L LAW 22, 32 (2011).

enactment of clawback statutes.[93] The clawback statutes deny recognition to a designated kind of American judgment and then seeks to neutralize its consequences by authorizing a claim under foreign law. Although seldom, if ever, enforced, clawback statutes represent an extreme form of the public policy exception to recognition of judgments from another country.[94] By legislation, the foreign country declares its abhorrence of an American judgment, although more symbolically than practically if past experience is any guide.

E. Beyond Ordinary Money Judgments

Several standard exceptions exempt from recognition particular kinds of judgments, in the absence of a special treaty or statute. By its terms, the 2005 Uniform Act does not cover judgments for taxes, the imposition of a fine or other penalty, and judgments in domestic relations cases.[95] As its full name implies, the Act only applies to "money judgments." The ALI proposed statute covers a broader range of judgments, with somewhat different exceptions. For a start, it reaches declaratory judgments and injunctions, subject to the caveat that they "may be entitled to recognition or enforcement under such procedures as the recognizing court deems appropriate."[96] As with all judgments, enforcement follows the procedure in F2, even when principles of full faith and credit require recognition according to the law of F1. Enforcement of declaratory judgments and injunctions, however, is discretionary with F2. The same is true of judgments for taxes, fines, and penalties.[97] Like the 2005 Uniform Act, the ALI proposed statute contains an exception for domestic relations cases, but adds an exception for bankruptcy cases and for arbitral awards and orders to arbitrate.[98] The last exception arises not from lack of enforcement, but because of enforcement under the separate provisions of the New York Convention on the Recognition and Enforcement of Foreign Arbitral Awards,[99] to be discussed in the next chapter.

The rationale for all these limits on coverage, which correspond to those in other countries, derives from special concerns about preserving the sovereignty of the enforcing state. The court in F2 goes further into the merits of the dispute, or requires a special treaty or

---

[93] *Id.* at 33–34.

[94] *Id.* at 34–35

[95] 2005 Uniform Act, *supra* note 34, § 3(b).

[96] 2005 Uniform Act, *supra* note 34, § 3(b)(3); ALI, *supra* note 82, § 2(b)(ii).

[97] *Id.* § 2(b)(i).

[98] *Id.* § 1(a).

[99] United Nations Convention on the Recognition and Enforcement of Foreign Arbitral Awards, June 10, 1958, 21 U.S.T. 2517, 330 U.N.T.S. 38.

statute, to enforce a claim by the plaintiff in such cases. This caution results from a combination of reasons derived from the continuing effects of the judgments in question or from their close connection to the exercise of sovereign power by either F1 or F2. Taxes, penalties, and fines are fundamental to government, in the sense that it can do little else without financial resources or the threat of punishment. How a government performs these essential functions could be the subject of cooperation with other governments, but it proceeds by special treaties and procedures that do not support general recognition of judgments.

Bilateral tax treaties promote international cooperation in reporting and collecting taxes, but only with limitations and qualifications. States resist commandeering when they might be held responsible for the tax policies and decisions of another nation. Each country's taxes are generally regarded as its own business. Erosion of this rule, to the extent it has occurred, has resulted from tax treaties rather than general statutes or judicial interpretation.[100] Enforcement of tax judgments, like enforcement of tax laws, otherwise rests with the taxing nation.

The same dynamics figure into the exclusion of penalties and fines. Criminal judgments fall entirely outside the scope of the statutes on recognition and enforcement of foreign judgments, and by extension, civil judgments for penalties and fines receive the same treatment. States cooperate in enforcement of criminal law less at the conclusion of a case, after a court has rendered judgment, than at the beginning, when treaties for extradition bring a defendant before the court for prosecution. Although convicted fugitives from justice can be extradited, typically extradition occurs at the commencement of the proceedings, particularly in nations like the United States, which do not generally allow trials in absentia.[101] Extradition treaties, like tax treaties, are bilateral agreements subject to qualifications and exceptions that narrow the range of crimes for which an individual can be extradited.[102] They stand at the opposite extreme, both in procedural context and in substantive content, from the general rules applied to recognition of judgments. Some countries, as noted earlier, have expanded the exclusion of fines to also exclude civil judgments for punitive damages. The United States is not among them, since the doctrine here confines penalties and

---

[100] AG of Can. v. R.J. Reynolds Tobacco Holdings, Inc., 268 F.3d 103, 113–15 (2nd Cir. 2001), *cert. denied*, 537 U.S. 1000 (2002).

[101] FED. R. CRIM. P. 43(a).

[102] CURTIS A. BRADLEY & JACK L. GOLDSMITH, FOREIGN RELATION LAW: CASES AND MATERIALS 553–57 (5th ed. 2014).

fines to those in favor of the government, but American courts have had few occasions to address this issue.[103]

Domestic relations implicate the sovereign interests of a country in protecting its own nationals whose status as married, single, or in custody of another is at stake. Judgments that determine custody, support, and alimony also require continuing supervision at the enforcement stage, requiring an investment of resources by F2 that it might not be willing to make to implement the family law policies of F1. International cooperation, as with tax issues, depends upon particular statutes and treaties, rather than general principles for recognition of foreign judgments.[104]

Injunctions generally pose the same problems of continuing enforcement. Under the usual rule of full faith and credit, the law of F1 determines recognition of FI judgments in F2, but the law of F2 determines the procedure for enforcement. As the Supreme Court has observed with respect to sister state injunctions, "[e]nforcement measures do not travel with the sister state judgment as preclusive effects do; such measures remain subject to the even-handed control of forum law."[105] What is true of enforcing sister state injunctions holds even more true for foreign injunctions. Unlike money judgments, foreign injunctions require continuing supervision and remain subject to equitable supervision. They cannot be enforced by a process as straightforward as finding assets of the defendant and selling them in satisfaction of a money judgment. The enforcement procedures in F2 predominate over the preclusive effect given by F1, so much so that foreign injunctions rarely are enforced at all.

A further reason for such hesitation comes from the mechanism for enforcement of injunction, which is by way of contempt. If a defendant disobeys an injunction, the court first holds the party in contempt and then imposes a sanction that may be either criminal or civil in nature. The distinction between the two forms of contempt depends nominally upon the punitive nature of criminal contempt, as a penalty for disobeying injunction, and the coercive nature of civil contempt, as an incentive to compel compliance with the injunction. Both forms of contempt, however, can land the disobedient party in jail or subject the party to large monetary penalties. These outcomes trigger in the enforcing state the same concerns as the exception for judgments imposing penalties and fines. Declaratory judgments raise similar concerns, although more indirectly because they can support an injunction followed by contempt sanctions. The prospect of using

---

[103] GARY BORN AND PETER B. RUTLEDGE, INTERNATIONAL CIVIL LITIGATION IN UNITED STATES COURTS 1110 (5th ed.).

[104] ALI, *supra* note 82, § 1, Reporters Notes 3(a).

[105] Baker v. General Motors Corp., 522 U.S. 222, 235 (1998).

RECOGNITION AND ENFORCEMENT
                           OF JUDGMENTS

coercive power in F2 to penalize a disobedient party from F1 might well lead courts to be reluctant to recognize foreign injunctions and declaratory judgments. Hence the ALI proposed statute makes recognition of such judgments discretionary rather than mandatory, even if all the other requirements of the statute are met.[106]

---

[106] ALI, *supra* note 82, § 2(a)(ii) (stating such judgments "may be entitled to recognition or enforcement under such procedures as the recognizing court deems appropriate").

Chapter VIII

ARBITRATION

Arbitration carries forward many of the themes from previous chapters. Arbitration agreements are simply one kind of forum selection clause, one that takes the claims within its scope to a private rather than a public forum. They ordinarily are accompanied by choice-of-law clauses, in order to identify the law that the arbitrator should apply to the dispute. If a government agrees to arbitration, it has by that means waived any defense of sovereign immunity. Arbitration itself has its own sets of procedures, usually adopted by reference in the arbitration agreement and covering such issues as prehearing motions, discovery, and evidence. A valid arbitration agreement supports a stay of any competing judicial proceedings and an injunction compelling arbitration. A valid award, if not otherwise satisfied, must be confirmed and enforced in judicial proceedings, resulting in a judgment usually entitled to recognition in other countries. Indeed, arbitration awards in some respects receive greater faith and credit than foreign judgments.

Arbitration presents an alternative and a challenge to traditional litigation. Arbitration allows the parties to tailor the means of deciding any dispute between them by selecting who will decide and according to what choice of substantive law. By contract, parties can dispel some of the uncertainty that surrounds international civil litigation, given the choice of courts and law available to parties in the absence of arbitration. In consumer and employment disputes in domestic law, critics of arbitration have argued that it allows large corporations to slant the playing field of dispute resolution in their own favor. Individuals, in these circumstances, face take-it-or-leave-it adhesion contracts that they seldom read and even more rarely understand. Corporations can exploit their position as repeat players to obtain advantages that they could not gain in litigation. Similar imbalances might be found in international contracts, but much less frequently because of the presence of business entities and other large institutions on both sides. Even in the presence of an imbalance in bargaining power, each party has the resources to protect itself, both in negotiating the arbitration agreement and in bringing a claim to arbitration. That does not free international arbitration from the need for judicial review, but it explains the trend toward strongly favoring enforcement of arbitration agreements and arbitration awards in transnational cases.

That trend also has a strong presence in domestic law, as decisions over the last several decades have expanded the power of arbitrators to decide questions of law, to dispense with procedural complexities, and to decide an increasing range of disputes. This trend in favor of arbitration shows little sign of retreating, although it may have crested as arbitration proceedings have become, in many respects, as contentious and elaborate as litigation. In transnational cases, however, arbitration has one distinct advantage that is absent in domestic cases. It establishes a structure, even if ad hoc and incomplete, which confers legitimacy through agreement of the parties and attempts to rise above the contingencies and allegiances of national legal systems. It envisages its own form of international adjudication in a microcosm. This chapter explores the extent to which international arbitration is successful in this task, first by considering the standard sources of arbitration in contracts and treaties, and the general standards for enforcing such agreements; second, by examining actions to compel arbitration and motions to stay litigation; and third, by examining the standards for confirming and enforcing arbitration awards. The chapter concludes by returning to this issue of legitimacy in arbitration.

A. Sources of Arbitration Law

Arbitration is a creature of contract, whether between parties in commercial dealings or between states in treaties. Hence it must conform to the principles of contract law and treaty interpretation. The Supreme Court has recently insisted that these two sources of law coincide with respect to international arbitration. At least as an initial matter, the same principles apply to arbitration under treaties as under contracts.[1] That approach yields a presumption that courts should decide questions of arbitrability: both the existence of an agreement to arbitrate and the range of disputes subject to arbitration.[2] Almost all other issues go to the arbitrator, with only limited review by the courts. That still leaves many fine distinctions and close questions in contested cases on the exact division of power between the arbitrator and the courts, to be discussed in subsequent sections of this chapter. But once a dispute falls within the scope of an arbitration clause, it becomes subject to the standard rules and practices of arbitration and to the overall structure of international and domestic law on enforcing arbitration agreements and awards.

The infrastructure of rules and practices for arbitration, and often the identity of the arbitrators themselves, comes from several prominent public and private institutions. The United Nations Commission on International Trade Law (UNCITRAL) and the

---

[1] BG Grp., PLC v. Rep. of Arg., 134 S.Ct. 1198 (2014).

[2] *Id.* at 1206–07.

International Centre for Settlement of Investment Disputes in the World Bank (ICSID) provide model procedures that can be used in ad hoc arbitration or adopted by other bodies—or in the case of ICSID, by agreement to the related Convention on the Settlement of Investment Disputes between States and Nationals of other States (ICSID Convention).[3] These public bodies also provide for appointment of arbitrators and require, for instance, that a majority of arbitrators come from states other than those of the parties to the dispute. A variety of private institutions create similar rules for arbitration, such as the American Arbitration Association (AAA), the International Chamber of Commerce (ICC), the London Court of International Arbitration (LCIA), and the Dubai International Arbitration Centre (DIAC). These institutions add to the array of standard procedures available to the parties and allow a range of control over both the crucial issue of the identity of the arbitrators and the procedures in arbitration, which often vary in complexity with the nature of the dispute.

Because arbitration is a creature of contract, the parties control the selection of the arbitrator. If there is a panel of three arbitrators, each party selects one arbitrator, and the arbitrators select a chair; or if the first two arbitrators cannot agree, the arbitral institution with which they are affiliated selects the chair. These methods of selection ensure a degree of independence and expertise of the arbitrator, as reflected in the arbitrator's reputation and experience. Precautions taken at this first step in the arbitration process can forestall challenges to the arbitration award later on grounds of partiality or corruption.[4] The arbitrator exercises broad power over the procedures used in the arbitration, usually with the acquiescence of the parties, in addition to resolving the merits of the dispute itself. The arbitrator may also choose the law applicable to the controversy if it is not specified by agreement.[5]

The goal of keeping arbitration efficient results in simplified procedures with no exact analogues to the intricacies of pleading or elaborate forms of discovery. The parties and the arbitrator must define the scope of the issues for arbitration and settle on administrative matters, such as the language to be used, the place to hold hearings, and the method of recording the proceedings. The parties can also agree to an exchange of documents and identification of witnesses, but usually they do so without the cumbersome requests, objections, and contentious depositions characteristic of

---

[3]   Convention on the Settlement of Investment Disputes Between States and Nationals of Other States, Mar. 18, 1965, 17 U.S.T. 1270, 575 U.N.T.S. 159.

[4]   Federal Arbitration Act, 9 U.S.C. § 10(a)(1), (2) (2012).

[5]   ANDREAS F. LOWENFELD, INTERNATIONAL LITIGATION AND ARBITRATION 407–09, 460 (3d ed. 2006).

American discovery. Avoiding these burdensome aspects of litigation is, in any event, the aspiration of modern arbitration practice, but as disputes become more complicated and the stakes rise higher, arbitral proceedings tend to grow longer and more complex as well. The parties rationally will invest more in arbitration if the investment gives them a better prospect of success in obtaining or avoiding a larger recovery. If both parties view the case in the same way, they will agree to the same procedures; even if they do not, the arbitrator has every incentive to ensure that the parties receive a full hearing on the merits. A thorough review of the relevant facts and law makes the arbitration award harder to overturn and more acceptable to the losing party.

Under all the standard procedures for international arbitration, the arbitrator's award must be reduced to writing and usually, unless the parties agree otherwise, supported by a statement of reasons.[6] The award is almost always preceded by one or more hearings to present evidence and arguments, another process that allows the record to be clarified and the disputed issues of law to be fully understood. This last point acquires particular significance if the applicable law is foreign and unfamiliar to one or more members of an arbitration panel. A hearing also allows for greater informality in the exchanges between the parties and the arbitrator, and it enhances the possibility that peripheral issues will be resolved by agreement.

A prevailing party must resort to judicial proceedings to enforce an arbitration award. Even preliminary relief can be obtained only through a court order—for instance, the freezing of a party's assets so that they are available to satisfy any resulting award. An arbitrator might have the power to make an interim award to this effect, but, like other awards, only a court can enforce it.[7] A court might also order an interim award without an arbitrator's decision, but judicial decisions are divided on the arbitrator's power to do so.[8] All judicial proceedings related to arbitration must conform to the superstructure of laws and treaties that determine when an agreement to arbitrate is valid and when an award is enforceable.

The principal source of such laws is the United Nations Convention on the Recognition and Enforcement of Foreign Arbitral

---

[6]   *Id.* at 404.

[7]   GARY BORN, INTERNATIONAL ARBITRATION: CASES AND MATERIALS 831–39 (2011).

[8]   *Compare* McCreary Tire & Rubber Co. v. CEAT S.p.A., 501 F.2d 1032, 1038 (3d Cir. 1974) (no power), *with* Carolina Power & Light Co. v. Uranex, 451 F. Supp. 1044, 1050–52 (N.D. Cal. 1977) (power in exceptional circumstances).

Awards, usually known as the New York Convention.[9] In the United States, the Convention has been implemented by amendments to the Federal Arbitration Act.[10] Some nations, particularly in Latin America, have not agreed to the Convention, but they have subscribed to the analogous terms of the Inter-American Convention on International Commercial Arbitration, known also as the Panama Convention.[11] Together, these sources codify American policies in favor of arbitration, and to the extent that they have received the approval of other commercial nations, they reflect the international consensus favoring arbitration. The same consensus emerges from the widespread acceptance of bilateral investment treaties (BITs), which typically incorporate arbitration by reference under the procedures established by ICSID. Awards under BITs are then subject to enforcement under the New York Convention. As an alternative to a BIT, an award might be made under the ICSID Convention, which provides that the award is enforceable as if it were already a foreign judgment.[12]

Both the New York Convention and the Federal Arbitration Act begin by defining the scope of covered arbitration agreements.[13] Each then imposes a duty to recognize those agreements and provide for an order compelling arbitration and staying or dismissing competing litigation.[14] The duty to recognize arbitration awards follows, subject to the exceptions listed in the Convention.[15] The duty to enforce agreements and awards will be taken up in the next sections of this chapter. The provisions on scope raise a few separate issues of their own.

The New York Convention applies only to arbitration awards rendered in other countries.[16] Awards rendered in the United States without significant contacts overseas come under separate provisions of the Federal Arbitration Act.[17] The Act's provisions for foreign awards apply to any "arbitration agreement or arbitral award arising out of a legal relationship, whether contractual or not, which is considered as commercial."[18] Although there must be an agreement to arbitrate, such agreement can cover claims that extend beyond

---

[9] United Nations Convention on the Recognition and Enforcement of Foreign Arbitral Awards, June 10, 1958, 21 U.S.T. 2517, 330 U.N.T.S. 38 [hereinafter New York Convention].

[10] 9 U.S.C. §§ 201–08.

[11] OAS/Ser. A/20, reprinted in 14 I.L.M. 336 (1975).

[12] LOWENFELD, *supra* note 5, at 459.

[13] New York Convention, *supra* note 9, art. I(1), (2); 9 U.S.C § 202 (2012).

[14] New York Convention, *supra* note 9, art. II; 9 U.S.C. §§ 203–06 (2012).

[15] New York Convention, *supra* note 9, arts. III–V; 9 U.S.C. § 207 (2012).

[16] New York Convention, *supra* note 9, art. I(1).

[17] 9 U.S.C. §§ 1–16, 208 (2012).

[18] *Id.* § 202.

contracts to statutes and the common law. The Act also provides for federal jurisdiction over claims for enforcement of arbitration agreements and awards, specifically allowing removal from state court to federal court.[19] These provisions make foreign commercial arbitration almost entirely a matter of federal law and federal judicial decisions. State law might govern the claims decided on the merits by the arbitrator, but the scope of the arbitrator's powers falls under the New York Convention as federal law implemented by the Federal Arbitration Act.[20] Hence the Act firmly establishes federal policy in favor of international arbitration and defeats any objection that an agreement to arbitrate "ousts" the courts improperly of jurisdiction. The role of courts, instead, is to assist in the process of arbitration and intervene only where necessary to preserve their integrity.

B. Injunctions, Stays, and Dismissal in Favor of Arbitration

Litigation preliminary to arbitration dovetails with questions of coverage. The terms of the agreement to arbitrate should govern these questions in the first instance. Judicial decisions took some time to concede to arbitrators the power to resolve questions other than those immediately raised by the contract between the parties. International cases were among the first to do so, taking their lead from decisions enforcing forum-selection clauses that referred disputes between the parties to the courts of another country.[21] Typically, arbitration clauses cover all disputes between the parties arising out of their contractual relationship, not just those supported by ordinary contract law.[22] Such broad terms of coverage echo the coverage of the New York Convention, which extends to any commercial relationship, "whether contractual or not."[23]

The argument against coverage according to the literal terms of the contract or the New York Convention rests on the role of some statutory claims as a protection for the weaker party in a contractual relationship. An admiralty case raised this issue when an insurer, subrogated to the claims of a cargo owner, brought an action for cargo damage under the Carriage of Goods by Sea Act (COGSA).[24] A central

---

[19] *Id.* §§ 203–07.

[20] "An action or proceeding falling under the Convention shall be deemed to arise under the laws and treaties of the United States." *Id.* § 203.

[21] *See* Mitsubishi Motors Corp. v. Soler Chrysler-Plymouth, Inc., 473 U.S. 614, 628–40 (1985); Scherk v. Alberto-Culver Co., 417 U.S. 506, 516–19 (1974).

[22] *E.g., Mitsubishi*, 473 U.S. at 617 (clause covered "[a]ll disputes, controversies or differences which may arise between [the parties] out of or in relation to Articles I-B through V of this Agreement or for the breach thereof").

[23] 9 U.S.C § 202.

[24] 46 U.S.C. § 30701 note (2012), formerly 46 U.S.C. App. § 1300 *et seq.*

provision of COGSA prohibits the vessel owners and other carriers of goods by sea from reducing their liability below the statutory floor for losses to cargo.[25] The insurer sued the carrier in federal court despite an arbitration clause that covered "[a]ny dispute arising from this Bill of Lading," arguing that sending the case to arbitration threatened to discount the carrier's liability below the floor established by the statute.[26] That threat was aggravated by the choice-of-law clause in the bill of lading providing for application of Japanese law to the dispute, which in turn was to be arbitrated in Japan.[27]

The Supreme Court found the risk of subverting the protective provisions of COGSA to be minimal. The bill of lading, as the contract between the cargo owner and carrier, did not explicitly reduce the carrier's liability below the statutory floor. Such an intent could only be inferred from the arbitration clause, but the New York Convention did not support any such suspicion of arbitration. On the contrary, the Convention was designed, along with the implementing legislation in the Federal Arbitration Act, to foster arbitration, even if it occurred in a foreign country. Arbitration could not be avoided based on the fear that it would "oust" the jurisdiction of American courts to protect cargo owners. According to the Court, "[i]t would also be out of keeping with the objects of the Convention for the courts of this country to interpret COGSA to disparage the authority or competence of international forums for dispute resolution."[28] Further support for this conclusion came from the origins of COGSA as implementing legislation for the Brussels Convention for the Unification of Certain Rules Relating to Bills of Lading,[29] better known as the Hague Rules. No other nation had interpreted the limitation on liability in its version of the Hague Rules to prohibit forum selection clauses, and in *Vimar Seguros*, Japan itself had enacted a version of the Hague Rules that would apply under the terms of the choice-of-law clause.[30] International uniformity both with respect to arbitration and with respect to the substantive law reduced the threat of compromising cargo interests. To the extent that any threat remained, it could be dealt with in proceedings to enforce the arbitration award where, if the award flagrantly violated

---

[25] *Id.* § 3(8), formerly 46 U.S.C. App. § 1303(8) (on Responsibilities and liabilities of carrier and ship—Limitation of liability for negligence).

[26] Vimar Seguros y Reaseguros, S.A. v. M/V Sky Reefer, 515 U.S. 528, 531–32 (1995) (citing old 46 U.S.C. App. § 1303 which has since been recodified as 46 U.S.C. § 30701).

[27] *Id.* at 531.

[28] *Id.* at 537.

[29] International Convention for the Unification of Certain Rules Relating to Bills of Lading, Aug. 25, 1924, 51 Stat. 233, 120 L.N.T.S. 155.

[30] *Vimar Seguros*, 515 U.S. at 536–37.

COGSA, it could be refused enforcement for being "repugnant to the public policy of the United States."[31]

The whole tone and tendency of the opinion in *Vimar Seguros* favored arbitration, as do domestic decisions expanding arbitration to reach statutory claims.[32] Similar decisions also have limited judicial review of arbitration awards, as discussed in the next section. In light of these developments, the suggestion in *Vimar Seguros* that any defects in the arbitration award could be remedied by judicial review of the award rings hollow. The same presumption that favors arbitration in the first place also favors enforcement of the resulting arbitration award. The weight of the decision rests upon a willingness to trust arbitration and to hold the parties to their agreement to submit to this process. Commercial parties, as in this case and in almost all those covered by the New York Convention, can do more to protect themselves in negotiations and as repeat players in arbitration than private individuals can in their roles as consumers or employees. The check provided by judicial refusal to enforce an agreement or an arbitration award functions less as general supervision of the arbitration process and more as a willingness to intervene when its integrity can be called into question.

A court still must determine that the parties have made an agreement to arbitrate and that the dispute in question falls within its scope. That determination falls under the ambiguous heading of "arbitrability," which might refer either to the power of courts to send a case to arbitration or the power of arbitrators to decide whether they can grant relief under the terms of the arbitration clause. The first set of issues, for the court, focus on the existence of an agreement to arbitrate. The second set, for the arbitrator, focus on the satisfaction of procedural prerequisites for arbitration. The distinction between the two kinds of issues can be contested, as it was in *BG Group, PLC v. Republic of Argentina.*[33] The majority and the dissent in that case divided over how to characterize a requirement that the party seeking arbitration first resort to local legal remedies before going to arbitration. The majority found it to be a procedural issue for the arbitrator, while the dissenters interpreted it as a condition on the party's consent to arbitration, in this case by a sovereign state as defendant. Although they disagreed on this issue, both the majority and dissenters recognized the need for courts to

---

[31] *Id.* at 540 (quoting RESTATEMENT (THIRD) OF FOREIGN RELATIONS LAW OF THE U.S. § 482(2)(d) (1986)).

[32] *E.g.*, AT & T Mobility LLC v. Concepcion, 563 U.S. 333 (2011); Gilmer v. Interstate/Johnson Lane Corp., 500 U.S. 20 (1991).

[33] 134 S.Ct. at 1206–08.

make the preliminary determination about whether the case would go to arbitration.

Analysis of this preliminary issue can lead to conceptual tangles about who, between the courts and the arbitrator, has the power to resolve the issue of arbitrability and under what law to do so. The power of courts to make this determination follows from the basic principle that courts always have "jurisdiction to determine jurisdiction."[34] So, too, they must have the power to determine whether they can keep a case and decide it on the merits, or stay or dismiss it in favor of arbitration. No other decision maker is in a position to provide this necessary check on the arbitration process. Arbitrators themselves cannot be given this power without eroding the basic requirement that arbitration be based on an agreement to arbitrate. Because arbitrators are not public officials, they have only the jurisdiction conferred upon them by agreement of the parties. Under American law, the agreement must contain "clear and unmistakable evidence" that the parties conferred this power on the arbitrator.[35] Other countries take a different approach, giving the arbitrator broader power to determine issues of arbitrability. Under the heading of "competence-competence," they allow the arbitrator to determine the scope of arbitral jurisdiction.[36] In the United States, the court always has the residual power to make this determination. Without a valid agreement to arbitrate, the arbitrators have no authority to resolve the dispute between the parties, and they amount to nothing more than officious intermeddlers appointed by, at most, one of the parties.

Determining the validity and scope of the agreement to arbitrate presupposes a choice of law question about which law should apply to the agreement. This too can lead to conceptual puzzles, often manipulated by the parties to achieve the outcome that they regard as favorable to their position. The law from several different states might affect the outcome of an international arbitration: the law of the place where the contract was formed, the law of the place of performance, the law chosen by a choice-of-law clause in the contract, the law of the place where a party seeks enforcement of the agreement to arbitrate, the law of the place of arbitration, and the law of the place where a party seeks to confirm or enforce an arbitration award. None of these sources of law is necessarily identical with any other, although they often coincide. Roughly speaking, the first three alternatives go to the substantive law

---

[34] In re Lodholtz, 769 F.3d 531, 534 (7th Cir. 2014), *as modified on denial of reh'g* (Dec. 4, 2014) (Posner, J).

[35] First Options of Chi., Inc. v. Kaplan, 514 U.S. 938, 939 (1995).

[36] GARY B. BORN & PETER B. RUTLEDGE, INTERNATIONAL CIVIL LITIGATION IN UNITED STATES COURTS 1168–70 (5th ed. 2011).

governing the dispute, while the last three go to the law governing procedure and remedies.

The parties can try to resolve the first set of questions by agreeing to a choice-of-law clause, but for the same reason that they cannot make an arbitration clause self-validating, immunized from judicial review of its existence, scope, and enforceability, the parties cannot pre-empt judicial determination of the validity of the choice-of-law clause. A court must initially determine that the choice-of-law clause is valid before it can refer to the law selected by the clause to determine the enforceability of the arbitration agreement or arbitration award. The arbitrator also has to make a similar determination before applying the law selected by the choice-of-law clause to the merits of the dispute. Conceivably, the court and the arbitrator could reach different results on these issues, but as a practical matter, the arbitrator's decision will be dispositive only if the court enforces the arbitration agreement or the arbitration award. Otherwise, if the agreement is unenforceable, the arbitrator will never get a chance to decide the issue, or if the award is unenforceable, the arbitrator's decision on the issue will count for nothing. Moreover, the potential disparity in the decisions of different courts, although real, has been diminished by the increasing uniformity of governing law in different countries, like that generated by the New York Convention and by the UNCITRAL Model Law on Commercial Arbitration. The presumption in favor of arbitration under the Convention will lead courts to enforce arbitration agreements most of the time, regardless of the law selected to determine this issue. As discussed in the next section, the same is true of enforcement of arbitration awards.

The second set of issues, on remedies and procedure, provides the framework for deciding the first set of issues on substantive law. If the case goes to arbitration, the arbitrator will decide most of these issues. In the absence of a choice-of-law clause, an arbitrator might need to undertake a full-fledged choice-of-law analysis, with all of the complications discussed in Chapter 2.[37] The arbitrator's decision begins with the terms of the agreement. By referring the dispute to arbitration in a particular place, and often under the rules of a particular institution such as the International Chamber of Commerce (ICC), the contract identifies the basic procedural rules governing the arbitration. These rules leave much latitude to the arbitrator to make particular procedural rulings, but they also address questions such as the parties' ability to resort to courts for interim relief or to set aside an award. Actions to set aside or confirm an award typically are filed in the place, or "seat," of arbitration, as

---

[37] LOWENFELD, *supra* note 5, at 407–09.

the UNCITRAL Model Law provides.[38] The model law also provides for the arbitrator's power to address choice-of-law issues as determined by the parties.[39] The parties' agreement, the law of the seat of arbitration, and the rules of the arbitral institution determine the context in which choice-of-law issues arise. These issues do circle back and affect interpretation of the agreement, but seldom influence the question of choice-of-law itself. The circularity, while conceptually puzzling, does not prevent the arbitrator from reaching a decision practically consistent with the agreement of the parties. In any event, courts do not generally review awards for errors in the arbitrator's choice-of-law analysis.[40]

Both the party seeking arbitration and the party seeking to avoid it can resort to the courts to test the enforceability of the agreement to arbitrate: the party seeking arbitration by filing an action for an injunction to compel arbitration; the party seeking to avoid arbitration by filing a lawsuit on the merits, which then typically elicits a motion by the opposing party to stay or dismiss the lawsuit, usually with the addition of a motion to compel arbitration. Neither of these lawsuits need be brought in the seat of arbitration, and the Federal Arbitration Act specifically authorizes injunctions to compel arbitration at any place where the parties' agreement provides, "whether that place is within or without the United States."[41] Alternatively, the party seeking to avoid arbitration can file a claim on the merits and, as in *Vimar Seguros*, in a forum (New York) distant from the place of arbitration (Tokyo). The Court there affirmed an order to compel arbitration and stay judicial proceedings. It did not consider the possibility of a dismissal because the district court had granted only a stay, reserving the possibility of a challenge to recognition and enforcement of any resulting award.[42] As discussed in Chapter 6 on parallel judicial proceedings, a stay constitutes the less intrusive remedy since it preserves ongoing judicial proceedings, allowing the court to take any necessary action after an arbitration award has been rendered. It dispenses with the need for either party to file a second action and revisit issues at the end of a case that were already litigated when the case was originally filed. To use the terminology of old decisions skeptical of arbitration, a court that stays its own proceedings is not entirely "ousted" of jurisdiction.

---

[38] UNCITRAL Model Law on International Commercial Arbitration art. 34, June 21, 1985, 24 I.L.M. 1302.

[39] *Id.* art. 28.

[40] LOWENFELD, *supra* note 5, at 406.

[41] Federal Arbitration Act, 9 U.S.C. § 206.

[42] *Vimar Seguros*, 515 U.S. at 540–41.

An injunction against other claims on the merits in other courts goes to the opposite extreme. Instead of a court holding off on its own decision, it interferes with another court by ordering the parties to cease their litigation there. Courts, however, rarely issue such countersuit injunctions in favor of arbitration, demonstrating the same restraint applied to countersuit injunctions generally. As also discussed in Chapter 6, courts enjoin competing proceedings only where necessary in aid of their jurisdiction or to protect and effectuate their judgments. A court that has ordered the parties to arbitrate their dispute conceivably could find it necessary to order them not to litigate elsewhere in order to protect and effectuate this judgment.

A court took this step in *Paramedics Electromedicina Comercial, Ltda. v. GE Medical Systems Information Technologies, Inc.*,[43] but the circumstances of the case reveal how narrow the grounds for issuing a countersuit injunction are. Technically, the Second Circuit held only that the district court had not abused its discretion in issuing the countersuit injunction.[44] The plaintiff, known as Tecnimed, had entered into an agreement with the defendant, known by the acronym of GEMS-IT, to distribute the latter's medical devices in Brazil. The agreements contained broad arbitration clauses, which GEMS-IT invoked, prompting a lawsuit by Tecnimed in New York to permanently stay arbitration. At the same time, Tecnimed brought an action in Brazil against GEMS-IT and a related Brazilian corporation. GEMS-IT removed the New York action to federal court and counterclaimed for an order compelling arbitration and an injunction against the Brazilian cases. The district court granted both injunctions.

The Second Circuit's reasoning in affirming the entry of these injunctions emphasized the strong policy in favor of arbitration and the duplication inherent in the Brazilian proceedings, which concerned the arbitrability of a dispute already sent to arbitration by the federal district court. The president of Tecnimed had frankly avowed that Tecnimed had filed the Brazilian action "to avoid being dragged into an arbitration process that GE had no right to force upon it."[45] The Second Circuit also expressed concern that the failure to issue an injunction now would just set up a conflict of judgments later, with the Brazilian court refusing to recognize an American judgment enforcing any resulting arbitration award and with an American court deciding whether or not to give any effect to such a Brazilian judgment.[46] The court characterized this problem in terms

---

[43]　369 F.3d 645, 654–56 (2d Cir. 2004).

[44]　*Id.* at 649.

[45]　*Id.* at 654.

[46]　*Id.*

of protecting the jurisdiction of the American court to enforce an arbitration award, but the opinion also has clear implications for protecting American judgments, initially in ordering arbitration and ultimately in enforcing any resulting award.

To be sure, the Brazilian court had suspended its own proceedings on the merits, complying in this respect with the New York Convention to which Brazil had recently become a signatory. The suspension, however, would have lasted only six months, and GEMS-IT had to continue to file pleadings in the Brazilian action. The gravamen of the objection to the Brazilian proceedings rested more on blatant forum shopping than on preserving respect for American courts. Tecnimed, after all, had begun the American litigation by filing a suit in New York to stay arbitration. After it lost that lawsuit, it tried to continue the litigation in Brazil, effectively shopping for some court that would take the case rather than let it go to arbitration. Similar attempts to shop for a favorable judicial decision after having suffered an unfavorable decision have led courts to find an exception to the usual principles of comity and respect for foreign courts. Multiple proceedings in different forums remain tolerable only so long as they are not deployed as a substitute for an appeal.

The European Union takes that rule a step further for competing proceedings within the union itself. The EU Court of Justice reached this conclusion in *Allianz SpA and Generali Assicurazioni Generali SpA v. West Tankers Inc.*,[47] extending the principle from the Brussels Regulation[48] that the court that first takes control over a matter has exclusive jurisdiction over it. Although the regulation does not explicitly cover arbitration, the Court reasoned that the principle of priority accorded to the first court prevents a second court from enjoining its proceedings, even if they should be referred to arbitration. That issue is for the first court alone to decide. This decision, like others that apply only among courts within the EU, illustrates the difference that a unified system of law can make in reconciling the conflict between parallel proceedings. All courts within the EU are bound by decisions of the Court of Justice and so a coordinating rule, like that within our federal courts that accords general priority to the first action filed, can work to simplify the decision-making process. Instead of two courts competing to have

---

[47] Case C-185/07, 2009 E.C.R. I-00663.

[48] Council Regulation (EC) No. 44/2001 of 22 December 2000 on Jurisdiction and the Recognition and Enforcement of Judgments in Civil and Commercial Matters, art. 27 2001 O.J. (L 12). For the pending changes in the regulation, *see* Regulation (EU) 1215/2012 of the European Parliament and of the Council of 12 December 2012 on jurisdiction and the recognition and enforcement of judgments in civil and commercial matters (recast), art. 29, Official Journal, OJ 20 December 2012, L 351/1.

priority over each other, and then to decide whether to defer to arbitration, only one court makes that decision.

C. Recognizing and Enforcing Arbitration Awards

Paradoxically enough, foreign arbitration awards have a firmer claim to recognition and enforcement under the New York Convention than do most foreign judgments. The latter lack a widely adopted treaty that assures their acceptance in other countries, while the former fall under the protection of the Convention and its implementing legislation in all the major trading countries of the world. The Convention also contains a narrower list of grounds for refusing to recognize awards, as compared to those for refusing to recognize judgments. The grounds for nonrecognition under the Convention are entirely permissive with the enforcing court, and they fall into three categories: failure to comply with the agreement between the parties, violations of public policy or restrictions on arbitration in the enforcing state, and procedural defects as a matter of due process or under the law of the place of arbitration.[49]

All three categories overlap to some extent, primarily because of the overriding importance of the agreement of the parties as the foundation for arbitration. If the parties cannot make such an agreement, or if the award does not comply with its terms, it need not be enforced. The complications arise, as they do with enforcing arbitration agreements by an injunction or stay, in deciding which issues are for the arbitrator and which are for the enforcing court. An overriding principle, which supports the presumption in favor of arbitration, puts the burden of proof on the party arguing that the award should not be enforced.[50] The exceptions to recognition are just that: exceptions that must be established to displace the presumption in favor of enforcing an award.

1. Agreement of the Parties

The agreement to submit a dispute to arbitration governs both what can be arbitrated, who conducts the arbitration, and how it is to be conducted. A court can refuse to recognize an award for failure to comply with the parties' agreement in any of these respects. An award is invalid if it "deals with a difference not contemplated by or not falling within the terms of the submission to arbitration, or it contains decisions on matters beyond the scope of the submission to arbitration."[51] Likewise, it can be refused recognition if "[t]he composition of the arbitral authority or the arbitral procedure was

---

[49] New York Convention, *supra* note 9, art. V.

[50] *Id.* art. V(1); III GARY B. BORN, INTERNATIONAL COMMERCIAL ARBITRATION 3651 (2d ed. 2014).

[51] New York Convention, *supra* note 9, art. V(1)(c).

not in accordance with the agreement of the parties."[52] Both provisions give considerable leeway to the arbitrator to interpret the agreement once the arbitrator is properly selected. Few decisions actually turn on selection of the arbitrator since the parties and arbitral institutions largely control this process.[53]

The leading decision in *Parsons & Whittemore Overseas Co., Inc. v. Societe Generale de L'Industrie du Papier (RAKTA)*[54] illustrates the overlap between the jurisdiction of the arbitrator and interpretation of the contract on the merits. The decision confirmed an award finding a breach of contract by Parsons & Whittemore, which concerned a construction project in Egypt interrupted by the Six-Day War between Israel and Egypt in 1967. A panel of arbitrators awarded damages to the buyer of the project, a firm known by the acronym "RAKTA." Among other objections, Parsons & Whittemore argued that the award went beyond the arbitrators' power to award damages and costs, principally because the award included damages for loss of production even though the parties' contract seemed to provide otherwise. The court held that this provision went to the merits, not to jurisdiction, and therefore was properly subject to the arbitrators' interpretation.[55] This line of reasoning accords with cases on domestic arbitration which endorse the principles that "ambiguities in the language of the agreement should be resolved in favor of arbitration"[56] and that an award is legitimate if "it draws its essence" from the parties' agreement.[57]

The same presumption in favor of the arbitrator's authority holds even more strongly on procedural issues, since the arbitrator has broad discretion to tailor the procedures to the particular dispute.[58] Courts defer to the arbitrator's interpretation and application of the procedures that the parties have agreed to, either in their contract or by reference to institutional rules of arbitration. Where they have not agreed, the law of the place of arbitration can fill in the gaps, but that law, too, usually recognizes the discretion of the arbitrator over procedure. For all these reasons, judicial review of procedure under this heading is limited to serious violations of the parties' agreement or the law of the place of arbitration.[59] Judicial review for denial of due process falls under a separate heading in the

---

[52] *Id.* art. V(1)(d).

[53] II BORN, *supra* note 50, at 1642.

[54] 508 F.2d 969 (2d Cir. 1974).

[55] *Id.* at 976–77.

[56] EEOC v. Waffle House, Inc., 534 U.S. 279, 294 (2002).

[57] United Steelworkers v. Enterprise Wheel & Car Corp., 363 U.S. 593, 597 (1960).

[58] II BORN, *supra* note 50, at 2144 54.

[59] III BORN, *supra* note 50, at 3561, 3582.

New York Convention, because it involves mandatory principles of procedural fairness that apply regardless of the parties' agreement or the law of the place of arbitration.[60]

Other headings also limit the autonomy of the parties—in particular, if the applicable law denies them capacity to enter into the arbitration agreement, or if the agreement is "not valid under the law to which the parties have subjected it or, failing any indication thereon, under the law of the country where the award was made."[61] It follows from the foundational role of the parties' agreement that it must be an agreement valid and enforceable by law. General principles of contract may make the agreement invalid, for instance, because of fraud, mistake, duress, lack of consideration, unconscionability, impossibility, and frustration.[62] As with decisions about whether to order arbitration, decisions to refuse recognition for lack of a valid contract involve a division of authority between the courts and the arbitrator. As a practical matter, if the arbitrator has considered the issue of validity, the courts will give some deference to that decision, with few exceptions.[63] Substantive principles of contract law, to the extent that they have been submitted by the parties to arbitration, constrain the arbitrator primarily through his or her own decision-making process and only secondarily by judicial review. More robust exceptions to recognition arise from inconsistency between the award and the public policy of the enforcing state, to be discussed next.

2.   Public Policy

Public policy figures in recognition of arbitration awards just as it does in recognition of judgments: as a narrow but powerful ground for refusing recognition. On both issues, the party arguing against recognition must show more than legal error. Otherwise, judicial review would displace the arbitration award with a *de novo* determination of the legal issues by the court. Public policy comes in two varieties under the New York Convention: if the dispute "is not capable of settlement by arbitration under the law" of the enforcing country; and if "recognition or enforcement of the award would be contrary to the public policy of that country."[64] Both versions of the public policy exception refer to the law of the enforcing country, not to the law governing the parties' agreement or to the law of the place of arbitration. The latter's public policy figures in another exception to recognition, when an "award has not yet become binding on the

---

[60]   New York Convention, *supra* note 9, art. V(1)(b).

[61]   *Id.* art. V(1)(a).

[62]   III BORN, *supra* note 47, at 3470.

[63]   *Id.* at 3477–82.

[64]   New York Convention, *supra* note 9, art. V(2).

parties, or has been set aside or suspended by a competent authority of the country in which, or under the law of which, that award was made."[65] An award need not be confirmed in that country to be recognized elsewhere, but if the award is not yet final or has been annulled by a court in that country, it need not be recognized elsewhere. Among the grounds for annulling an award is violation of public policy.

The first form of public policy picks up where contract principles leave off and identifies particular claims, like those under protective statutes that specify mandatory terms for contractual relations, and which the enforcing country reserves for judicial enforcement. The New York Convention recognizes a defense to enforcement of arbitration agreements on this ground,[66] and as discussed earlier, the Supreme Court considered such an argument in *Vimar Seguros*, but held that the statutory claim there could be decided by an arbitrator rather than a court. Countries exclude from arbitration a laundry list of typical claims on disparate subjects, such as criminal cases, domestic relations and inheritance, bankruptcy, and trade sanctions. These claims touch upon public rights or the rights of third parties not involved in the arbitration process. Other countries, but not the United States, exclude antitrust claims, consumer claims, and employment claims from arbitration.[67] Because these claims can be defined categorically, they rarely pose problems of interpretation in determining whether they are subject to arbitration. A divorce or custody case also falls under this exception.

Awards contrary to public policy do not identify themselves as readily. Although narrow, this exception is open-ended. It was invoked in *Parsons & Whittemore* on the ground that the breach of contract there occurred simultaneously with the Six-Day War, and the breaching party argued that it could not complete the contract, which was to be performed in Egypt, because continued work on it would violate American foreign policy. The Second Circuit rejected this expansion of the public policy exception, finding that the exception applied "only where enforcement would violate the forum state's most basic notions of morality and justice."[68] The current position of the United States on foreign relations with Egypt did not meet this test. International arbitration could not survive if courts based their enforcement decisions on second-guessing their nation's foreign policy.

---

[65] *Id.* art. (V)(1)(e).

[66] *Id.* art. II(1).

[67] III BORN, *supra* note 50, at 3696.

[68] *Parsons & Whittemore*, 508 F.2d 969.

Another leading case also illustrates the narrowness of the foreign policy exception. In *Baxter International, Inc. v. Abbott Laboratories*,[69] the arbitrators had resolved a complicated intellectual property and antitrust dispute with a decision that effectively limited the American market for a widely used anesthetic to a drug produced under a single process patent, excluding competition from the same drug made by a different process. The losing party argued that the arbitrators' decision effectively required a violation of the antitrust laws, but over the dissent of one judge, the Seventh Circuit rejected this argument. First, other antitrust claims could go to arbitration without violating public policy. They were not excluded on the ground that they raised issues that only courts could resolve. Second, once the claims went to arbitration, a decision allegedly condoning or ordering an antitrust violation could not be distinguished from one that simply erred in interpreting the antitrust laws. Since an error of law does not amount to a violation of public policy, the losing party's objection to the arbitration award had to be rejected.[70] Against the argument that the prevailing party could then continue to violate the antitrust laws with impunity, the Seventh Circuit noted that third parties, including the federal government, were not bound by the arbitrators' decision or the court's own decision on enforcement. They remained free to bring their own antitrust actions.

Attempts to expand the public policy exception have also taken the form of arguments for review based on "manifest disregard of the law."[71] Courts have undertaken review on this ground by implication under § 10 of the Federal Arbitration Act, which provides for vacating domestic arbitration awards.[72] This section does not, however, apply to foreign arbitration awards which, by § 207, limits judicial review to "the grounds for refusal or deferral of recognition or enforcement of the award specified in the said Convention."[73] For this reason, some courts, like the Second Circuit in *Parsons & Whittemore*, have doubted that this ground applies to foreign arbitration awards.[74] Even the courts that accept review for "manifest disregard of the law" tend to construe it narrowly, for the same reason that courts narrowly construe the exception for public policy: Otherwise, it would lead to plenary judicial reconsideration of the merits.[75] The two

---

[69]   315 F.3d 829 (7th Cir.), *cert. denied*, 540 U.S. 963 (2003).

[70]   *Id.* at 831.

[71]   *Parsons & Whittemore*, 508 F.2d at 977.

[72]   9 U.S.C. § 10; Wilko v. Swan, 346 U.S. 427, 436 (1953).

[73]   9 U.S.C. § 207.

[74]   *See, e.g.*, Int'l Trading and Indus. Inv. Co. v. DynCorp Aerospace Tech., 763 F. Supp. 2d 12, 28 (D.D.C. 2011).

[75]   *E.g.*, Lagstein v. Certain Underwriters at Lloyd's, London, 607 F.3d 634, 641 (9th Cir. 2010), *cert. denied*, 562 U.S. 1110 (2010).

standards of review represent, at most, a difference in emphasis. As usually interpreted, the public policy exception emphasizes how important the public policy at issue is, while the implied exception for "manifest disregard of the law" emphasizes how clear the inconsistency with public policy is. Both elements figure into decisions that undertake substantive review of an arbitration award for consistency with public policy.

A similar form of review can take place in the courts of the state where the arbitration was held. The courts there can be asked to annul or confirm the award. The Federal Arbitration Act, for instance, allows for such actions to be brought in the "court for the district and division which embraces the place designated in the agreement as the place of arbitration if such place is within the United States."[76] The difficult question concerns the effect to give to a judgment annulling the award. The New York Convention permits courts in another country to refuse to recognize or enforce the award for this reason.[77] Yet principles of comity and preclusion might go further and require the court to follow the judgment of the foreign court. American decisions are divided on this question.[78] The entire weight of the argument turns on the word "may" in the New York Convention. The Convention allows but does not require the court in the enforcing state to refuse recognition on the enumerated grounds.[79] The converse problem does not arise for awards confirmed in the state of arbitration, since the Convention plainly allows nonrecognition on any of the enumerated grounds, regardless of prior judicial decisions. The balance to be struck here, as on other issues of international arbitration, lies between the policy favoring arbitration and the policy preserving the sovereignty of the enforcing state. A suitable compromise would lead courts to recognize a foreign judgment of annulment if it accorded broadly with their own grounds for refusing to enforce an award.

3. Procedure

Procedural issues in arbitration can emerge in a variety of different guises. As noted earlier, they can arise as asserted violations of the parties' agreement or of the law of the place of arbitration. They could also be cast as issues of public policy, to the extent that the latter embrace procedural principles in addition to substantive policies. When procedural issues acquire independent significance, however, they do so as a variation upon the "international concept of due process." As discussed in the previous

---

[76] 9 U.S.C. § 204.

[77] New York Convention, *supra* note 9, art. V(1)(e).

[78] *See* III BORN, *supra* note 50, at 3629–46.

[79] New York Convention, *supra* note 9, art. V(1), (2).

chapter, this concept constitutes a ground for refusing to recognize a foreign judgment. Under the New York Convention, the concept is framed as a claim that the losing party "was not given proper notice of the appointment of the arbitrator or of the arbitration proceedings or was otherwise unable to present his case."[80] As with international due process, not just any deviation from accepted procedures in the courts of the enforcing country will do. Arbitration has, as its characteristic feature, less formal and more flexible procedures than those followed in court. The question posed by this exception is when those procedures depart too far from accepted principles of procedural justice.

The Second Circuit in *Parsons & Whittemore* briefly addressed this question in rejecting the argument that the losing party was denied an opportunity to be heard because the arbitrator did not postpone a hearing to accommodate the schedule of its expert.[81] In all probability, that objection would have been held insufficient even if the claim had been tried in court, since the losing party made hardly any showing of good cause for postponement. The Federal Arbitration Act lists more serious procedural objections: "where the award was procured by corruption, fraud, or undue means," "where there was evident partiality or corruption in the arbitrators," or "where the arbitrators were guilty of misconduct" in various forms prejudicial to the rights of the parties.[82] This provision of the Act directly applies only to domestic arbitration, but similar grounds for refusing to recognize an award have been subsumed under the procedural exception in the New York Convention.[83] As with the public policy exception, this exception is theoretically broad but practically narrow. It encompasses a wide range of procedural objections, but these seldom prove to be successful in overturning an award. The Supreme Court has made notice and opportunity to be heard fundamental to American conceptions of due process, and so it is around the world. Without a chance to make a case or offer a defense, a party has no assurance that its side of a dispute has been heard at all. This possibility poses a particular risk in arbitration, where the arbitrator as a private decision maker can be held accountable only through the processes of arbitration and judicial enforcement. The latter, through review of procedural objections, provides a necessary check on the integrity of the former. Even if it seldom proves to be successful, the prospect of a procedural objection on the grounds of fundamental fairness forces arbitrators and arbitral institutions to maintain the integrity necessary to preserve their parties' trust. If

[80] *Id.* art. V(1)(b).
[81] *Parsons & Whittemore*, 508 F.2d at 975–76.
[82] 9 U.S.C. § 10 (2012).
[83] III BORN, *supra* note 50, at 3276–81, 3492–95, 3507–32.

the integrity of arbitrators were called into question, their reputation would suffer irreparable damage, and the parties would soon seek other arbitrators or other means of resolving their disputes.

D. Arbitration and Legitimacy

The growth of arbitration holds lessons at every level for the legitimacy of international dispute resolution: from particular arbitration agreements, to private institutions that facilitate arbitration, to treaties that provide for and enforce it, to judicial decisions that have given it a presumption of validity. These lessons communicate one basic message: Consent to international norms can go hand in hand with development of customary international law. The two sources of law often are opposed to one another, but the open-ended terms of the treaties, statutes, agreements, and rules that govern international arbitration leave much room for judicial interpretation. Instead of contrasting positive law created by agreement and legislation with natural law declared by courts, the law of arbitration merges the two in a way that enhances the authority of both.

Agreements to arbitrate can be subject to abuse, as can awards pursuant to those agreements. A party with overweening bargaining power can impose unconscionable terms for resolving disputes on the other party to the contract. The informality of the arbitration process can descend into partiality toward one party and unfairness toward the other—hence the need for a residual power of judicial review despite the strong presumption in favor of arbitration. Far from detracting from the authority of arbitrators, the possibility of judicial review does the opposite. It gives arbitration credibility by assuring that cases in which it appears to have gone wrong will receive a second look. Arbitration needs to serve as more than a black box that generates results regardless of the legal merits and procedural fairness.

Likewise, at the level of treaties and statutes, the law of arbitration has taken the approach of reconciling differences through consent rather than overriding them by commands. The New York Convention stands out among the treaties on arbitration as one that commits the signatory nations to enact implementing legislation that meets its basic requirements. Model legislation sponsored by UNCITRAL and codes of procedure adopted by public and private arbitral institutions have much the same effect. All of these sources of law stop short of compelling national or party compliance, but instead induce agreement by treaties, by adoption of uniform national law, or by contract. The pervasive adoption of bilateral investment treaties with provisions for arbitration according to ICSID procedures also promotes uniformity without coercion. None of this is to say that these treaties or codes resolve all the tensions inherent in international commerce and investment. Outstanding differences inevitably remain, as do objections to all these instruments of dispute resolution. Yet those instruments do accomplish a singularly important goal: They channel disputes to forms and procedures that promote a peaceful, if not entirely satisfactory, resolution of differences.

The role of arbitrators and courts in this process should be viewed as complementary rather than competing. Arbitrators play a large role in developing the customary law of arbitration through their broad power over the substance and procedure of arbitration. Courts contribute to development of the law through their published decisions and their ability to alter ongoing trends. The combined efforts of arbitrators and courts can reinforce one another if each pays attention to what the other naturally focuses on: The arbitrator can look beyond the agreement of the parties to the network of laws in which it is embedded, and courts can defer to the agreement of the parties when it is consistent with the applicable law. In a microcosm, arbitration presents all of the issues in international civil litigation and the possibilities for resolving them. It depends upon consent at every level by parties, institutions, and nations, which in turn generates widely accepted principles that arbitrators and courts can use to resolve concrete disputes. It also holds out the prospect of reconciling the sovereign interests of different countries and the competing rights of private individuals and firms. These are the central issues in international civil litigation. Arbitration, with its increasing prevalence, shows one way to answer them.

CONCLUSION

As this book reveals, the subject of international civil litigation presents challenges at several different levels, from the most technical and concrete, such as the precise means of discovery in other countries, to the most abstract and general, concerned with the relationship between sovereignty and individual rights. At each level, the challenge raises the question of whether international civil litigation is a genuine subject, rather than the accidental confluence of legal doctrines originating elsewhere. If it represents no more than points of accidental intersection of principles more fully and deeply developed in other fields, it would be better to study those principles independently. This book has tried to show that this view of the subject, if it was ever valid, has lost its hold as transnational cases have proliferated in our courts, in courts overseas, and before arbitrators. The growth in the quantity of cases has led to a need for an increase in quality in imposing a coherent structure on existing doctrine. Existing law provides the resources for discovering the themes that cut across and unify otherwise discrete areas of doctrine, but it does not often make those themes explicit. Issues such as jurisdiction and recognition of judgments, sovereign immunity and human rights, service of process, and discovery overseas traditionally have been related to one another, but they also are related to seemingly distant issues. Jurisdiction, for instance, figures prominently in the analysis of sovereign immunity, which is framed in jurisdictional terms, and enforcement of judgments plays an important role in finding assets to seize in order to deter and compensate for human rights violations.

International civil litigation draws from international law, domestic law, and the law of other nations to resolve these interconnected issues. Treaties form the basis for international arbitration, for process to be executed overseas, and for protection of human rights. Customary international law fills in the gaps not yet governed by multilateral conventions and bilateral treaties. All these forms of international law must be received into domestic law by judicial decisions or by ordinary lawmaking processes, which, in the United States, are under the control of Congress and the President. These branches of government give political accountability to the most salient and important forms of international laws. Treaties must be ratified by the President with the advice and consent of two-thirds of the Senate.[1] If the treaty is not self-executing, it must be implemented by legislation passed by Congress. Purely judge-made law, like the act-of-state doctrine, must be accommodated to these

---

[1]   U.S. CONST., art. II, § 2, ¶ 2.

democratically responsible forms of lawmaking, as it now is in the Foreign Sovereign Immunities Act.[2] Reception of customary international law often has a basis in legislation, as it does, for instance, in the Alien Tort Statute.[3] "International law is part of our law,"[4] not only because of judicial decisions recognizing customary international law. More often, international law becomes part of our law through treaties and legislation that define, implement, and constrain its scope. The law of other countries also comes into play at numerous points, most directly in choice-of-law decisions selecting foreign law to govern a dispute. Foreign law also is implicated across a range of other issues, such as *forum non conveniens*, stays and countersuit injunctions, and recognition of judgments. By definition, international civil litigation crosses international boundaries and therefore raises the possibility of applying foreign law.

As the questions presented in international cases become more concrete, they become more closely related to one another. Judicial decisions in this field do not simply follow the implications of principles developed elsewhere, although they must be consistent with those principles. International litigation shapes and qualifies those principles so that, in their modern form, they can no longer be considered the product only of domestic cases. Personal jurisdiction provides the best example of this tendency. Most of the hard problems, and all of the Supreme Court's recent decisions on this issue, have an international dimension. The restrictions on personal jurisdiction, and on the related concept of national sovereignty, now depend to a significant degree on how these doctrines are deployed in international cases. The same holds true for choice of law and the limits on the extraterritorial application of domestic law. Sovereignty has been both extended and eroded as the possibility has grown that the law of one nation might apply within the boundaries of another. However courts resolve this issue, they have made the concept of sovereignty different from what it was. So, too, courts have altered the terms in which they assert subject-matter jurisdiction, which initially depends upon the arguable application of American law to the controversy or upon the identification of parties as falling within some other recognized heading of American jurisdiction. The very ambiguity in the term "jurisdiction"—referring to the power of courts over the parties or over the controversy or the power of the forum to apply its law—reveals how interconnected all these issues are. Jurisdiction in the modern world cannot be analyzed independently of international cases.

---

[2]   94 Pub. L. No. 583, 90 Stat. 2891 (1976) (codified at 28 U.S.C. §§ 1330, 1332, 1391(f), 1441(d), and 1602–11 (2012)).

[3]   28 U.S.C. § 1650 (2012).

[4]   The Paquete Habana, 175 U.S. 677, 700 (1900).

Recognition of judgments and enforcement of arbitration awards reveals the same interconnections, currently derived based on several different sources of law. Recognition of foreign judgments, unlike recognition of domestic judgments, depends upon state law and, in most states, on some variant of the Uniform Foreign-Country Money Judgments Recognition Act.[5] State law invokes international notions of comity, resulting in a pattern of recognition of foreign judgments not very different from the pattern for domestic judgments under the Full Faith and Credit Clause.[6] A foreign judgment might be denied recognition because it is "repugnant to the public policy" of the enforcing state, but in fact, courts seldom refuse recognition of foreign judgments on this ground. The reliance in these cases on the "international concept of due process" reveals the influence of constitutional law as developed in domestic cases. A foreign court rendering a judgment must comply with the basic principles of American due process, even if it does not strictly conform to all the requirements of American legal doctrine.

Arbitration takes the interaction with domestic law in a different direction, away from state law and the indirect influence of the Constitution, to the New York Convention[7] and the Federal Arbitration Act.[8] International arbitration follows the accelerating trend in domestic law in favor of arbitration and assures enforcement of awards as a matter of federal law. The parallels with recognition of foreign judgments remain, but result in a presumption in favor of enforcement that is, if anything, even stronger. In addition to the New York Convention, other treaties and international arbitral institutions fill in the law of arbitration and reinforce the significance of arbitration in the international sphere. The connection with other areas of international civil litigation ranges from choice of law and choice of forum, almost invariably specified in an arbitration agreement, to the use of stays and injunctions in aid of arbitration.

The Foreign Sovereign Immunities Act exhibits yet another perspective on the development of international civil litigation. Foreign sovereign immunity grew out of the same principles of comity that dictated respect for foreign judgments, but over the course of the twentieth century, it went from being a purely judicial doctrine to one dependent on the views of the State Department and legislation enacted by Congress at the time. Accompanying these changes in the sources of the law, sovereign immunity itself became narrower, excluding commercial activity and, in recent decades,

---

[5]   Uniform Foreign-Country Money Judgments Recognition Act of 2005.

[6]   U.S. CONST. art. IV, § 1.

[7]   United Nations Convention on the Recognition and Enforcement of Foreign Arbitral Awards, June 10, 1958, 21 U.S.T. 2517, 330 U.N.T.S. 38.

[8]   9 U.S.C. §§ 201–08 (2012).

human rights violations. The law has gone from general immunity for foreign sovereigns to protecting commercial and property rights and then to protecting human rights. In the process, it has raised issues of jurisdiction and territorial contacts, as well as issues over the scope of the exceptions to sovereign immunity. The statute, for instance, leaves the interpretation of the central exception for "commercial activity" largely in the hands of the courts because the statute defines the term in circular fashion, as "either a regular course of commercial conduct or a particular commercial transaction or act."[9] The result has been continuing mutual influence of judicial decisions and legislative activity, making the limits on sovereign immunity a durable, if changing, feature of the law. Several other exceptions, some very detailed, allow enforcement of human rights against foreign sovereigns.[10] Principles of sovereignty, individual rights, and political accountability through legislation and executive action all come together in the Foreign Sovereign Immunities Act.

Even such mundane issues as service of process and discovery implicate the same fundamental issues. Restraint on any form of legal process sent overseas derives from the concerns of foreign sovereigns over control of official acts within their territory. Yet service of process is an essential component of notice and opportunity to be heard, as is discovery of the evidence needed to support or defeat a claim. Treaties and international agreements on both aspects of procedure have received the endorsement of the political branches of government, and the traditional form of discovery through "letters rogatory" goes through the State Department. The practicalities of litigation depend upon making good on these essential steps in modern litigation. It is necessary to look no further than the erosion of bank secrecy laws to see the dramatic effect of disclosure of information on litigation and law enforcement generally.

The strategic interests of the parties also cast a unifying structure over the issues taken up in this book. Deciding where to sue starts with issues of jurisdiction, but readily implicates issues of choice of law, access to evidence, and the enforceability of judgments. The forum court tends to apply its own law, and if it cannot, it might well entertain a motion to dismiss for *forum non conveniens*. Where the evidence is determines how effective discovery will be, and if it is found in or near the forum, litigation there will be correspondingly easier and less expensive. If the defendant also has assets in the forum, any resulting judgment can be enforced there, without the complications of recognition overseas. And even if foreign enforcement is necessary, the reputation of the initial forum and

---

[9]   28 U.S.C. § 1603(d) (2012).

[10]   *Id.* §§ 1604(a)(5), 1605A.

integrity of its procedures determines the likelihood of recognition in another country. Plaintiffs choose the court in which to sue with all these issues in mind, and defendants object to the plaintiffs' choice for equal and opposite reasons.

At the theoretical end of the spectrum of legal issues, international civil litigation has not served as a passive receptacle for ideas developed elsewhere, but instead has adapted and redefined these ideas to meet the needs of an increasingly interconnected world. Sovereignty itself has acquired new meaning as it has been contested in courts, whether by the expanded scope of personal jurisdiction, the extraterritorial reach of domestic law, or the restrictions on sovereign immunity. Individual rights form the basis for all kinds of civil litigation, but in the international sphere, they have taken an increasingly prominent role in litigation. The increased prominence of human rights most clearly exemplifies this trend, building upon the pervasive respect for property and contract rights and tort claims in international litigation. International law no longer is concerned mainly with resolving disputes between states, or what traditionally has been called "public international law." It now also extends to disputes involving private firms and individuals (what could be called, varying a traditional term for choice of law, "private international law"). So, too, the need for political accountability takes a distinctive form in international litigation, with the power that the President and Congress have traditionally exercised over foreign relations. The courts in this subject cannot act by themselves, as illustrated by the chilly reception that the act-of-state doctrine received after it was formulated by the Supreme Court. The doctrine was first narrowed by Congress, and then by the Court itself, and presently appears to be subject to an exception for commercial activity based on an analogy to the Foreign Sovereign Immunities Act.

The heterogeneity of these sources is a virtue, not a vice, of international civil litigation, as is the variety of fields from which this subject draws the content of the applicable legal rules. The different sources and content allow a degree of flexibility that a more homogenous set of rules would deny, enabling judges to adapt and develop the law as needed for the cases that they see and the context in which those cases arise. International civil litigation is not frozen into a single mold drawn from a single source of lawmaking. No one denies the changing nature of international relations, commerce, and investment, and the need for the law to change with it. The law must have the resources to adapt and influence these developments. International civil litigation is perfectly positioned to do so because it reflects both the changing landscape of international law and the need to reshape the law to meet the pressing issues of our time.

Providing a forum for the principled resolution of transnational disputes remains the essential function and the unifying ambition of this field.

TABLE OF CASES

INDEX

Nonparty witnesses, 108
Personal jurisdiction, 108–09
Restatement (3d) of Foreign
    Relations Law, 110
Secrecy laws, 115
Tax investigations, 115

Diversity Jurisdiction
Subject-Matter Jurisdiction, this index

Domicile
Aliens, 70–71
Diversity jurisdiction, 70–71
Venue, 119

Due Process
Arbitration award challenges, 183–85
Choice of law, 56–48
Extraterritoriality, 49
Full faith and credit, 47, 142–43
International due process, 153–54, 157
Personal Jurisdiction, this index
Quasi in rem jurisdiction, 46
Recognition and Enforcement of
    Judgments, this index
Service of process, 27–28, 97

Enforcement of Judgments
Recognition and Enforcement of
    Judgments, this index

***Erie* Doctrine**
    Generally, 3
Act of state doctrine, 92, 95
Forum selection clauses, 126
International law, 92, 95
Recognition and enforcement of
    judgments, 145–47

Evidence and Witnesses
Discovery, this index
Forum non conveniens, 121–22, 125

Expropriation
Act of state doctrine, 77, 87
Foreign Sovereign Immunities Act
    exception, 83
Human rights violations, 77, 84

Extraterritoriality
    Generally, 48–57
Antitrust laws, 48–53
Choice of law clauses, 57–59
Comity, 49
Conduct-and-effects test, 50–51, 53–
    57, 111–12
Direct and substantial effect in U.S.,
    51–53
Due process challenges, 49
Effects doctrine, 50–51, 53–57, 111–13
F-cubed transactions, 53–54
Human rights litigation, 54–57
Public and private enforcement of
    securities laws, 54

Restatement (3d) of Foreign Relations
    Law, 110
Securities laws, 53–57
SPEECH Act of 2010, 147–48, 151–52
Universal jurisdiction, 17, 89–91

Federal Arbitration Act
Generally, 167, 169, 173, 174, 179, 188

Federal Common Law
Admiralty, 69–70
Authority to create, 74
Choice of forum clauses, 70
Civil rights litigation, 89
Erie doctrine, 74
Forum non conveniens, 123
Forum selection clauses, 70
International law, 87
Recognition and enforcement of
    judgments, 145–47
Separation of powers, 93–95

Federal Question Jurisdiction
Subject-Matter Jurisdiction, this
    index

Federalism
Erie Doctrine, this index
Federal-state parallel proceedings,
    126–30, 132–33

Foreign Corporations
Diversity jurisdiction, 70–71
Personal jurisdiction, 18–21
Service of process, 28, 102–04
Venue, 119

Foreign Sovereign Immunities Act
    Generally, 76–91
Absolute or restrictive immunity, 76–
    84
Act of state doctrine compared, 75,
    94–95
Alien Tort Statute, 88–89
Aliens' claims, 63–66, 88–89
Commercial activities exception, 76–
    84
Constitutionality, 63–66
Corporations as instrumentalities,
    83–86
Effects in U.S., 79–82
Exceptions to immunity, 76–84
Expropriation exception, 82–83
Human rights litigation, 83–84
Jurisdiction, 65–66, 78
Restrictive or absolute immunity, 76–
    84
Retroactivity, 82–83
State court litigation, 64
State Department suggestions of
    immunity, 77–78
Tate letters, 77–78
Terrorism exception, 83–84